MISSIOLOGICAL
RESEARCH

MISSIOLOGICAL RESEARCH

Interdisciplinary Foundations, Methods, and Integration

Marvin Gilbert, Alan R. Johnson, and Paul W. Lewis
EDITORS

WILLIAM CAREY
LIBRARY

Published by William Carey Library, an imprint of William Carey Publishing
10 W. Dry Creek Circle
Littleton, CO 80120 | www.missionbooks.org
Melissa Hicks, copyeditor
Joanne Liang, interior design

William Carey Library is a ministry of Frontier Ventures
Pasadena, CA 91104 | www.frontierventures.org

Library of Congress Cataloging-in-Publication Data

Names: Gilbert, Marvin, editor. | Johnson, Alan R., editor. | Lewis, Paul W., PhD, editor.
Title: Missiological research : interdisciplinary foundations, methods, and integration / Marvin Gilbert, Alan R. Johnson, and Paul W. Lewis, editors.
Description: Pasadena, CA : William Carey Library, 2018. | Includes bibliographical references. |
Identifiers: LCCN 2017048389 (print) | LCCN 2017048851 (ebook) | ISBN 9780878086528 (ebook) | ISBN 9780878086337 (pbk.)
Subjects: LCSH: Missions--Research.
Classification: LCC BV2063 (ebook) | LCC BV2063 .M545 2018 (print) | DDC
266.0072--dc23
LC record available at https://lccn.loc.gov/2017048389

23 22 21 20 19 Printed for Worldwide Distribution

CONTENTS

UNIT 1: FOUNDATIONAL ISSUES IN MISSIOLOGICAL RESEARCH

UNIT 2: THEOLOGICAL RESEARCH IN MISSIOLOGICAL INQUIRY

UNIT 3: QUALITATIVE RESEARCH

UNIT 4: QUANTITATIVE AND MIXED METHODS RESEARCH

UNIT 5: THEOLOGICAL AND EMPIRICAL INTEGRATION

APPENDICES

PREFACE

Missiological research is a true joy for those engaged in the world of missions, especially the researchers. In light of this joy, this text is the outgrowth of felt needs within the Global Missions Department at the Assemblies of God Theological Seminary (AGTS) at Evangel University, Springfield, Missouri. Many students begin their doctoral studies in missiology without a strong background in empirical research methodology; others possess a limited biblical-theological background. And most have never fully engaged the complexity of interdisciplinary inquiry. This text is designed to address these needs for these students.

Initially Marvin Gilbert and Alan R. Johnson undertook the compilation of the original rendition of the volume for two reasons. First, faculty saw the need to aid their doctoral students as they studied research methodology. Then they also needed a reference tool that they could consult during the initial proposal writing process that would help them start thinking about how to link research questions with appropriate methods. However, after students started working with the first edition, and faculty members discussed the usefulness of the original materials, the editors determined that some key additions, modifications, and inclusions were desired (such as the inclusion of a section, with supportive appendices, on biblical-theological methodologies). It was at this point that Paul W. Lewis joined the editorial team. With insights and suggestions from the AGTS Intercultural Studies Department faculty, doctoral students, and other colleagues, this volume has come to fruition.

As with any work of this size, many contributed to this volume by investing long hours and hard work. First, we would like to express our appreciation to AGTS, and its Global Missions Department in particular for its support for this volume. Second, we would like to express our gratitude to the Assemblies of God World Missions (AGWM) (USA), through whom all three editors and most of the writers have grown in passion for, and understanding of, missions as their field of labor. Third, we would like to express our thanks to those who helped in editing, copying, and related activities needed to produce this manual, especially David G. Clark (PhD) who gave of his time and expertise to make this a better work, and Stephanie Leder who editorially helped to refine the work. Finally, we give all praise and honor to our Lord for His great salvation: the goal and reason for missions.

Marvin Gilbert, EdD, Alan R. Johnson, PhD, and Paul W. Lewis, PhD, editors

CONTRIBUTORS

Daniel E. Albrecht (PhD, Graduate Theological Union) *Dean and Professor of William Jessup University at the San Jose campus, San Jose, California*

Dr. Albrecht has been a teacher and writer specializing in spirituality and ritual studies. Formerly he was the Professor of Christian History and Spirituality at Bethany College in Santa Cruz, CA, where he was on faculty from 1981-2011. He is noted for his research in ritual studies, including his book, *Rites in the Spirit: A Ritual Approach to Pentecostal/Charismatic Spirituality.* Among his other research interests and publication topics are Christian Spirituality, Pentecostal Spirituality, Spiritual Development, Historical and Biblical Spiritualties.

Rob Bartels (JD, Cleveland State University) *Associate Professor of International Studies at Evangel University, Springfield, Missouri*

Dr. Bartels teaches Government, History, and Anthropology courses in the Social Sciences Department. He also serves as faculty adviser for CORD – the married-students fellowship, and as a faculty sponsor on Evangel's international study tours. His involvement with these tours has taken him around the globe, from China to Europe to South Africa. He formerly chaired and is a current member of the Faculty Affairs Committee at Evangel University.

Robert D. Braswell (PhD, Florida State University) *Dean of Research at Pan-Africa Theological Seminary, Springfield, Missouri*

Dr. Braswell has served with the Assemblies of God World Missions since 1990 and in Africa since 2004. Previously, he led the Assemblies of God Bible College in Dodoma, Tanzania, and directed the Centre for Postgraduate Studies at Global School of Theology–Western Cape in Cape Town, South Africa. His research interests include quantitative methods and Q Methodology, especially as applied to missiological research.

John L. Easter (PhD, Assemblies of God Theological Seminary) *Vice Chancellor of Pan-Africa Theological Seminary; Associate Professor of Intercultural Studies at Assemblies of God Theological Seminary, Springfield, Missouri*

Dr. Easter is a missionary educator in Africa. In 2001, he established and directed All Nations Theological Seminary, an Intercultural Studies graduate studies program, for mobilizing African national churches as sending missionary bodies. He now serves as the Executive Vice President of the Pan-Africa Theological Seminary, the Director of Africa's Hope, and the Executive Director for the Association of Pentecostal Theological Education in Africa. In 2010, he became the first recipient of the PhD degree at AGTS. His research interests are in biblical theology, missions, and cross-cultural education.

Marvin Gilbert (EdD, Texas Tech University) *Doctor of Ministry program director at Southwest Assemblies of God University, Waxahachie, Texas*

Dr. Gilbert, a retired missionary educator with the Assemblies of God World Mission, has served at the East Africa School of Theology, the West Africa Advanced School of Theology, and Global School of Theology in Cape Town, South Africa. Currently he is contributing to the development of research methods courses for the Pan-Africa Theological Seminary and Southwestern Assemblies of God University. His professional passion is empowering his students to conduct ethical, Kingdom-relevant research that employs best-practice methodologies.

A. Elizabeth (Beth) Grant (PhD, Biola University) *Associate Professor of Intercultural Studies at Assemblies of God Theological Seminary, Springfield, Missouri*

Dr. Grant has served with her husband as an Assemblies of God missionary to India and Eurasia for forty years. She and her husband are the co-directors of Project Rescue, a ministry to survivors of sex trafficking. She also served as the chairperson for the Network for Women in Ministry for the Assemblies of God (USA) from 1999–2010. In 2009 she became the first woman elected to the Executive Presbytery of the national Assemblies of God (USA). Dr. Grant's passion for intercultural missional education has taken her to seminary classrooms in India, Europe, and the United States.

Mark A. Hausfeld (DMin, Northern Baptist Theological Seminary) Past *President and Professor of Urban and Islamic Studies at Assemblies of God Theological Seminary, Springfield, Missouri*

Dr. Mark Hausfeld became president of the Assemblies of God Theological Seminary at Evangel University on July 1, 2015 and stepped down May 2017. He has more than thirty years of pastoral and missionary experience, both in the United States and abroad. Dr. Hausfeld has a passion for developing creative access evangelism. His focus has centered on discipleship and church planting in urban settings in North America and restricted contexts in Central Asia and far-reaching global Muslim communities.

Alan R. Johnson (PhD, Oxford Centre for Missions Studies, University of Wales) *2006–2007 J. Philip Hogan Professor of World Missions; Associate Professor of Anthropology at Assemblies of God Theological Seminary (AGTS), Springfield, Missouri*

Dr. Johnson is a veteran missionary to Thailand, having served there since 1986. His work has always sought to integrate both church planting and ministry to the whole person. In 2009, he authored *Leadership in a Slum: A Bangkok Case Study*, based on his dissertation at the Oxford Centre for Mission Studies: University of Wales. In addition to his adjunct teaching assignment at AGTS, he works with small churches in the Bangkok region and in ministry with urban poor. His current research interest is the social influence processes in Thai culture.

Anita L. Koeshall (PhD, Fuller Seminary) *2010–2011 J. Philip Hogan Professor of World Missions; Associate Professor of Intercultural Studies at Assemblies of God Theological Seminary, Springfield, Missouri*

Dr. Koeshall teaches Intercultural Studies (ICS) at the Assemblies of God Theological Seminary and trains cross-cultural workers to exegete culture and to develop life strategies in new contexts for Assemblies of God World Missions. She has served for more than three decades as an advisor and trainer of student leaders with Students for Christ–Europe, a student ministry she and her husband John pioneered. Dr. Koeshall holds a PhD in Intercultural Studies from Fuller Theological Seminary.

Paul W. Lewis (PhD, Baylor University) *Associate Dean, Admissions and Program Coordinator of the Intercultural Doctoral Studies and Professor of*

Historical Theology and Intercultural Studies at Assemblies of God Theological Seminary (AGTS), Springfield, Missouri

Dr. Lewis and his wife Eveline have over two decades in intercultural ministry, including ministering among International Students in the USA, and for eleven years in Northern Asia with Assemblies of God World Missions (USA). In 2006, he became the Academic Dean of Asia Pacific Theological Seminary in Baguio, Philippines until March 2012. In 2012, Dr. Lewis joined the faculty at AGTS. He is also the current editor of the *International Journal of Pentecostal Missiology*. His passion is the intersection of theology, history, and missions.

Johan Mostert (DPhil, University of Pretoria) *Professor Emeritus of Community Psychology at Assemblies of God Theological Seminary, Springfield, Missouri*

Dr. Mostert has served as a pastor, counselor, and director of the National Welfare Department of the Apostolic Faith Mission in South Africa for more than three decades. He is widely recognized as a leading authority on local church response to the global AIDS pandemic. His passion as a teacher is to train counselors who will respond to human suffering wherever it is found with biblical and psychological skill and Spirit-led compassion.

Warren B. Newberry (DTh, University of South Africa) *Associate Professor of Missions (retired) at Assemblies of God Theological Seminary, Springfield, Missouri*

Dr. Newberry, now retired, served for over forty years as a missionary educator, having taught regularly at the Caribbean School of Theology Graduate School, Asia Theological Center for Evangelism and Missions (Singapore) and All Nations Theological Seminary (Malawi). He continues to supervise doctoral students' research at AGTS.

DeLonn L. Rance (PhD, Fuller Seminary) *2008–2009 J. Philip Hogan Professor of World Missions; Professor of Intercultural Studies, Director of Intercultural Doctoral Studies, and Global Missions Department Chairperson at Assemblies of God Theological Seminary, Springfield, Missouri*

Dr. DeLonn L. Rance serves as the Director of Intercultural Doctoral Studies, Chair of the Global Missions Department, and Associate Professor of Missions and Intercultural Studies at the Assemblies of God Theological Seminary. For twenty years as a missionary in El Salvador, he fomented missionary vision and missiological education throughout Latin America. His passion is for missions mobilization and missionary formation.

Charles E. Self (PhD, University of California–Santa Cruz) *Professor of Church History at Assemblies of God Theological Seminary (AGTS), Springfield, Missouri*

Prior to his joining the faculty at AGTS, Dr. Self served for thirty years in various pastoral roles—including senior pastor—and concurrently taught for twenty-eight years at the following schools: Bethany University, AGTS (adjunct), Western Seminary (adjunct), George Fox University, and Continental Theological Seminary in Brussels, Belgium. In 2007, Dr. Self led the establishment and development of AGTS West in collaboration with the Northern California–Nevada District Council and Bethany University. His research interest is in the integration of history, theology, missions, and whole life discipleship with a focus on the impact of Christianity in indigenous cultures.

INTRODUCTION

Marvin Gilbert, EdD, Alan R. Johnson, PhD,

and Paul W. Lewis, PhD

Welcome to the Kingdom-impacting world of missiological research. Research has been described as a means of systematic inquiry into a problem —a problem that states, in so many words, that valuable information is unknown, but not unknowable. Phrased differently, research is a respected means of resolving our collective, but personally experienced, ignorance. For a missiologist, research is a respected means of resolving ignorance about how the Church works in the cross-cultural context.

This volume, then, is meant to be a tool for engaging in sound missiological research practices. Every doctoral student in intercultural studies must master the best-practice research methods in at least two disciplines. The biblical-theological research chapters provide concise explanation of the wide variety of theologically oriented methods of inquiry. These are followed by chapters devoted to empirical research. The final section of this work focuses on the challenge of integrating findings from these two distinct approaches to research.

Many of the chapters contain a distillation of established research methodology, including theological research methods, authored by faculty members writing within the strength of their prior learning and experience. A few of the chapters present new models for, and perspectives on, interdisciplinary missiological research. *All* the chapters are short and succinct: almost all contain fewer than 1,100 words of instructional content.

The back matter of all but a few chapters contains resources for additional reading and exploration: textbooks and key journal articles, websites, and one journal article with its abstract. The journal article illustrates the chapter's focus and underscores—perhaps subtly—the importance of scholarly journals in missiological research.

Twenty-five appendices and a glossary both supplement and illustrate some of the chapters' content. Fourteen of the appendices relate to and enrich the presentation of the empirical methods; the remaining appendices augment the chapters focused on biblical-theological research. Appendix 18 is particularly noteworthy, as it consists of an extensive bibliography of the theological research resources identified in chapters 14 through 21.

Research, in general, is conducted for the academy; it expands the body of knowledge by either generating new theory or evaluating existing theory. Missiological research, in particular, is conducted for both the academy *and* the Church. May your research become a blessing to both domains!

A fundamental question is "How to use this volume?" First, this volume is partially meant to be an introduction of the vast array of missiological research methodologies. This includes the social science/empirical research methods, which can also be helpful to many students or researchers in various other related fields of research (e.g., Business). Further, the work presents an introduction to the usage of biblical and theological inquiry. This section will be especially useful for the missions practitioner who is less familiar with the biblical-theological methods for the related components of their missiological research.

Second, this volume provides an overview of the array of methodologies together. This allows the student or researcher to see in one work the various issues and methods available. This will prove especially helpful for those who are in the process of starting their research; they can investigate and decide on which method(s) works best for their study.

Third, this volume serves as a reference volume. It is hoped that as a missiological researcher plummets the depth of his or her research, this volume will be used repeatedly for introductions and clarifications concerning various methodologies (such as a specific method used in an important journal article), for understanding the parameters, benefits, and limits of certain methodologies, and as a source/resource for future missiological research. It is understood that these essays are introductory only, yet they are supplemented with pertinent bibliographical resources. Thus, this text will also serve as a reference, enabling the researcher to delve deeper into each methodology. It is our hope that these chapters will become a valuable tool and oft-used resource for current and future missiological research!

UNIT 1
Foundational Issues in Missiological Research

1
INTERDISCIPLINARY RESEARCH[1]
An Epistemological Framework
Marvin Gilbert, EdD

Research in any discipline follows established procedures, utilizes reliable tools and resources, and advances within a defined epistemological framework. Historians see the world through a historiographer's "lenses." Theologians conduct research within an exegetical and hermeneutical worldview. And both social and natural scientists embrace principles and procedures that form a scientific epistemological framework.

Missiological and applied-ministry researchers face a unique challenge. They must utilize more than one epistemological framework—exegetical/hermeneutical and empirical/scientific—while mastering a variety of otherwise disparate investigative methodologies. This challenge extends to the process of analyzing the results, which must be integrated and synthesized in a credible interdisciplinary manner. Such adroit, flexible researchers can contribute much to both the Church and the academy by overcoming the natural tendency to value one research domain over the other.

This chapter introduces the essence of an epistemological framework designed to facilitate interdisciplinary research. For theologians without a strong background in social science research (SSr), this framework may be uncomfortable initially, in that empirical research methodologies are

---

1. The term "interdisciplinary" is preferred to the term "multidisciplinary" in this text. Within a *multidisciplinary* relationship, cooperation between the relevant disciplines "may be mutual and cumulative, but not interactive" (Augsburg 2005, 56). Augsburg's quotation describes fairly well the actual practice of investigation within each discipline involved in a given missiological study (e.g., theological reflection and anthropological case study). Nonetheless, both the content and (to some extent) the methodology used in each discipline must be influenced by the other. The creative, integrative conclusions reached at the end of the study must draw upon the findings produced by research within each discipline. For these reasons, the term "interdisciplinary" is the preferred descriptor.

placed on par with methods of biblical exegesis and theological reflection (B/Tr). This integrative framework in *no way* implies that empirical findings are as important as God's Word. It *does* imply, however, that the Truth of the Word rightly divided and the truth of empirical research credibly executed can be effectively integrated to challenge, empower, and guide the Church in the pursuit of God's mission.

BASIC PRINCIPLES OF RESEARCH

As its title implies, this text focuses on the social science domain of interdisciplinary research. Before discussing the epistemological framework itself, a quick review of four basic SSr principles may be helpful to the reader.

Best practice. Best practice is a discipline-specific benchmark for credible research (and other professional activities). A best-practice commitment to research within each discipline is essential, though the specific expression of best-practice varies considerably from one discipline to another (e.g., best-practice in Old Testament exegesis differs sharply from best practice in ethnographic research).

Objective. The data generated by social science research, either words or numbers,[2] are characterized by their objectivity. Uncontrolled bias and prejudice *cannot* be allowed to influence the findings. Conclusions reached in best-practice SSr are fact-driven; empirical findings, not preconceived ideas, inform those conclusions.

Observable (empirical). Observation is foundational to all SSr. This dependence on careful, systematic observation is captured by the term "empirical": the "positivist" tradition in social science research (Bernard 2011a). Empirical research is, thus, limited to what can be observed and measured by the researcher. In the data-gathering stage, guesswork and pre-existing beliefs play little, if any, role.[3]

---

2. See chapter 22 titled, "The Nature of Data."

3. Intuition and guesswork do play a role in some stages of grounded-theory and other types of qualitative research, in which the methodology emerges over time during the study.

Replicable. Replicability proposes that the findings presented in a given research report[4] should be found again (within some chance fluctuations) if the original study was repeated—replicated—by another researcher. A true replication requires the second researcher to use the same methodology and to follow exactly the same procedures under the same conditions, that is, using the same "operational definitions" (Bernard 2011b).

Epistemological Principles:

The following epistemological principles compose the essence of a workable interdisciplinary epistemological framework.

Sequential operations. SSr and B/Tr cannot be conducted simultaneously. While the results of B/Tr can inform the content of a SSr questionnaire, administering the resultant questionnaire cannot be done while exegeting a New Testament passage.

Mutually exclusive (i.e., discipline-specific) **methodologies.** A given SSr study can employ multiple methods (e.g., a mixed qualitative and quantitative design), yet a given research method cannot be effectively applied to both B/Tr and SSr.

Mutually exclusive data sets. SSr and B/Tr cannot be conducted on the same data set.[5]

Mutually exclusive analyses. SSr methods cannot be used to analyze data gathered by B/Tr methods (and vice versa). For example, principles of exegesis cannot be used to analyze interview transcripts.

Revelatory Truth. B/Tr yields revelatory data (RD): this is the domain of Truth.

Empirical facts. SSr yields empirical data/findings (ED/F): this is the domain of fact.[6] SSr offers empirically justified, fact-based conclusions, but not Truth. All SSr conclusions are to some extent relative and tentatively held because of the inescapable influences of bias and chance fluctuation in the data.

---

4. Often presented in scholarly journal articles, monographs, and papers presented at professional meetings.

5. With the possible exceptions of higher criticism and linguistic analysis of the biblical text.

6. At best, truth with lower-case "t".

Location of primary SS data. With some exceptions,[7] a missiological researcher cannot capture original (i.e., primary) data in the social science collection of an academic library. That collection contains two types of secondary data: (a) previously published ED/F, and (b) guidelines for best-practice SSr methodology.[8] Primary social science data are located in the "field"; the term "field research" is often used in the social science literature.[9]

Evidence of high-quality research. The evidence of credible, high-quality research in the social science collection cannot be directly applied to the B/Tr collection, and vice versa:

1. The quality of SSr is benchmarked against best-practice reliability and validity standards (Bernard 2011b).
2. The quality of B/Tr is benchmarked against best-practice trust and truth standards.

SYMBOLIC REPRESENTATIONS

This chapter concludes with a symbolic presentation of key statements in the epistemological framework. (The legend at the end of the table explains two unusual symbols.)

SSr ≠ B/Tr	These two broadly defined approaches are neither identical nor interchangeable in a given study.
SSr + B/Tr = interdisciplinary research framework	Missiological research IS interdisciplinary.
SSr ⟶⊣ RD SSr ⟶⊣ Truth	Social science research *cannot* yield revelatory data (RD) or Truth.
SSr ⟶ factually, apparently true, findings (at best)	The "apparently true" characteristic is established by validity and reliability evidence.

---

7. For example, library science research may focus on library-user behavior, historical documents and artifacts, demographic databases, and meta-analysis of published findings for future theory-building efforts.

8. Published articles from credible academic journals utilize best-practice methodology; if they did not, the articles would not be accepted for publication.

9. Data located in the field are "dirty" data; they must be located and extracted from real-life contexts.

B/Tr ➞⊣ ED/F	Biblical/Theological research cannot yield ED/F.
RD + ED/F integrative conclusions (and theoretical implications)	The goals of credible missiological research include the development of integrative conclusions and either (a) the application of an existing theory, or (b) the development of a new theory.
Theory ➞ Truth	Theory is not Truth; future studies can lead to the rejection of seemingly irreproachable theories.

Legend: ≠ not equal to; cannot be equated
      ➞⊣ a blocked process: impossible connection or linkage

REFERENCES AND RESOURCES FOR ADDITIONAL READING

Augsburg, Tanya. 2010. *Becoming Interdisciplinary: An Introduction to Interdisciplinary Studies.* 2nd ed. Sunnyvale, CA: Kendall/Hunt.

Bernard, H. Russell. 2011a. "Anthropology and the Social Sciences." In *Research Methods in Anthropology: Qualitative and Quantitative Approaches,* 1–22. 5th ed. Alta Mira, CA: AltaMira Press.

———. 2011b. "The Foundations of Social Research." In *Research Methods in Anthropology: Qualitative and Quantitative Approaches,* 23–53. 5th ed. Alta Mira, CA: AltaMira Press.

Craib, Ian, and Ted Benton. 2010. *Philosophy of Social Science: The Philosophical Foundations of Social Thought.* 2nd ed. New York: Palgrave Macmillan.

Repko, Allen F., ed. 2008. *Interdisciplinary Research: Process and Theory.* Thousand Oaks, CA: Sage Publications.

Strober, Myra. 2010. *Interdisciplinary Conversations: Challenging Habits of Thought.* Palo Alto, CA: Stanford University Press.

WEBSITES OF INTEREST

National Institute of Health—Common Fund
      https://commonfund.nih.gov/interdisciplinary/
The National Academies Press—Facilitating Interdisciplinary Research
      http://www.nap.edu/catalog.php?record_id=11153

JOURNAL ARTICLE WITH ABSTRACT

Porter, Alan L., and Ismael Rafols. 2009. "Is Science Becoming more Interdisciplinary?: Measuring and Mapping Six Research Fields over Time." *Scientometrics* 81:719–45. doi: 10.1007/s11192-008-2197-2.

In the last two decades there have been studies claiming that science is becoming ever more interdisciplinary. However, the evidence has been anecdotal or partial. Here we investigate how the degree of interdisciplinarity has changed between 1975 and 2005 over six research domains. To do so, we compute well established bibliometric indicators alongside a new index of interdisciplinarity (Integration score, aka Rao-Stirling diversity) and a science mapping visualization method. The results attest to notable changes in research practices over this 30-year period, namely major increases in number of cited disciplines and references per article (both show about 50% growth), and co-authors per article (about 75% growth). However, the new index of interdisciplinarity only shows a modest increase (mostly around 5% growth). Science maps hint that this is because the distribution of citations of an article remains mainly within neighboring disciplinary areas. These findings suggest that science is indeed becoming more interdisciplinary, but in small steps—drawing mainly from neighboring fields and only modestly increasing the connections to distant cognitive areas. The combination of metrics and overlay science maps provides general benchmarks for future studies of interdisciplinary research characteristics.

2
EPISTEMOLOGICAL FRAMEWORKS IN QUALITATIVE RESEARCH

Alan R. Johnson, PhD

Researchers conduct their inquiry into the external world of phenomena outside themselves; they do so holding particular views of reality that include what exists (ontology), and how people come to know that reality (epistemology). This dynamic combination of ontology and epistemology provides the framework in which they conduct their inquiry. That framework, in turn, impacts the status of the knowledge they produce.

Research methods are the specific practices used to attain knowledge of particular phenomena (Krauss 2005, 758–59). In contrast, the nature of that knowledge and the claims researchers can make from it are directly related to epistemology. In general, epistemological concerns center on the nature, origins, and sources of what constitutes knowledge.

A number of nuanced positions can be identified in the literature concerning the nature of reality and how humans know it.[1] These positions generally align themselves between two major epistemological poles. Specific research methods tend to cluster in "streams" flowing between those poles. This chapter briefly examines these two major poles, labeled here the "realist position" and the "anti-realist position." This essay then argues for a hybrid position that incorporates strengths from both poles. The chapter concludes with guidelines for moving from epistemology to specific research methods.

The realist position
The realist position is associated with the positivist research epistemology that has developed principally in the natural sciences, and is often associated with the use of quantitative methods. Empirical realism is based on

---

1. See Schwandt 1994 for a useful overview.

the beliefs that (1) a real world exists, (2) humans have direct perceptual access to that real world, (3) words can, with reasonable clarity, refer to real objects in the world, and (4) true statements correspond with how things truly are in the world (Knight 2002, 23–24). Thus, the positivist paradigm is based on the belief that researchers can exteriorize reality, remain detached from it, and can understand their observations of real events by logical analysis (Krauss 2005, 761). The goal of positivist research is to explain phenomena, predict future events, identify regularities, and establish causal relationships.

The anti-realist position

The other major epistemological pole is often labeled the "anti-realist" position, and is associated with the qualitative research paradigm. It is also referred to as the "naturalistic," "interpretivist," or "constructivist" position. Broadly stated, this view argues that reality is constructed, not discovered; reality is viewed a social artifact, a product of mind and language (Knight 2002, 24). Rather than remaining detached and objective, the overriding goal in the positivist paradigm, qualitative researchers typically interact directly with their research participants (i.e., human subjects) throughout their data-gathering activities. The very fact that such qualitative inquiry is occurring changes both the researcher and the research participants.

Knowledge at the anti-realistic pole is established through meanings attached to the phenomenon being studied. This implies that knowledge is context- and time-dependent. It also implies that qualitative research findings are a creation of the inquiry process itself. A strongly held constructivist position concludes that there is no single truth; all "truths" are relative, since all are human constructions (Schwandt 1994, 200).

CRITICAL REALISM AS A MEDIATING POSITION

The positivist paradigm is powerful and dominates the natural sciences and parts of the behavioral sciences. Aspects of this paradigm are appealing to missiological researchers who eagerly embrace belief in absolute truth. Even so, the assumptions of the realist position are vulnerable when applied to human thought and action (Kaboub 2008, 343; Knight 2002, 24). So the question must be posed: Does a philosophical position allow for a conception of absolute truth while allowing for human meaning construction? Stated differently, is it possible to hold an epistemological position that avoids the problems associated with (1) naïve realism, with its "snapshot" views of alleged reality, and (2) the interpretivist/constructivist view that posits the existence of multiple realities or "truths"?

One answer to this critically important question requires a pragmatic modification of the realist position to address its weaknesses. Such a pragmatic position on ontology and epistemology holds that realism is a fair description of some aspects of the world, while the rest is observer-relative (Knight 2002, 26). A "naïve" realist position sees a single reality within which a detached, unbiased researcher seeks to discover objective truth or "metaphysically explored true meaning" (Krauss 2005, 765). In contrast, a "critical-realist" position embraces multiple *perceptions* of a single mind-independent reality (Krauss 2005, 765). By adopting critical realism, a researcher acknowledges that reality exists, yet his or her understanding of reality is only a social construct that must be continually tested against the real (Knight 2002, 27). Kaboub (2008) calls this a "critical multiplism," arguing that this perspective is "based on the belief that no one approach is ever sufficient for developing a valid understanding of a phenomenon" (343).

Krauss explained an important difference between the realist positivist position and critical realism. While the concept of reality in realism extends beyond consciousness, it is not fully knowable. As a result, it is perceived in different ways by different people:

> The critical realist agrees that our knowledge of reality is a result of social conditioning and, thus, cannot be understood independently of the social actors involved in the knowledge derivation process. However, it takes issue with the belief that the reality itself is a product of this knowledge derivation process. The critical realist asserts that real objects are subject to value laden observation. (Krauss 2005, 761–62)

Both reality and value laden observations of that reality operate in two different dimensions: Krauss labeled the first dimension "intransitive" because it is relatively enduring. The second dimension is transitive and changing.

Schwandt, T. A. 1994. "Constructivist, Interpretivist Approaches to Human Inquiry." In *Handbook of Qualitative Research*, eds. Norman K. Denzin and Yvonna S. Lincoln, 118–37. Thousand Oaks, CA: Sage Publications.

WEBSITES OF INTEREST

Christian Smith: University of Norte Dame
        https://www3.nd.edu/~csmith22/criticalrealism.htm
Critical Realism
        http://www.criticalrealism.com/

JOURNAL ARTICLE WITH ABSTRACT

Vasilachis de Gialdino, Irene. 2009. "The Ontological and Epistemological Foundations of Qualitative Research." *Forum: Qualitative Social Research* 10, no. 2, http://www.qualitative-research.net/index.php/fqs/article/view/1299/3163 (accessed November 27, 2013).

The purpose of this paper is to describe the most relevant features of qualitative research in order to show how, from the Epistemology of the Known Subject perspective I propose, it is necessary to review first the ontological and then the epistemological grounds of this type of inquiry. I begin by following the path that leads from the Epistemology of the Knowing Subject to the Epistemology of the Known Subject, proposed as a new and non-exclusive way of knowing. I pass on to describe the primary and secondary characteristics of qualitative research, expressing the need for an ontological rupture. Finally, cognitive interaction and cooperative knowledge construction are considered as two fundamental features in the process of qualitative research grounded on the Epistemology of the Known Subject.

3
THE CHALLENGES AND PITFALLS OF INTERDISCIPLINARY RESEARCH

Beth Grant, PhD

An increasingly complex world struggles to cope with diverse problems, some on a global scale. This calls for a unique approach to research: one that merges the insights and perspectives of multiple disciplines and leads to integrative understanding and ideas. A growing number of academic institutions now offer interdisciplinary studies, with instruction and research focused on this need. The nature and dynamics of interdisciplinary research (IR) itself still need to be thoroughly examined, however, in order to "raise the bar" for academic credibility in this new approach to research.

UNDERSTANDING INTERDISCIPLINARY RESEARCH

Three key adjectives, described below, characterize this dynamic yet still emerging approach to research.

Heuristic. Repko (2008) defined IR as "a decision-making process that is heuristic, iterative, and reflexive" (137). Its heuristic nature refers to the assistance it offers in discovering knowledge. This discovery process illuminates the contributions of the relevant disciplines: their unique approaches to, and perspectives of, various topics. The second aspect of this heuristic decision-making process is the integration of the various disciplinary insights, leading to greater understanding or discovery.

Iterative. Integration is at the core of all interdisciplinary activity, including research. Integrative synthesis is unique to interdisciplinary, as compared to disciplinary research, facilitating an interdisciplinary understanding of the topic under investigation. This synthesis is not a linear process. IR is characterized by re-visiting and re-assessing earlier steps in the research process as more data are gleaned. Because of this iterative repetition of designed sequences, no specific formula exists for accomplishing it.

Reflexive. The reflexive characteristic of IR highlights the constant need for self-awareness on the part of the researcher. The researcher must acknowledge and challenge her biases to avoid skewing the research process and the conclusions that follow.[1]

CHALLENGES

IR offers significant advantages, bringing multiple perspectives, research tools, and understandings to bear on complex problems. As with all research methodologies, however, it has its own unique challenges. Seven of these are highlighted here:

1. Early on, a researcher must decide how many disciplines, with their unique perspectives and methods, are most relevant to the research topic and problem. A preliminary literature review within the chosen disciplines will indicate a given discipline's relevance and validity to the research topic or problem.

2. A researcher must decide where and how to position his or her own research as it relates to one or more academic disciplines, theories, streams of inquiry, and ideologies (Clandinin and Connelly 2000, 135–36). When working across disciplines, this critically important step must become even more intentional and methodical.

3. There is no one way to engage in IR, no formula exists to ensure success. Therefore, IR demands an even greater intentionality in research design and approach; the data-gathering and data-analysis methodologies used must be designed with care. Otherwise, the interdisciplinary researcher only confirms the concerns of those who question the credibility of IR. For example, Lattuca argues that interdisciplinary researchers are viewed as being focused lightly on multiple disciplines without any depth of insight and knowledge of any one discipline (2001, 122–24).

4. The IR must balance the depth of disciplinary research with the breadth of IR. This challenge is apparent, for example,

---

1. See chapter 6 in Repko (2008).

in how a researcher approaches the literature search. A traditional disciplinary research project entails in-depth literature search within a given academic discipline. In contrast, an interdisciplinary literature search requires equally rigorous investigation in several relevant disciplines.

5. Current library cataloging is designed by disciplines, supporting disciplinary, rather than interdisciplinary, literature researches. The interdisciplinary researcher must search diligently across the library system to find information relevant to the research topic.

6. Unfortunately, the researcher as student has often not been taught how to integrate new knowledge with previously learned concepts. As a result, the process of integration—inherent to the entire interdisciplinary research process—is often new cognitive territory.

7. When exploring a research problem from the perspectives of several disciplines, a researcher inevitably encounters conflicting insights and theories. The IR challenge is to identify the conflicts and their sources, then create commonalities in the integrative process. This "interdisciplinary common ground" is reached as the researcher brings out potential commonalities underlying the conflicting insights between disciplines, a process that leads to potential reconciliation and integration (Repko 2008, 272).

PITFALLS FOR RESEARCHERS DOING INTERDISCIPLINARY RESEARCH

Novice interdisciplinary researchers face several pitfalls that can threaten the validity of their research efforts. Four of these are identified in this section.

Limited focus. Some researchers tend to focus on specific insights rather than disciplinary sources. This pitfall can result in researchers generating a large amount of data and corresponding insights from only one or two disciplines, leaving untouched potentially pertinent data and insights from other equally relevant disciplines. It can also make the researcher less creative and less open to new, unanticipated findings.

Seduction by a secular discipline's literature. Repko (2008) identified the challenge of "becoming seduced by existing literature" (178). This describes the tendency of researchers to accept a particular discipline's perspective of a problem or topic to be studied and even subconsciously making that the baseline of their understanding. That single-discipline baseline is then used to evaluate the perspectives and insights from all other research disciplines. This hinders interdisciplinary researchers' creativity and objectivity, and curtails the opportunity to discover new valid interdisciplinary insights.

Seduction by theological literature. The literature-seduction pitfall, acknowledged by secular researchers, has its own unique expression among theologians and missiologists. This latter group of IR scholars views biblical Truth as their baseline for understanding and evaluating all other truth. This commitment to the theological literature may, unfortunately, disqualify the work of theologians and missiologists in some secular scholars' minds. In any case, it makes it imperative that researchers who hold biblical Truth highly be stringent in their (1) IR design, (2) implementation of multiple methodologies, (3) evaluation of data, and (4) conclusions that reflect a commitment to an interdisciplinary perspective. Missiological studies, by nature IR, must stand up to the academy's scrutiny.

Limited recognition of assumptions. Given the threat posed by the preceding pitfalls, it is important for a missiological researcher to acknowledge early on his or her Scripture-is-dominant "bias." This acknowledgement must be included in the list of assumptions provided at the start of a report of findings. Maintaining an open objective mind to the insights of other disciplines remains the goal of credible missiological research; such insights inform the research process and lead to a more appropriately nuanced understanding of the topic.

REFERENCES AND RESOURCES FOR ADDITIONAL READING

Clandinin, D. Jean, and F. Michael Connelly. 2000. *Narrative Inquiry: Experience and Story in Qualitative Research.* San Francisco, CA: Jossey-Bass Publishers.

Lattuca, Lisa R. 2001. *Creating Interdisciplinarity: Interdisciplinary Research and Teaching among College and University Faculty.* Nashville, TN: Vanderbilt University Press.

Repko, Allen F. 2008. *Interdisciplinary Research: Process and Theory.* Thousand Oaks, CA: Sage Publications.

Silverman, David, and Amir Marvasti. 2008. *Doing Qualitative Research: A Comprehensive Guide.* Thousand Oaks, CA: Sage Publications.

Wan, Enoch. 2005. "The Paradigm and Pressing Issues of Inter-Disciplinary Research Methodology." *Global Missiology* 2 (January). http://ojs.globalmissiology.org/index.php/english/article/viewFile/97/281 (accessed October 17, 2011).

WEBSITES OF INTEREST

Association for Integrative Studies
      http://www.units.muohio.edu/aisorg/
Interdisciplinary Studies Project
      http://www.pz.harvard.edu/interdisciplinary/index.html

JOURNAL ARTICLE WITH ABSTRACT

Sá, Creso M. 2008. "'Interdisciplinary Strategies' in U.S. Research Universities." *Higher Education: The International Journal of Higher Education and Educational Planning* 55: 537–52. doi 10.1007/s10734-007-9073-5.

In the context of increasing support for interdisciplinary modes of research, many in the policy, scientific, and academic communities propose that universities should change structurally to reduce the barriers to investigation that involves researchers from multiple disciplines. This paper examines "interdisciplinary strategies" in U.S. research universities—deliberate efforts to spur collaborative research across traditional departmental and disciplinary boundaries, including the creation and adaptation of university policies, practices, and structures. It identifies and analyzes the use of incentive grants to initiate new interdisciplinary units, the establishment of "campus-wide institutes" that steer campus investments in interdisciplinary areas, and new modes of faculty hiring and evaluation.

4
THE FOUR-PHASE MODEL OF MISSIOLOGICAL RESEARCH

Marvin Gilbert, EdD

The four-phase model[1] of missiological research organizes the various research tasks into four phases of investigation. These phases are *not* mutually exclusive, nor are they totally sequential. Rather, they are major "landmarks" in the sometimes-meandering journey from topic-selection to problem-resolution.

This interdisciplinary model differs significantly from those presented in single-discipline research texts. Single-discipline research is comparatively simple, no matter what methodological complexity may be involved in a study. The fact that two disciplines are involved complicates the tasks in substantial ways. For example, a skilled library researcher and New Testament exegete must also function as a skilled field researcher when addressing social science research questions.

The most complicated aspect of interdisciplinary research is the interface between the divergent arenas of investigation. The section entitled, "Synergistic Interaction" addresses briefly this unique interaction, emphasizing the role played by phase 1 findings in the later phases of research.

THE FOUR PHASES

The four phases of investigation are:

Phase 1. The interdisciplinary researcher produces a thorough review of the theological and biblical literature germane to the study's problem. In this phase, the researcher will also engage in exegetical study and theological reflection. All activity in this phase is library-centered: biblical and theological collections are tapped, including theological journals and internet resources.

Phase 2. Like phase 1, phase 2 is library-centered in the empirical literature sections; the conventional holdings and a variety of media and

---

1. See Appendix 1 titled, "The Four-Phase Model of Missiological Research."

special collections are tapped. The focus is on both content and methodology; the interdisciplinary researcher must identify and evaluate (and later utilize) research methods reported in credible academic journals and other primary research reports.

Phase 3. Empirical (i.e., field) research characterizes phase 3. The researcher creatively applies (1) *content* gleaned in phase 1, and (2) *content* and *methodology* gleaned in phase 2. New data are generated in phase 3; these data may be quantitative or qualitative or a mixture of the two. In any case, phase-3 data must be analyzed using best-practice procedures, ideally supported by relevant software packages.

Phase 4. Phase 4 is, without question, the most challenging. Paul Leedy (Leedy and Ormrod, 2009) argues that this is where true research takes place. Successful completion of phase 4 requires an integrative synthesis of findings from the first three phases. The researcher must employ critical and creative thinking skills, whether the objective is (1) the generation of new theory, (2) the critical evaluation of an existing theory, or (3) practical recommendations for organizational change.

SYNERGISTIC INTERACTION

A unique feature of the four-phase model is the application of findings from one phase to one or more other phases. For example, phase 1 findings are obviously used to address theological research questions flowing from the statement of the problem. However, they *also*:

- Inform to some extent the scope of library research in phase 2 (and vice versa).
- Inform to some extent the content of phase 3 methodology (e.g., the content of a ministry-centered questionnaire).
- Contribute to the integrative synthesis that characterizes phase 4.

This synergistic interaction ought to characterize each new phase of research, culminating in the integrative phase 4.

CONCISE SUMMARY OF THE FOUR-PHASE RESEARCH PROCESS

These four phases define the essence of interdisciplinary missiological research. The table presented on the following page summarizes what is accomplished by each research task and each phase of such an interdisciplinary investigation.

The overarching goal in all research phases, steps, and activities is the resolution of the research problem.[2] If the research problem can be definitively resolved, the study itself will be judged a success. And findings from a successful study can be published for the benefit of both the academy and the Church, influencing the future activities of both.

(Developmental Task) Phase of Research	Basic Question	What It Identifies	Tools and Resources	Characterized By
Topic	What is my general area of interest?	The general focus / scope of the study	• Missiological engagement • The literature • Felt need/curiosity	Brevity and clarity
Problem (Statement of)	What do I not know now?	The hole ("lacuna") in the body of: • theory & praxis knowledge (PhD) • praxis knowledge (DMiss)	• Critical thinking • Self-editing skills • Critical review by others	Precision in wording, resulting in a carefully crafted sentence; researchable in scope
Purpose (Statement of)	Why am I seeking to resolve the problem	Motivation for pursuing the study: • missiological motivation • personal motivation	• Critical thinking • Prayer • Personal and ministry reflection	Personal passion mixed with missional intent, academic rigor, and intellectual honesty
Phase 1: Biblical/theological literature review, plus exegesis	What does God say about the topic? [Discovering what is true, in the process of resolving one or more research questions]	Insights and findings from the biblical and theological literature germane to the problem	• EBSCO/ATLAS • Google Scholar • Original language tools	Best practice in library research, biblical exegesis and theological reflection

---

2. The statement of the problem is typically introduced in the first chapter of the dissertation or project, or early in an academic journal article.

(Developmental Task) Phase of Research	Basic Question	What It Identifies	Tools and Resources	Characterized By
Phase 2: Social science literature review	What have social scientists written about the topic? [Discovering what is already known about the people/context being studied, in the process of resolving one or more research questions]	Insights and findings from the social science literature germane to the problem (and to the research methodology needed to resolve it)	• EBSCO/ATLAS • Google Scholar • Internet (e.g., Electronic Theses and Dissertations [ETD's] information databases)	Best practice in library research, identifying and critically interacting with all relevant social science content and methodology
Phase 3: Empirical (field) research	What can I learn about the topic? [Discovering what no one knows about the people/context being studied, in the process of resolving one or more research questions]	Insights and findings from original (i.e., "dirty") data generated by original empirical research	Established qualitative / quantitative methods identified in phase 2*	Best practice in unbiased (valid and reliable) empirical investigation
Phase 4: Integrative reflection	What can I conclude from my interdisciplinary investigation?	The missiological and ecclesiastical significance of the entire study	• Critical thinking skills • Prayer and meditation • Critical review by others	• Integrative insights • Recommendations for future research • impact on the writer

The *content* of phase 3 research will normally be informed by the results of phases 1 and 2, while the *methodology* used in phase 3 will be largely informed by the results of phase 2.

REFERENCES AND RESOURCES FOR ADDITIONAL READING

Creswell, John W. 2008. *Research Design: Qualitative, Quantitative, and Mixed Methods Approaches.* 3rd ed. Thousand Oaks, CA: Sage Publications.

Creswell, John W., and Vicki Plano Clark, eds. 2008. *Designing and Conducting Mixed Methods Research*. 2nd ed. Thousand Oaks, CA: Sage Publications.

Hermans, Chris A. M., and Mary E. Moore, eds. 2004. *Hermeneutics and Empirical Research in Practical Theology: The Contribution of Empirical Theology by Johannes A. van der Ven*. Leiden: Brill.

Lattuca, Lisa R. 2001. *Creating Interdisciplinarity: Interdisciplinary Research and Teaching among College and University Faculty*. Nashville, TN: Vanderbilt University Press.

Leedy, Paul, and Jeanne Ormrod. 2009. *Practical Research: Planning and Design*. 9th ed. Upper Saddle River, NJ: Prentice Hall.

Tashakkori, Abbas, and Charles B. Teddlie. 2010. *SAGE Handbook of Mixed Methods in Social & Behavioral Research*. 2nd ed. Thousand Oaks, CA: Sage Publications.

WEBSITES OF INTEREST

Research Proposal Guide
> http://researchproposalguide.com/

University of Minnesota: The Graduate School-Writing and Research Support:
> http://www.grad.umn.edu/gradwriting/writingandresearch.html

JOURNAL ARTICLE WITH ABSTRACT

Johnson, R. Burke, and Anthony J. Onwuegbuzie. 2004. Mixed Methods Research: A Research Paradigm Whose Time has Come. *Educational Researcher* 33, no. 7: 14–26. doi: 10.3102/0013189X033007014v.

The purposes of this article are to position mixed methods research (*mixed research* is a synonym) as the natural complement to traditional qualitative and quantitative research, to present pragmatism as offering an attractive philosophical partner for mixed methods research, and to provide a framework for designing and conducting mixed methods research. In doing this, we briefly review the paradigm "wars" and incompatibility thesis, we show some commonalities between quantitative and qualitative research, we explain the tenets of pragmatism, we explain the fundamental principle of mixed research and how to apply it, we provide specific sets of designs for the two major types of mixed methods research (*mixed-model* designs and *mixed-method* designs), and, finally, we explain mixed methods research as following (recursively) an eight-step process. A key feature of mixed methods research is its methodological pluralism or eclecticism, which frequently results in superior research (compared to monomethod research). Mixed methods research will be successful as more investigators study and help advance its concepts and as they regularly practice it.

5

THE FOUR-PHASE MODEL IN ACADEMIC CONTEXT

Marvin Gilbert, EdD

The four-phase model of interdisciplinary research can be employed in a variety of missiological and ministerial research contexts, including the research required by postgraduate degree programs. In this chapter, the model is graphically applied to the requirements of the Doctor of Missiology[1] project. The model's details, presented in Appendix 2, can easily be adapted to the requirements of any interdisciplinary dissertation, thesis, or project.

THE FOUR-PHASE MODEL ORGANIZED BY PROJECT CHAPTERS

Each of the four phases informs the content of at least one chapter in a missiological dissertation or doctoral project. Given the unique nature of each interdiscipinary study, determining in advance the exact number of chapters is not possible.

Chapter 1. Chapter 1 contains many of the details first presented in the research proposal or prospectus. Of central importance is the presentation of the study's (1) topic, (2) statement of purpose, (3) statement of the problem, and (4) research questions.[2] These key statements are supplemented by statements of the study's limitations, delimitations, assumptions, and definitions.

Chapters reporting phase 1 and 2 research. In the next two or more chapters, the results of phase 1 and phase 2 research are presented. These chapters may be organized by phase number (e.g., chapter 2 reports the results of phase 1 research; chapter 3 reports the results of phase 2.) Alternatively, the writer may prefer to organize those chapters creatively by

---

1. Or Doctor of Applied Intercultural Studies (or related degrees) like offered by the Assemblies of God Theological Seminary in Springfield, Missouri.

2. The research questions could include (or be replaced by) qualitative or quantitative hypotheses.

major topics that emerge during the library research. In any case, the number of chapters, two minimum, associated with research in phases 1 and 2 should reflect the study's breadth of scope and complexity.

Chapters reporting phase 3 research. These chapters, normally two, center on the empirical research phase of the study. Typically, the first of these chapters describes the research methodology used to capture the data needed to resolve the research questions associated with phase 3. The second chapter presents the data generated and discusses the findings. The data-analysis techniques used may vary widely; they are primarily differentiated by the qualitative or quantitative nature of the data and the software packages utilized. If the findings are extensive or particularly complex, more than one chapter may be required.

The final chapter. The final chapter in the project is typically the product of phase 4 research. Phase 4 is a highly inductive process in which data generated by phases 1, 2 and 3 are analyzed from an interdisciplinary perspective. This chapter presents a creatively organized, integrative conclusion. It is the most difficult chapter to write; its content cannot easily be described prior to the writing process. This observation notwithstanding, the chapter should contain (1) an overview of the findings from phases 1 through 3, (2) a synthesis guided by critical thinking, (3) recommendations for the Church, mission, school or other institution, and (4) recommendations to the academy for future research. Normally all this information can be presented in a single chapter.[3]

ARROWS AND THE FOUR-PHASE MODEL

The graphic image presented in Appendix 2 contains a number of solid and dashed arrows. Each style of arrow represents a unique process within a given phase of research. The purpose of the various arrows is intended to be self-evident in the context of the model. Even so, a brief overview may be helpful to the reader.

Solid black arrows. Solid black arrows extend downward from the "Statement of the Problem" box to the three "Research Question(s)" boxes.

---

3. Should the presentation of two chapters seem advantageous, the writer should feel free to develop them.

These arrows indicate that all research questions grow out of the problem statement.[4]

Solid gray arrows. The 75%, 50%, and 25% gray *solid* arrows extending upward represent research activities in phases 1, 2, and 3, respectively. These arrows represent activity focused on resolving one or more research questions. When extended downward, the gray arrows represent the writing activity needed to produce the various chapters in the project.

Dotted gray arrows. The 75%, 50%, and 25% gray *dotted* arrows extending upward from the three "Research Question(s)" boxes represent the data that emerge from the first three phases of research:

1. 75% gray represents the biblical-theological data produced in phase 1.
2. 50% gray represents previously published findings from the social science literature generated and summarized in phase 2.
3. 25% gray symbolizes the new empirical data generated in phase 3.

Note that all three types of data then contribute to the final chapter: the product of phase 4's integrative analysis and reflection.

THE LIBRARY AND THE LIBRARY "ANNEX"

A unique feature of the graphic model (in Appendix 2) is the crucial role played by the library. All activity in phases 1 and 2 take place within the library. The biblical and theological collections of the library[5] traditionally are in their own section of the library, while the social science collections are usually designated in a different section of the library.

Synergistic interaction between the both sections of the library (i.e., these two disciplines), and ultimately other disciplines as well, should characterize library research. For example, a phase-2 researcher (in the social science section of the library) might discover that a lack of forgiveness is associated with mental illness among a given people group. That discovery should lead the research back to the biblical-theological section

---

4. In essence, all four phases of the research model introduced in the preceding chapter "hang" on the problem statement. The resolution of the problem is the goal of all research activities.

5. The library's collection, as envisioned by this model of research, extends to the wealth of information available on the internet.

of the library—back to phase 1 research—to discover what Scripture says about a lack of forgiveness. Similarly, a study of hope in the New Testament should lead the researcher back to the other section to discover what social and medical scientists have reported about the role of hope within the various institutions of society.

The library "annex," an extension of the biblical-theological section of the library, is the "venue" for original exegetical and theological research. In the annex, a phase 1 researcher goes beyond the limits of conventional literature searches and reviews. Original research occurs in the library annex, research on par with the empirical research conducted in phase 3. The separate solid red arrow passing through the library annex graphically represents the importance of this research; its contribution to problem-resolution is significant. No interdisciplinary study is complete without this original exegetical investigation and theological reflection. Research in the annex is essential.

REFERENCES AND RESOURCES FOR ADDITIONAL STUDY

Academic Coach. *21 Dissertation Tips.* http://successfulacademic.typepad .com/successful_academic_tips/2005/11/dissertation_ti.html.

Batacan, John Matthew. 2010. "The Experience of Wellness During the Dissertation Process of Recent PhD Graduates: A Heuristic Study." PhD diss., University of Idaho.

Bloomberg, Linda D., and Marie F. Volpe, eds. 2008. *Completing Your Qualitative Dissertation: A Roadmap from Beginning to End.* Annotated ed. Thousand Oaks, CA: Sage Publications.

The Education Dissertation: A Guide for Practitioner Scholars. Thousand Oaks, CA: Corwin Press.

Single, Peg Boyle. 2009. *Demystifying Dissertation Writing: A Streamlined Process from Choice of Topic to Final Text.* Herndon, VA: Stylus Publishing.

WEBSITES OF INTEREST

Dissertation Planning and Writing
    http://dissta.com/
Writing and Presenting Your Thesis or Dissertation
    http://www.learnerassociates.net/dissthes/

JOURNAL ARTICLE WITH ABSTRACT

Blum, Lawrence D. 2010. The "All-but-the-Dissertation Student and the Psychology of the Doctoral Dissertation." *Journal of College Student Psychotherapy* 24, no. 2: 74–85.

Completion of the dissertation is an important milestone and often a major obstacle for PhD candidates, some of whom become and remain all-but-the-dissertation students. All-but-the-dissertation students usually disappoint both themselves and their departments. Thus, it is important to understand the psychology of the dissertation. A review of doctoral dissertations on the topic of dissertation completion is followed by a discussion of developmental conflicts that frequently influence dissertation difficulties and then a presentation of the dynamic psychotherapy of a patient struggling to complete a dissertation. Problems in both external reality and internal fantasy are noted. The importance of understanding specific developmental conflicts and individual dynamics in treatment of this population is emphasized.

6
THE LIBRARY IN INTERDISCIPLINARY RESEARCH
Content and Methodology

Beth Grant, PhD

The significance of the library in interdisciplinary research cannot be overemphasized. Other scholars will eventually ask a researcher how his or her research contributes to the academy. By initially investing time and effort in thorough interdisciplinary library research, the researcher will know where his or her work fits into the corpus of the literature and why. That knowledge will strategically inform the entire project.

CONTENT: WHAT TO LOOK FOR IN THE LIBRARY RESEARCH PROCESS[1]

For a novice interdisciplinary researcher, both the library and associated research processes may seem overwhelming, leading to the question, "Where do I start?" Librarians and service staff may not be able to answer to that question, since library training has traditionally been based on cataloguing by academic disciplines, not topics.[2] A novice researcher who is not yet sure how to frame the relevant questions may be unable to effectively communicate what he or she actually needs.[3]

This chapter focuses first on the kinds of resources available in the library and their specific contributions to interdisciplinary research. This information is summarized in the subsequent table, followed by guidelines for library research, with basic steps for the process.

---

1. See chapter 4 titled, "The Four-Phase Model of Missiological Research," especially phases 1 and 2: both are library-centered.

2. Witt and Rudasill noted the need for more interdisciplinary training for library service staff in order to re-think research and better serve researchers working across disciplines (2010, 40).

3. See Case's "Taylor's Typology of Information Needs" regarding how library researchers frame their questions of library staff in asking for help (2007, 72).

RESOURCES AND STRATEGIES FOR SUCCESSFUL LIBRARY RESEARCH

Before beginning library research, a scholar should clearly identify the central research problem. Otherwise, library research can be confusing, wasting both time and energy on non-essential—even irrelevant—activities. A precisely articulated research problem provides the essential "road-map" for strategic library research.

Category of Library Resources *	Value to Interdisciplinary Research
Books	• Provide more context, background, and history than articles: A good starting point • Sources for theory and concepts on which research may build across disciplines • Kinds: scholarly books, monographs, reports of major research studies, chapters by recognized scholar-researchers on topic
Journal Articles	• Periodical literature and journals publish scholarly research findings • Sources for more recent scholarly studies • Help develop lists of relevant sources
Professional Data Bases	• Cross-academic disciplines • Keywords to classify may change when crossing disciplines (use subject headings) • Examples: ERIC, EBSCO, Academic Search Complete, H-NET, JSTOR, ATLA
Scholarly Research Papers	• Dissertations • Government documents • Professional academic papers

* See chapter 7 titled, "Social Science Resources for Enriching the Literature Review."

Three possible strategies to library-research navigation as described by Repko (2008, 31–32):

1. Traditional keyword searching method. This method typically includes the options of entering the author, title, other keyword or subject. If an author or title are not known, keywords or subject can be used; these will yield multiple "hits." The researcher can then examine the resources based on both the relevance to the problem and the academic discipline(s) represented.

2. Boolean search strategy. This approach is helpful in narrowing the number of relevant options when the keyword

approach yields a large number of hits. The Boolean search strategy refines and limits the search through "and", "or" and "not." The basic Boolean formula is:

_____ *(search term)* and _____ *(search term)* and (or)
_____ *(search term)*

Using the word "not" in the formula allows the researcher to glean even more precise results.

3. Federated searching approach. This strategy is especially effective for interdisciplinary library research, as it allows access to multiple databases in a single key-stroke. Instead of logging into multiple databases, the library researcher must only open or log into one (the federated search tool), construct one search, and evaluate one set of results.

SPECIFIC STEPS IN SUCCESSFUL LIBRARY RESEARCH

A researcher should begin by reading sources that provide a broad overview of the problem to determine if sufficient literature exists to justify further inquiry. While narrowing the search for relevant resources, the interdisciplinary researcher must intentionally select sources from several disciplines. Maintaining an interdisciplinary perspective on the literature does not happen without this commitment.

Resources that address the topic in a cursory way have some value. Cursory references provide linkages to other disciplinary theories and concepts. These, in turn, can lead to interdisciplinary insights for the researcher and enrich the final literature review.

As the researcher continues to read, he or she must begin organizing pertinent information and insights distilled from the literature. This organization should make the information easily accessible as the research process continues. In particular, the following relevant information should be recorded for each source chosen: (1) author's name and publication date, (2) disciplinary perspective reflected in the work, (3) pertinent insight(s) and seminal quotations, (4) theory employed in the work, (5) the research method used, (6) the kind of data reported by author to support findings, and (7) the author's epistemology.

The interdisciplinary researcher's goal in library research is not to amass the largest possible quantity of sources. It focuses, rather, on the quality and relevance of the sources chosen, in light of the research problem. The ability to accurately assess resource quality and determine significance across several disciplines develops slowly; it requires a substantive amount of time given to the process of interdisciplinary library research. The skill to discern what information is most appropriate and most relevant comes with practice.[4]

INTERDISCIPLINARY INFORMATION-SEEKING SKILLS FOR LIBRARY RESEARCH

Recent studies have documented that researchers have difficulties accessing needed information when they are investigating outside their primary field of study. O'Connor and Newby (2011, 224–29) investigated the research needs and behaviors of interdisciplinary researchers for the purpose of developing an information literacy course for interdisciplinary graduate students. They identified and documented specific information-seeking needs and behaviors that characterize interdisciplinary researchers.[5]

Some skills needed by both disciplinary and interdisciplinary library researchers are similar. Interdisciplinary researchers, however, require more time in the library in order master the skills unique to each discipline. They must also gather more information to provide a substantial literature foundation for their topic. Being aware of these distinctive factors can enhance the success of novice interdisciplinary researchers and minimize the impact of the potentially paralyzing question, "Where do I start?"

REFERENCES AND RESOURCES FOR ADDITIONAL READING

Case, Donald Owen. 2007. *Looking for Information: A Survey of Research on Information Seeking, Needs and Behavior.* 2nd ed. London: Academic Press.

---

4. Case (2007, 8) argued that simply gathering information in research does not necessarily lead to being an informed researcher, as there is no shortage of information.

5. See Appendix 3, "Interdisciplinary Researchers' Needs and Behaviors."

Creswell, John W. 2009. *Research Design: Qualitative, Quantitative, and Mixed Methods Approaches*. 3rd ed. Thousand Oaks, CA: Sage Publications.

O'Connor, Lisa, and Jill Newby. 2011. "Entering Unfamiliar Territory: Building an Information Literacy Course for Graduate Students in Interdisciplinary Areas." *Reference & User Services Quarterly* 50, no. 3: 224–29. http://blog.rusq.org/wp-content/uploads/2011/04/Information-Lit.pdf (accessed September 24, 2011).

Repko, Allen F. 2008. *Interdisciplinary Research: Process and Theory*. Thousand Oaks, CA: Sage Publications.

Witt, Steven W., and Lynne M. Rudasill, eds. 2010. *Social Science Libraries: Interdisciplinary Collections, Services, Networks*. The Hague: International Federation and Library Associations and Institutions.

WEBSITES OF INTEREST

Association of College and Research Libraries
        http://www.ala.org/ala/mgrps/divs/acrl/index.cfm
Association of Research Librarians
        http://www.arl.org/
Journal of Librarianship and Information Science (Articles reflect the most recent issues and developments in the field of library science)
        http://lis.sagepub.com/

JOURNAL ARTICLE WITH ABSTRACT

Newell, William H. 2007. "Interdisciplinary Research and Writing: A Guide." *Issues in Integrative Studies* 25: 84–110. http://www.units.muohio.edu /aisorg/PUBS/ISSUES/25_newell.pdf (accessed October 19, 2011).

This article examines the current challenges of library-based interdisciplinary research and writing within the larger context of the theory and practice of interdisciplinarity. Based upon experience with college seniors researching and writing year-long interdisciplinary projects and informed by the literatures on library science and interdisciplinary studies, the essay identifies the underlying sources of those challenges, the implications for the teaching of interdisciplinary subjects, and the consequences for inter-disciplinary scholarship at a critical time in the maturation of the field. The paper employs a pragmatic approach informed by the foundational literature of the field.

7
SOCIAL SCIENCE RESOURCES FOR ENRICHING THE LITERATURE REVIEW

Marvin Gilbert, EdD

A literature review is foundational to research reports, including theses, dissertations, and doctoral projects. It tells the reader what has been (1) discovered in previous investigations, and (2) accepted as the theoretical and philosophical underpinnings on a topic. In short, a well-written literature review gives the reader a working understanding about a given area of research.

Equally important, a well-crafted literature review allows the reader to grasp easily where the "hole" is in the body of knowledge. A study presented to the academy is justified, in part, if the researcher is able to say, with support from the literature, "We know these things from previous studies, but we do not know about *this* area or issue."[1]

TWO CHARACTERISTICS OF AN ADEQUATE LITERATURE REVIEW

Two characteristics, among others, describe in general terms an adequate literature review in most graduate academic contexts. Not included are the quality of the writing, the referencing, and the formatting, all of which contribute to the perceived adequacy of a literature review. The emphasis here is on the scope of the review and the depth and breadth of the sources reviewed.

Scope. Generally, literature reviews for masters' theses are required to be *complete* or *comprehensive*. Enough of the precedent literature is reviewed to create a clear understanding of the field (sub-discipline) and unique topic the thesis is exploring. In contrast, literature reviews for doctoral dissertations should be *exhaustive*. The researcher explores the topic in

---

1. This general rule excludes the rarely executed replication studies, a principle of good science that is—perhaps unfortunately—rarely practiced in the real world of research.

great depth; the review is broad enough to demonstrate complete mastery of the literature.

Variety of media types. As students advance through increasingly challenging degree programs, they learn how to interact with sophisticated scholarly research. Emerging researchers find that book-dominated literature reviews are inadequate. Attempts to comprehend the current state of the literature using only textbooks are doomed, no matter how recent their copyright dates.[2] The delay between writing a chapter and having the entire book published is often three to five years. Textbooks summarize a given topic well, but their content is always somewhat—not reflecting the cutting edge in a given discipline. Thus, a comprehensive and balanced literature review must rely on information extracted from the following list of scholarly media:

- Scholarly books. Books are the most common citation in pre-doctoral literature reviews.
- Scholarly journals.[3] These are often the source of the most current information, and the most thoroughly screened or reviewed information.
- Websites of professional organizations and related resources. These web sites offer unique sources of information, often including current research reports and theoretical articles.[4]
- Discipline-specific dictionaries. These reference resources offer a rich source of information for those seeking to define unique terms and grasp their significance within a given discipline. Appendix 5 lists discipline-specific dictionaries of interest to missiologists.
- Discipline-specific encyclopedias and other reserve-collection resources (e.g., academic yearbooks, monograph collections). In many cases, these under-utilized works are

---

2. This is especially true of those fields dependent upon empirical research. Such fields are dynamic; the current state of knowledge remains in flux.

3. These are sometimes called "academic" journals because the articles published in them are being presented to the academy. The journals themselves are often published by research universities.

4. See Appendix 4 for websites of particular interest to Pentecostal researchers; note especially the site for the Society for Pentecostal Studies.

a rich source of information about the theories, general findings, and influential people in a discipline.[5]

- Electronic theses and dissertations. Many universities now offer open access to their electronic theses (masters-level) and dissertations (doctoral-level) collections (ETDs). Finding a recently published dissertation on a topic related to one's research is a gift![6]

Appendix 8, "Sources of Quotable / Citable Information for Post-graduate Scholars," presents a quick-reference guide for sources that are citable in a reference list.

OPEN-ACCESS JOURNALS

Scholarly open-access (O-A) journals are available free online. The primary advantage of O-A publishing is that the content is available to readers everywhere with minimum delay; no affiliation with an academic library is required. This advantage benefits both authors and readers.

Major directories of O-A journals have emerged recently, notably the *Directory of Open Access Journals* (DOAJ) and the *Open J-Gate*. Each has its own standards and procedures for listing journals. Articles in the major O-A journals are included in the standard bibliographic databases for their subject. As a quick indicator of how rapidly peer-reviewed O-A journals have grown, on May 22, 2011, the number listed in the DOAJ was 6,523. Listed in the table below is sample of the O-A journals presented in Appendix 9.[7]

Asian Journal of Pentecostal Studies	ttp://www.apts.edu/index.cfm?menuid=94&parentid=54
Journal of Religion and Popular Culture	http://www.usask.ca/relst/jrpc/
Research and Practice in Human Resource Management	http://www.usask.ca/relst/jrpc/

---

5. See Appendix 6 for a list of discipline-specific encyclopedias of interest to missiologists.

6. See Appendix 7 for a list of universities and portals offering searchable ETD collections.

7. See Appendix 9 for a more extensive list of O-A journals of interest to missiologists.

Cyber Journal for Pentecostal-Charismatic Research	http://www.pctii.org/cyberj/
Current Issues in Comparative Education	http://www.tc.columbia.edu/cice/index.html

Almost all academic disciplines have launched their own journals. In many fields, such as higher education, multiple journals now exist for publishing research. In fact, the growth of some O-A journals was directly linked to the frustration experienced by scholars unable to publish their research. Responding to this frustration, institutions, universities, and professional organizations began launching new journals, often the O-A type.

DISCIPLINE-SPECIFIC DICTIONARIES AND ENCYCLOPEDIAS

Discipline-specific dictionaries and encyclopedias merit special discussion in the context of developing exhaustive literature reviews. Unused by most undergraduate students, these reference works offer unique definitions and discipline-rich overviews of key topics, personalities, theories, and (in some cases) synopses of the current state of research and knowledge.

As an example of the usefulness of such resources, the *Encyclopedia of Social and Cultural Anthropology* (Barnard and Spencer) defines unique terms such as "French anthropology," "Malinowski," "cultural materialism," and "shamanism." As defined in this work, these terms include valuable insights and quotable information not found in most standard dictionaries. The researcher struggling to locate pivotal definitions in the literature should begin with a dictionary that is truly capable of defining them. This saves the researcher valuable time and energy.

REFERENCES AND RESOURCES FOR ADDITIONAL READING

Bailey, Jr., Charles W. 2010. *Transforming Scholarly Publishing Through Open Access: A Bibliography.* Seattle, WA: Create Space.

Galvan, Jose L. 2015. *Writing Literature Reviews: A Guide for Students of the Social and Behavioral Sciences.* 6th ed. Glendale CA: Pyrszak Publishing.

LEADERSHIP WEBSITES OF INTEREST: EXAMPLE OF DISCIPLINE-SPECIFIC WEB RESOURCES

Center for Creative Leadership
        http://www.ccl.org/leadership/
Educational leadership resources
        http://coe.fgcu.edu/faculty/valesky/links.html
The Greenleaf Center for Servant Leadership
        http://www.greenleaf.org/

JOURNAL ARTICLE WITH ABSTRACT

Craig, Iain D., Andrew M. Plume, Marie E. McVeigh, James Pringle, and Mayur Amin. 2007. "Do Open Access Articles Have Greater Citation Impact?: A Critical Review of the Literature." *Journal of Informetrics* 1: 239–48. doi: 10.1016/j.joi.2007.04.001.

The last few years have seen the emergence of several open access options in scholarly communication which can broadly be grouped into two areas referred to as "gold" and "green" open access (OA). In this article we review the literature examining the relationship between OA status and citation counts of scholarly articles. Early studies showed a correlation between the free online availability or OA status of articles and higher citation counts, and implied causality without due consideration of potential confounding factors. More recent investigations have dissected the nature of the relationship between article OA status and citations. Three non-exclusive postulates have been proposed to account for the observed citation differences between OA and non-OA articles: an open access postulate, a selection bias postulate, and an early view postulate. The most rigorous study to date (in condensed matter physics) showed that, after controlling for the early view postulate, the remaining difference in citation counts between OA and non-OA articles is explained by the selection bias postulate. No evidence was found to support the OA postulate per se; i.e. article OA status alone has little or no effect on citations. Further studies using a similarly rigorous approach are required to determine the generality of this finding.

8

PRIMARY AND SECONDARY SOURCES

Charles E. Self, PhD

This chapter introduces the types of materials demanded by interdisciplinary research, with an emphasis on historical inquiry. It also offers some insights on how a cohesive analysis emerges—although no published work is exhaustive—even if the task is tiring. Choices must be made, and some information invariably remains at the archaeological dig, the archival bin or obscure library, or buried as the millionth listing in the Google index. Selectivity is essential, and is not to be equated with subjectivity. If it were, all history would be mere chronicle and compilation.

In light of this, it is important to recognize that vast amounts of data are available via the internet and other media. However, neither the historical accuracy nor the trenchant analysis of this data are guaranteed. Researchers must be able to weigh the relative value of these materials, eventually deciding to include or exclude them from the resultant study. In particular, interdisciplinary researchers access input from widely divergent fields, including archaeology, anthropology, biological science, psychometrics, sociology, history and other disciplines. What all of these have in common is the availability of primary and secondary documents.

Primary and secondary documents are technical terms, not descriptions of relative worth. In historical research, thorough secondary narratives close to events may be more germane to the subject than bits and pieces of knowledge emerging from primary sources. Integrity in research demands consideration of all relevant sources. Historical researchers, in particular, must demonstrate a willingness to adjust their guiding hypotheses and, in humility, hear from other experts in the field, even while forging new insights for the discipline.

SOURCE SELECTIVITY IS ESSENTIAL

The key to historical inquiry is reasonable breadth and depth, combined with a consideration for all major perspectives. For example, the history of missions in nineteenth-century Belgian Congo must include the narratives of missionaries, public documents, journals of the oppressor and oppressed, and a host of other available evidence. Combined, these sources can paint a picture of the complex cultural, economic, religious, and political realities of this tragic period. Notice the assessment term, "tragic," in the previous sentence. This term is carefully chosen after years of research on the topic, including an evaluation of the narratives of Belgian, Congolese, and third-party observers. Some materials from this era extol the benighted rule of King Leopold II and the economic benefits to Belgian citizens (along with the privilege of the Congolese becoming "civilized" through their laborious servitude). However, the evaluations of most historians unveil a complex set of narratives punctuated by prophetic calls by missionaries for justice.

In the following sections, brief descriptions of primary and secondary documents are offered, along with insights for their incorporation into research and writing. Much historical work is tedious. In the midst of the necessary data mining, however, veins of "gold" are occasionally unearthed, yielding new understanding.

What surprises many newer scholars are the commonalities of human persons and societies across time. From within a wide range of societies, scholars discover art, family, religion, social order, food gathering, cultivation, tool-making, and other modes of existence with commonalities in regards to all humanity. Solid research also reveals (1) the extent to which human societies advance and decline, and (2) evidence that political, social and technological advances can be arrested and subverted. Simply put, human history is complex! This is why books are published on the same persons or subjects as new information comes to light with new insights or perspectives.

DISTINGUISHING PRIMARY AND SECONDARY SOURCES

Many historical materials are a mixture of primary and secondary material. An eyewitness account of an event as it unfolds (primary) may contain interpretive elements and personal judgments (secondary material). The following is a definition accepted in most academic circles. It is a summation of several published definitions:

> Primary sources are artifacts, texts, and other materials that were created during the era under study. Secondary sources are created after the events and contain more interpretive elements. These secondary sources become works consulted by other interpreters.

Primary materials

Primary source materials can be classified in one of seven distinct categories:

1. Audio, video, and written journals concomitant with events
2. Autobiographies, oral histories, testimonies, interviews
3. Transcriptions of interviews with participants in the events under study
4. Relevant archival materials contemporaneous to the events
5. Records, statistics, and surveys by public and private agencies
6. Documents that were socially important
7. Other items that place the learner in the contemporaneous timeframe.

Secondary materials

These source materials are also diverse:

1. Biographies, narratives, and other written accounts composed later than the events themselves
2. Interpretive reports concerning statistics and trends
3. Archaeological materials[1]
4. Later fictional and non-fictional writings that describe and interpret the events and issues under study.

---

1. If they can be dated with precision, archeological materials become primary sources.

THE IMPORTANCE, RELIABILITY, AND SUBSTANCE OF HISTORICAL MATERIALS

No human being is a completely unbiased observer; however, careful evaluation of the nature of the accounts and the method used to collect the data will increase the account's reliability. For example, transcripts of interviews conducted within hours or days of an event may vary from testimonies—legal or personal—given months or years after. This does not mean the later accounts are unreliable. Still, the longer the time gap is between the event and record of it, the greater the opportunity for interpretive issues to influence the narrative. In contrast, immediate impressions can be affected by predispositions, impact-shock, and other factors. This is why multiple sources are invaluable.

The veracity and significance of a particular event increases with multiple attestations by primary and secondary sources. Sometimes a lone observation of narrative can transform understanding. For such to happen, however, that observation must be at least indirectly verified by other data and narratives. Discovering new sources is both a painstaking and rewarding work. If the subject is a newer one, or the hypothesis has never been tested, the need for fresh sources increases. Sometimes the same material seen with "new eyes" produces breakthroughs in understanding.

As all historical material is evaluated, the honest scholar keeps the two horizons of knowledge in perspective. The first is the epistemological framework of the participants themselves. The second is the researcher's personal context and motives. With a solid literature review complete and awareness of primary sources available, the diligent inquirer can reasonably hope to unveil solid knowledge and develop meaningful analysis built on facts rather than mere supposition.

REFERENCES AND RESOURCES FOR ADDITIONAL STUDY[2]

Galgano, Michael J., J. Chris Arndt, and Raymond M. Hyser. 2013. *Doing History: Research and Writing in the Digital Age.* Boston, MA: Cengage Learning.

---

2. Historical research is treasure hunting with purpose. It is an opportunity to align events, information, people, and movements and then see processes that yield insights. We can research with integrity, though we will never exhaust the

Iggers, Georg G. 2005. *Historiography in the Twentieth Century: From Scientific Objectivity to the Postmodern Challenge.* 2nd ed. Middletown, CT: Wesleyan University Press.

Rosenthal, Joel T. 2001. *Understanding Medieval Primary Sources: Using Historical Sources to Discover Medieval Europe.* New York, NY: Routledge. (an exemplary text)

WEBSITES OF INTEREST

University of Illinois. Finding Secondary Sources
    www.library.illinois
    .edu/ugl/secondarysources.html
Virginia Tech University. Primary, Secondary and Tertiary Resources
    www.lib.vt.edu/help/research/primary-secondary-tertiary.html
Yale University. Primary Sources
    www.yale.edu/collectionscollaborative/primarysources/
    primarysources.html.

---

information available. The aim is representative material, not every scrap of possibly relevant data. The following is a select list of places beyond libraries and research institutes where treasures are found:

Civic/government record offices—local and national. These can be challenging, but if you have relationships with locals and communicate your positive aims, historical documents can be forthcoming.

University archives can have a wide array of holdings for research.

Religious community records—churches, temples, mosques and synagogues are often repositories of history.

Cultural centers—they have beautiful front rooms and even more extensive back rooms.

Museums have curators and scholars that will share insights and materials with qualified colleagues.

Headquarters of political parties contain surprising amounts of information.

Denominational leaders and offices are great sources of oral and written records.

Leading local and national oral historians, elders, and experienced leaders will open new vistas through effective interviewing.

Alliances, networks, and other agencies that promote cooperation—both public and private—will often have valuable records.

JOURNAL ARTICLE WITH ABSTRACT

Cannadine, David. 2002. "Perspectives: One Hundred Years of History in Britain."
    www.history.ac.uk/makinghistory/resources/articles/making_history.html
    (accessed April 25, 2014).

This article began as one of the lectures to celebrate the hundredth anniversary of the founding of the British Academy, which was delivered at the University of Sheffield on 14 March 2002 by the author. [Cannadine contends that the last half of the twentieth century is the greatest period of history writing ever.]

9

INTEGRATIVE CRITICAL ANALYSIS

Marvin Gilbert, EdD

A METHODOLOGICAL LACUNA: A NOUN IS NOT A VERB

Research methodologies do not exist in an investigative vacuum; they exist only to generate the data needed to answer or resolve research questions.[1] This principle applies even to those research questions focused on the precedent literature.

In the case of fresh empirical and even exegetical-theological research, the link between research question[2] and research method must be clear and well supported by the methodological literature. This question-method linkage vanishes, however, when a researcher tries to explain how he or she will answer a research question focused on the precedent literature.

The topics addressed in literature-focused research questions may be quite varied: from contemporary views of prosperity to the colonial history of a South American people group. A skilled interaction with a relevant body of literature is clearly required to answer such questions. The resulting literature review is, however, a *product* of inquiry, not the *method* of inquiry. Stated differently, a literature review is a noun, not a verb. What, then, is the verb? What research method can produce a well-crafted and comprehensive literature review?

Several useful texts inform researchers about literature reviews, describing a variety of activities and strategies.[3] These texts do not, however, identify a specific method of inquiry; a methodological lacuna exists in both theological and empirical research texts. This chapter attempts to address this lacuna by proposing the phrase "integrative critical analysis"

---

1. And hypotheses in the case of quantitative research.
2. Or hypothesis.
3. See, for example, the sources listed under References and Resources for Additional Reading.

(ICA) as a methodological framework for those activities and strategies needed to produce a credible review of precedent literature.

INTEGRATIVE CRITICAL ANALYSIS AND QUALITATIVE META-ANALYSIS

This previously unnamed research method has a solid foundation in the research literature. *Quantitative* researchers, particularly in the hard sciences such as medicine and biochemistry, use meta-analysis to reexamine a given stream of quantitative research over several years. The objective of a *quantitative* meta-analysis is to "summarize the results of multiple studies," typically combining the quantitative data reported in a plethora of small-sample studies to generate statistically supported trends (Walker, Hernandez, and Kattan 2008, 431).

Meta-analysis has also been applied to *qualitative* data reported in a large group of studies on the same topic.[4] Inductive reasoning and well-established methods of qualitative analysis, rather than statistical analysis, informs this method of inquiry. Essentially ICA facilitates an *interdisciplinary* qualitative meta-analysis of the precedent literature, challenging the researcher to summarize synergistically and strategically what a diverse collection of scholars have discovered and reported to the academy.

INTEGRATIVE: KNOWLEDGE SEGREGATION IS NOT ALLOWED

A missiological researcher must master the literature generated within multiple disciplines. He or she will initially apply ICA to one discipline: perhaps the discipline representing the researcher's greatest strength in previous graduate training. Even *within a single discipline*, however, the precedent literature contains divergent opinions, schools of thought, theologies or philosophies, and biases. By applying ICA, a researcher can develop a comprehensive understanding of that single body of knowledge.

The primary strength of ICA, however, lies in the integration of the findings reported in *multiple* bodies of knowledge. Gestalt psychologists assert that the whole is greater than the sum of its parts. Similarly, a missiological researcher must develop *greater-than-the-parts* integrative insights into diverse, missiologically relevant bodies of knowledge. This

---

4. See, for example, the journal article cited at the end of this chapter.

"synergistic interaction"[5] in pursuit of an interdisciplinary grasp of the literature is foundational to ICA.

Beth Grant's perspective on interdisciplinary library research is noteworthy in this context.[6] She argues that the researcher must strive for quality sources, not the mere accumulation of citations. The problem (and its research questions) must determine the relevance of a given source. Grant warned that "the ability to accurately assess resource quality and determine significance across several disciplines develops slowly; it requires a substantive amount of time given to the process of interdisciplinary library research." ICA, bluntly stated, is a demanding, time-consuming method of inquiry.

CRITICAL: DO NOT BELIEVE EVERYTHING YOU READ

"Critical," the second word in ICA, denotes the researcher's application of critical thinking skills while interacting with the literature. In brief, a critical thinker:

- identifies and challenges assumptions (particularly the assumptions of other writers),
- remembers the importance of context (e.g., the academic discipline or school of thought),
- imagines and explores alternatives to current norms and styles of behaving and thinking,
- embraces a reflective skepticism (especially when interacting with the world of ideas),
- justifies his or her beliefs (e.g., all summaries-conclusions are fully supported by the data),
- strives for objectivity (e.g., attempting to disprove pre-research beliefs and assumptions).

As is evident in these six characteristics, ICA is a research methodology ideally suited to extracting meaning from the precedent literature. ICA insists on comparisons, striving to identify and explicate both agreement and disagreement *within* and *between* disciplines.

---

5. See chapter 4, "The Four-Phase Model."

6. See chapter 6, "The Library in Interdisciplinary Research: Content and Methodology."

Missiological research, by its very nature, is a process of interdisciplinary inquiry; a process that extends to interdisciplinary bodies of literature. Remembering the importance of context, a critically thinking missiological researcher applies ICA to both the relevant biblical-theological and the social science literature, without being easily convinced by one theological or empirical position, or another. Employing ICA, the researcher (1) reads extensively the literature in multiple disciplines, (2) masters comprehensively those diverse literature sources, and (3) resists emphatically the temptation to believe everything he or she reads.

ANALYSIS: THREE GOALS DEFINE THE CHALLENGE OF ICA

The first goal of ICA is the creation of a big-picture overview of the literature. This overview empowers the reader to grasp the complexity of the interdisciplinary literature. Literature reviews generated by ICA, typically two or more, must enhance the reader's understanding of the relevant fields of study. The resulting big-picture conclusions must always be supported by specifics: the definitions, detailed findings, and theories (or theologies) embraced by various disciplines and schools of thought within those disciplines.

The second goal of ICA is strategic sequencing in the literature review. A prosecuting attorney presents trial evidence strategically; exhibit 13 is of greater strategic value to the case than is exhibit 3. This does not imply that exhibit 3 has no value. It does mean, however, that the earlier evidence becomes foundational to the more critical evidence presented later in the trial. In the same way, a literature reviewer must present evidence strategically, not randomly. An ICA-generated literature review builds a "case" that is based squarely on published findings and theories (i.e., the "evidence").

A strategically crafted literature review *never* reads like a lengthy annotated bibliography, in which source after source are reviewed sequentially. Rather, the review should systematically and strategically lead the reader from limited knowledge of the reviewed topic to some depth of understanding of the bodies of knowledge involved. This is possible only when the researcher (1) thoroughly masters the relevant literature, (2) writes with a strategic plan in mind, and (3) communicates said plan in a reader-friendly manner. A researcher using ICA strives to empower the reader to reach evidence-based conclusions that build convincingly throughout the review.

The third goal of ICA is identifying what *does not* appear in the literature. This inductive process benefits from the researcher's strategic sequencing of the literature. A researcher uses ICA to build a credible case for new research by distinguishing between what the academy knows and what it does not yet know: "A well-crafted literature review allows the reader to grasp easily where the 'hole' is in the body of knowledge."[7] That hole or lacuna, strategically described in the conclusion of a literature review, justifies the need for a new study.

The difference between *analyzing* and *reporting* the literature is enormous. Mere reporting or reciting what others have discovered is never adequate. An integrative critical analysis of published literature is a process of true discovery; that process is as significant to the total research effort as are the fresh empirical findings and exegetical analysis that typically follow such an analysis of the literature.

REFERENCES AND RESOURCES FOR ADDITIONAL READING

Dubber, Markus D. 2014. "Critical Analysis of Law: Interdisciplinarity, Contextuality, and the Future of Legal Studies." *Critical Analysis of Law: An International & Interdisciplinary Law Review* 1, no 1. http://ssrn.com/abstract=2385656.

Galvan, Jose L. 2015. *Writing Literature Reviews: A Guide for Students of the Social and Behavioral Sciences.* 6th ed. Glendale CA: Pyrszak Publishing.

Machi, Lawrence A., and Brenda T. McEvoy. 2012. *The Literature Review: Six Steps to Success.* 2nd ed. Thousand Oaks, CA: Corwin Press (A Sage Company).

Ridley, Diana. 2012. *The Literature Review: A Step-by-Step Guide for Students.* 2nd ed. London, UK: Sage Publications.

Walker, Esteban, Adrian V. Hernandez, and Michael W. Kattan. 2008. "Meta-Analysis: Its Strengths and Limitations." *Cleveland Clinic Journal of Medicine* 75: 431–39. doi: 10.3949/ccjm.75.6.431.

---

7. From chapter 1, "Interdisciplinary Research: An Epistemological Framework."

WEBSITES OF INTEREST

University of Minnesota-Duluth. Guidelines for Writing
a Literature Review
http://www.duluth.umn.edu/~hrallis/guides/researching
/litreview.html

University of South Carolina at Chapel Hill. Literature Reviews
http://writingcenter.unc.edu/handouts/literature-reviews/

JOURNAL ARTICLE WITH ABSTRACT

Wu, Wen-Hsiung et al. 2012. "Review of Trends from Mobile Learning Studies: A Meta-Analysis." *Computers & Education* 59: 817–27. doi:10.1016/j.compedu.2012.03.016.

Two previous literature review-based studies have provided important insights into mobile learning, but the issue still needs to be examined from other directions such as the distribution of research purposes. This study takes a meta-analysis approach to systematically reviewing the literature, thus providing a more comprehensive analysis and synthesis of 164 studies from 2003 to 2010. Major findings include that most studies of mobile learning focus on effectiveness, followed by mobile learning system design, and surveys and experiments were used as the primary research methods. Also, mobile phones and PDAs are currently the most widely used devices for mobile learning but these may be displaced by emerging technologies. In addition, the most highly-cited articles are found to focus on mobile learning system design, followed by system effectiveness. These findings may provide insights for researchers and educators into research trends in mobile learning.

10
THEORY DEVELOPMENT

Alan R. Johnson, PhD

In the next chapter entitled, "Theory in Missiological Research," the notion of building middle-range theories is introduced as a goal of missiological research. The process of developing theory is bound closely to what Knight (2002) labels "sensemaking" (meaning understandings of the research topic, situation and questions) and "claimsmaking." In this view, research is a systematic inquiry to answer questions that have been posed, these answers, in turn, should be seen by others as "a plausible and careful set of answers" (Knight 2002, 1). Theory development essentially involves "connecting those understandings to ideas that are discussed" in academic communities, among practitioners or in policy making circles (2002, 3).

Researchers seek to create accounts for phenomena in the social world that better fit empirical data than other accounts and thus are more plausible and defensible. These sensemaking accounts take the form of theory that is not causal or probabilistic but rather looks for configurations, patterns, and factors and how and under what circumstances they interact.

A BRIEF HISTORY OF THEORY DEVELOPMENT IN THE SOCIAL SCIENCES

To comprehend the history of theory in the social sciences requires an historical perspective on contested areas of research traditions that became known today as sociology and anthropology. In the stream that became sociology, the research subject was one's own society. Research was conducted within a positivist worldview that assumed neutral observers could discover objective data. Quantitative approaches produced probabilistic theories, while descriptive and comparative work developed broad orienting frameworks to account for social phenomena. The research stream that became anthropology focused on the radical "other," with a holistic view of smaller scale societies. Anthropology's assumptions were still positivist, but the product tended to be descriptive and lacking in theoretical development. Its primary research method was (and still is) based in ethnographic participant observation, seeking explanation of what people do and how they see the world.

A reaction against macro-theoretical perspectives in the social sciences led to the search for middle-range theories rooted in empirical data. Researchers developed grounded theory (GT) in the medical sociology field seeking to develop theory rooted in data from specific settings. Today, grounded theory[1] is the most cited qualitative research method in the social sciences, and is best viewed as a family of methods where there exists a spectrum of methodologies and presuppositions regarding the status of data (see Bryant and Charmaz 2007).

The contrast between macro-level and middle-range theories can be understood in terms of levels of abstraction. Rather than addressing highly abstract notions like "post-modernism" or "enlightenment," mid-level chunks of culture (e.g., marriage, divorce, taken-for-granted understandings, and grading practices) become the focal point for developing explanations of how these things work (Berger 1995, 10–11). This makes middle-range theories and middle levels of abstraction highly appropriate for missiological research due to the missiological researcher's focus on real-life ministry settings.

THE PROCESS OF THEORY DEVELOPMENT

The way in which theory is developed is bound up with the methods used for analyzing qualitative data. Theory is the abstract expression of how sense is made of the data.[2] Theory emerges as a qualitative researcher immerses himself or herself in the data:

- discovering themes, clusters, and cases;
- discerning conditions, interaction among the actors, strategies and tactics, and consequences;
- looking for mediators in a chain of causes, counter-examples, indicators of analytical concepts indicators that would

---

1. See chapter 28 titled, "Grounded Theory hod" for more details.
2. Chapter 32 titled, "Qualitative Data Analysis," develops this concept in more detail.

falsify a concept (see Miles and Huberman 1994; Strauss and Corbin 1987, 27–28).

The researcher then takes the results of this analysis and couches it in terms that reveal the relationships between the various factors. The resulting explanation illuminates particular phenomena and, where possible, shows something about causality and the ability to predict future action from the theoretical model.

David Martin (1978), a sociologist of religion, offers a good example of this abstract framing of a general theory in social science. Two salient statements from his work are relevant here:

- "In circumstance X this or that development Y tends to occur, or more broadly that in the complex of historical circumstances a, b, c, a development p, q, r, tends to occur, with these and these appropriate qualifications" (1978, 2).
- "Theory has a purely conditional form: if x and y are present then z is likely to this or that extent. Often I cannot even hope to indicate what that extent is, and there are a lot of situations where it is difficult to be certain how far x is operative or y, or indeed some other factor" (1978, 14).

Notice how a set of relationships is proposed and qualified within certain circumstances. Martin encouraged the work of theoretical development, even though due to the high complexity of social relationships the researcher is often unable to capture everything. Martin (1978) notes, "the attempt at theory is not rendered useless by the fact that the scope of explanation is limited or something's left unexplained. What is needed is some indication of the crucial nexus of relevant factors and some hint as to their likely relationships" (14).

EXAMPLES OF MISSIOLOGICAL THEORY

Theory development is precisely what the researcher tries to do in missiological research development. Examining problem areas about which little is known, seeking to elucidate relevant factors and how they are connected. In addition, missiologists and mission practitioners trust and rely on the work of the Holy Spirit at each critical point in this process: seeking the guidance of the Spirit in what to study, in the following analytical process, and in shaping missiologically relevant theory. Finally, field workers need the guidance of the Spirit when applying fresh theoretically grounded insights to improve missiological praxis.

The following two examples illustrate theory development from two different missiological writings. The first is an explicit attempt at theory development, in which DeLonn Rance in his doctoral dissertation examined the activity of the Holy Spirit in calling missionaries in the El Salvadoran context (2004). His interview data show how the Spirit "initiates, motivates and sustains the entire missionary enterprise" (2004, 252). From his findings, he developed four major factors in the work of the Spirit in that context. The factors of missionary call, missionary empowerment, missions structures, and Salvadoran contextual factors are described in detail. These define the universe of elements that interrelate in the El Salvadoran missionary experience. Rance's model of how the Spirit is at work can now be applied to other contexts.

The second example shows how missiological writing discuss concepts and relationships that are theoretical in nature, but are not explicitly framed as theory. For example, Ralph Winter's development of the E and P scales (Winter and Koch, 2002). The E scale looks at cross-cultural evangelism from the perspective of the evangelist. The scale assesses increasing complexity as the evangelist moves farther and farther away from her own cultural setting. The P scale assesses the same process from the perspective of people in the existing church, in terms of the evangelism's cultural relevancy to them. The abstract constructs of the E and P scales can be applied to analyze what is happening on the ground from any starting point among any people. These scales can explain why people of different cultural backgrounds living geographically proximate to Christians have trouble receiving and responding to the gospel. The scales can also predict people's responses, based on the cultural relevance of the version of faith of existing bodies of believers and the sensitivity of the evangelist.

These two examples illustrate the importance of having theory development as a goal for missiological researchers. The strength of theory development lies in its application to other contexts. Moving past mere descriptions to the formulation of more abstract concepts, configurations, and factorial relationships, the researcher makes it possible for others to apply research findings in new settings. Thereby empowering those who follow to solve problems on a new plane of understanding.

REFERENCES AND RESOURCES FOR ADDITIONAL READING

Berger, Bennett M. 1995. *An Essay on Culture: Symbolic Structure and Social Structure*. Berkeley, CA: University of California Press.

Bryant, Anthony, and Kathy Charmaz. 2007. "Introduction. Grounded Theory Research: Methods and Practices." In *The SAGE Handbook of Grounded Theory*, edited by Anthony Bryant and Kathy Charmaz. 1–28. London: Sage Publications.

Knight, Peter T. 2002. *Small-scale Research: Pragmatic Inquiry in Social Science and The Caring Professions*. London: Sage Publications.

Martin, David. 1978. *A General Theory of Secularization*. Oxford: Blackwell.

Miles, Matthew, and A. Michael Huberman. 1994. *Qualitative Data Analysis*. 2nd ed. Thousand Oaks, CA: Sage Publications.

Rance, DeLonn Lynn. 2004. "The Empowered Call: The Activity of the Holy Spirit in Salvadoran Assemblies of God Missionaries." Ph.D. diss., Fuller Theological Seminary.

Strauss, Anselm. 1987. *Qualitative Analysis for Social Scientists*. Cambridge: Cambridge University Press.

Winter, Ralph, and Bruce A. Koch. 2002. "Finishing the Task: The Unreached People Challenge." *International Journal of Frontier Missions* 19, no. 4: 15–25.

WEBSITE OF INTEREST

Sociology 401: Primer in Theory Construction, n.d., http://www.soc.iastate.edu/sapp/soc401theory.html. Accessed Nov. 9, 2011

JOURNAL ARTICLE WITH ABSTRACT

McKinley, William. 2010. "Organizational Theory Development: Displacement of Ends?" *Organization Studies* 31, no. 1: 47–68. doi: 10.1177/0170840609347055.

In this essay I argue that organization theory has witnessed a significant displacement of ends over the last thirty years. Whereas in the 1960s and 1970s the dominant goal of the discipline was achieving consensus on the validity status of theories, today the overriding goal appears to be development of new theory. Formerly new theory development was considered a means to the end of attaining consensus on theory validity, but was not the only activity deemed necessary to accomplish that goal. In addition, instrumental standardization and replication were viewed as important. The contemporary displacement of ends toward new theory development creates the paradox that organization theory today is both epistemologically simpler (in terms of the intellectual activity deemed desirable) and more complex theoretically than it was thirty years ago. I discuss the advantages and disadvantages of the displacement of ends toward new theory development in organization theory, and offer some possible remedies that are designed to reallocate priorities and resources toward the instrumentation, theory testing, and replication components of the research process. I also propose an agenda of future research in the history and sociology of organization science that would study the displacement of ends hypothesized here, with a view to improving our understanding of how organization theory has evolved and how its knowledge could be made more useful to managers.

11

THEORY IN MISSIOLOGICAL RESEARCH

Alan R. Johnson, PhD

In social science, the term "theory" is used with widely divergent meanings. In order to speak clearly about theory in the social sciences, it is necessary to start with how theory is understood in the natural sciences.

THEORY AS A VARIED CONSTRUCT

"A scientific theory is an attempt to bind together in a systematic fashion the knowledge that one has of some particular aspect of the world of experience" (Ruse 2002, 870). In this sense a theory provides abstract explanation of observed facts and the ability to predict what will happen based on application of the theoretical model to empirical settings.

Kaplan and Manners provide some important distinctions to keep in mind when thinking about theory in scientific research, particularly in the social sciences (1972, 11–14). Simply put, theories encapsulate what happened and why it happened. They explain facts already known and can lead to new facts. In this sense, a theory is a kind of generalization. Kaplan and Manners (1972) state, "A generalization is a proposition that relates two or more classes of phenomena to each other" (11–12). Unlike empirical (or inductive) generalizations (which label the regularities of nature and identify the kinds of relationships in the observed phenomena), theoretical generalizations account for why such regularities hold, leading to new facts and opening new lines of research. See the first chart which summarizes the key terms and critical differences relevant to theories.

Term	Definition	Level/degree of Abstractness	Remarks
Descriptive statements	Refer to events in a specific space-time context	High generality, low in abstractness, low in explanatory power	Describe a concrete phenomena
Empirical generalizations	Refer to relationships that hold under specified conditions irrespective of time and place		Discover laws of nature
Theoretical generalizations	Refer to highly abstract relationships under which empirical generalizations and descriptive statements provide examples of special instances	Low generality, highly abstract, high explanatory power	Construct theories, use and operationalize abstract terms that refer to non-observables (e.g., social cohesion, anomie, class)

It is helpful, then, to think of theory in the social sciences in terms of a continuum of use. This continuum ranges from theories that closely resemble those used in the natural sciences to theories that are less strict in their formulation. The following table, based on Kaplan and Manners (1972), summarizes this continuum. It starts with the natural science model and progresses to ways in which the term "theory" is used in social science fields.

Domain of Usage	Definition/ Characteristics	Example	Remarks
1. Theory as used in natural science	Given one or more empirical general-izations - laws and series of facts you can logically deduce the phenomena to be explained.	Rusting of metal. Metal of a particular class rusts under these conditions, you can predict; or if you have rusted metal you can explain why in terms of the conditions.	Deductive systems require universal laws. Prediction and expla-nation are equal.

Domain of Usage	Definition/Characteristics	Example	Remarks
2. Scientific definition of sociological theory	"A set of interrelated propositions that allows for the systematization of knowledge, explanation, and prediction of social life and the generation of new research hypotheses" (Ritzer 2000, 5, footnote 1).	Given condition A there is a strong tendency or low probability that B will occur.	The lack of universal laws in social science means that explanations come from statistical generalization and thus are probabilistic (1972, 15). Therefore, the boundary conditions and limits to the situation must be made clear.
3. Concatenated (or factor) and pattern theories	Showing how component parts, laws, generalizations enter into a network of relations and thus have an identifiable pattern or configuration (1972, 15–16).	Explaining the origins of capitalism by looking at technological, economic, social structural, ideological and personality factors.	A patterning form of explanation. The patterning allows the researcher to show how various cultural elements relate to a larger system; one can express these relationship in propositional forms.
4. Sociological theories in the broad sense	Influential theories with a wide range of application, dealing with centrally important issues that have stood the test of time (Ritzer 2000, 5). Theoretical orientations or perspectives which provide the background for understanding and evaluating both facts and explanations (Calhoun 1996, 432–33).	Anomie, Protestant work ethic, functionalist explanations.	One cannot observe all the facts; they are filtered by theoretical considerations. Descriptions vary with the conceptual or theoretical framework used to capture them (1972, 21–22).

Domain of Usage	Definition/ Characteristics	Example	Remarks
5. Other uses of theory in social science literature (Thomas and James 2005, 5–6).	Epistemological presupposition, developed argument, craft knowledge.	What we see as objective facts are socially constructed through language and our worldview. For example, the physical fact of a flood, once it is put into language becomes a social construction, as an act of God, caused by global warming, a curse of disobeying the gods, and so on.	This is "theory" in the loosest sense and not related to abstract relationships and explanation.

THEORY PRODUCTION AS THE GOAL OF THE THESIS

In what sense then does the missiological researcher develop theory as a product of his or her work? Here a helpful distinction is to think of macro-theory, like gravity or quantum mechanics in physics, with mid-range theory that provides explanation for a specific social setting. Robert Merton coined this notion of mid-range theory, proposing sociological theories of the middle range as a position between total theoretical systems to cover all aspects of life and a theoretical descriptive work or minor hypotheses (1968, 39–40).[1]

> Middle-range theories may seem to be similar to general, total theories in the sense that they also involve abstractions. However, unlike those in the general theories, the abstractions in theories of the middle range are firmly backed up by observed data. Middle range theories have to be constructed with reference to phenomena that are observable in order to generate an array of theoretical

---

1. The source of this material on mid-range theory and the quote that follows from the same source was originally found at http://ssr1.uchicago.edu/PRELIMS /Theory/thmisc2.html accessed on 13 Oct 2011 in an article on sociological theory. The site was part of The Society for Social Research and dated 2007. This link is now dead. The original source for the material and quote can be found in Merton 1968, Chapter 2 "On Sociological Theories of the Middle Range," 39–40.

problems as well as to be incorporated in propositions that permit empirical testing. (Merton 1968, 39)

Examples in the field of sociology include theories of reference groups, of social mobility, of role-conflict, of the formation of social norms, among others. In missiological research, the kind of theory generated falls into this notion of middle range as it is empirically generated, focuses on specific settings, and the forms of explanation used are either probabilistic from statistical generalization or the pattern type.

THEORY AS A FRAMEWORK FOR CAPTURING DATA

Another way in which theory enters into missiological research or research of any kind, is as a framework for understanding data gathered to answer the research questions. In this sense, it is the theoretical framework for the research. One way to illustrate this is to think of a sieve that catches things of a certain size and lets other things through. As the theoretical framework of understanding in a piece of research changes, this allows different information to be "caught." For example, when studying the subject of missionary attrition through the frames of various disciplines, the findings and claims one can make change with each discipline. The disciplines of psychology, theology, anthropology, and economics all yield different kinds of answers and influence the kind of theoretical account created as a product of the research.

THEORY AS A FRAMEWORK FOR INTERPRETING DATA

While research is generally embedded in a theoretical perspective to help guide the data collection and interpretation, instances arise where the research will reveal things that lie outside the scope of that perspective. Knight encourages researchers early in the process to raise their awareness of theories, positions, and views that can be brought to bear on their emerging collection of data (2002, 183). At this point specific theory can be drawn upon to help create an explanative account of what is happening. In such cases the researcher reviews the various theoretical options for understanding this kind of data and then shows which one best accounts for the material.

THE IMPORTANCE OF THEORY IN MISSIOLOGICAL RESEARCH

Why is theory generation important in missiological research? Simple description and guess work in real-life settings are neither acceptable nor helpful. Missiological research can lend great insight into understanding why and how people in various contexts respond to the gospel and develop into mature communities of faith. Understanding why that has worked or not worked in various circumstances has eternal implications. Therefore, seeking patterns, regularities and explanations that will allow a continual refinement and improvement of praxis is essential. This is not merely a technical procedure, but is guided by the Spirit to know how to apply new understandings and the power of the Spirit in order to break through intractable problems that will be revealed by the missiologist's work.

REFERENCES AND RESOURCES FOR ADDITIONAL READING

Kaplan, David, and Robert Manners. 1972. *Culture Theory*. Englewood Cliffs, NJ: Prentice-Hall.

Knight, Peter T. 2002. *Small-Scale Research: Pragmatic Inquiry in Social Science and the Caring Professions*. London: Sage Publications.

Merton, Robert. 1968. *Social Theory and Social Structure*. New York: Free Press.

Ritzer, George. 2000. *The McDonaldization of Society*. Thousand Oaks, CA: Pine Forge Press.

Ruse, Michael. 2005. "Theory." In *The Oxford Companion to Philosophy*, 870–71. Oxford: Oxford University Press.

Thomas, Gary, and David James. 2005. "Reinventing Grounded Theory: Some Questions about Theory, Ground and Discovery." http://www.education.bham.ac.uk/aboutus/profiles/inclusion/thomas_gary/grounded%20theory%20paper%20for%20students.doc. Accessed October 21, 2011.

JOURNAL ARTICLE WITH ABSTRACT

Southern, Stephen, and James Devlin. 2010. "Theory Development: A Bridge between Practice and Research." *The Family Journal* 18, no. 1: 84–87.

Theory development is an intentional process by which marriage and family counselors may bridge the gap between research and practice. The theory building process includes inductive and deductive forms of reasoning, qualitative and quantitative approaches to knowledge development, and diffusion of innovations. Grounded theory provides an accessible method for bridging the gap. Theoretical orientation development is a lifelong process involving the interaction of personal and professional influences in theory selection and elaboration. Examination of personal values and values implicit in theories afford opportunities for ongoing professional development.

12

ETHICAL RESEARCH WITH HUMAN SUBJECTS

Johan Mostert, DPhil

Lapses in research ethics have become front-page news in recent times. All three of the following stories dominated headlines in the first half of 2011:

- The German Minister of Defense was obliged to resign after University of Bayreuth officials discovered that his PhD was largely plagiarized. Karl-Theodor zu Guttenberg was stripped of his doctorate; his subsequent resignation became a major embarrassment to the government of Chancellor Angela Merkel and the Christian Democratic Union party.

- A state investigation in Georgia revealed that teachers and principals in dozens of Atlanta public schools doctored the test papers of their students, falsifying the children's academic progress. The report, released by the Governor, showed that the department emphasized test results "to the exclusion of integrity and ethics."[1]

- After a fifteen-year legal battle, Pfizer Pharmaceuticals began paying out millions of dollars in compensation after the Nigerian government sued it for a botched 1996 clinical trial in that nation. The pharmaceutical giant had failed to obtain adequate informed consent from the parents of the meningitis-stricken children, and did not adequately protect the subjects from potential harm. Eleven children died and many more were harmed.

---

1. http://www.usatoday.com/news/nation/2011-07-06-Atlanta-schools -standardized-test-cheating_n.htm.

ETHICAL VIOLATIONS AND ATTEMPTS TO CORRECT THEM

Atrocities and clear violations of ethical principles have, unfortunately, marred the history of research with human subjects. The most infamous of these violations was the experimental medical research by the Nazis, using imprisoned Jews as human guinea pigs. More recent ethical abuses are, in some ways, equally troubling. The US government remained involved in the Tuskegee Syphilis Study from 1929 to 1972. In this study, poor, uneducated African American men in Alabama suffered and died after they were experimentally infected with syphilis and left untreated. The researchers involved published their findings for over forty years.

The international research community has responded to unethical researchers by developing clearly worded research guidelines. The Nuremburg Code and the Declaration of Helsinki of the World Health Organization (WHO) stopped unethical research in the West. This closed door, unfortunately, led some researchers to find Majority World locations that would allow ethically questionable experimentation. This shift forced the medical establishment to unmistakably condemn such practices, spotlighting the ethics of clinical research regardless of location (Angell 1997).

Missiological research does not involve potentially dire physical consequences, as have some medical and pharmacological trials. Little imagination is needed, however, to envision missiological research having serious emotional, spiritual, and social impact. The ethical guidelines developed by the international research community reflect an appropriate, universally applicable moral code. The guidelines are, in fact, standards that inform the way that missiologists should do research. In the United States, these guidelines have been codified in Federal Regulations that are designed for the protection of human subjects by the Department of Health and Human Services.[2] Professional associations, such as the American Psychological Association, point their researchers to these regulations.

PRINCIPLES OF ETHICAL RESEARCH FOR MISSIOLOGISTS

Missiological research is typically guided by the research ethics of the seminary, university, or agency that endorses a study. Before engaging in

---

2. http://www.hhs.gov/ohrp/humansubjects/guidance/45cfr46.html.

research involving people, a researcher must obtain the approval of the endorsing institution's Institutional Review Board (IRB). The researcher must provide accurate information about the proposed research protocol. Once a given protocol receives IRB approval, the researcher must ensure that the study is conducted accordingly. The following is a succinct summary of the principles of ethical research normally required by an IRB.

Avoidance of plagiarism. Researchers never present the work of other authors as their own work. Similarly, researchers never present their own previously published work as original research in another publication (self-plagiarism).

Voluntary participation. All persons who participate in the research must do so freely as volunteers. Financial payments, if used in the study, should only compensate participants fairly for their time.

Informed consent. Researchers must secure signed and dated informed consent from their participants, indicating all were appropriately informed about (and understood) their rights. Those rights include the right to not participate in the first place, and the right to withdraw from a study in progress without loss of benefit or services.[3]

Protection of participants. Researchers must ensure that participants are protected from harm, both in the process of conducting the research and in the manner in which the research findings are made known to the public. This extends to safeguarding the research data.

Anonymity. Researchers are committed to providing anonymity for their research participants. This applies to both data collection and data storage. It should be impossible for anyone (including the researchers themselves, in complex study designs) to connect specific data to a particular research participant.

Confidentiality. Information obtained from research participants must always be kept secure, unavailable to all unauthorized persons. This principle extends both to those involved in the study and those who are not, even if they gave informed consent for the participant to be involved (e.g., parents or legal guardians of minor children).

Honest reporting. Researchers do not fabricate data and will faithfully report their findings, even when those findings are negative or do not support their hypothesis. Researchers avoid making false or deceptive

---

3. See Appendix 10, "Informed Consent Essential Content."

statements based on their data. They do not allow vested interests (e.g., their employers, research funders, or organizations in which they hold membership) to distort, suppress, or alter their findings. In addition, researchers honestly and fairly acknowledge any technical limitations, shortcomings, or failures encountered in their studies.

A SPECIAL NOTE ABOUT THE USE OF DECEPTION IN RESEARCH

Deceptive or misdirecting techniques have occasionally been used to obtain scientific data from participants, particularly in the fields of psychology and sociology. If the value of the potential knowledge outweighs the impact of deception in a given study, the IRB *may* approve the research. Even so, the missiological researcher must acknowledge that deception is, by definition, unethical, and contextually unwise.

Where deception or misdirection has been used, researchers are obligated to debrief the participants about the nature of the deception at the earliest possible opportunity. They must also provide participants with the option to withdraw their data from the study (i.e., have their data deleted).[4]

REFERENCES AND RESOURCES FOR ADDITIONAL READING

Adler, Emily S., and Roger R. Clark. 2015. *An Invitation to Social Research: How it's done.* 5th ed. Stamford, CT: Cengage Learning.

Angell, Marcia. 1997. "The Ethics of Clinical Research in the Third World." *The New England Journal of Medicine* 337:847–849.

Dunn, Dana S. 2009. *Research Methods for Social Psychology.* West Sussex, UK: Wiley-Blackwell.

Neuman, William L. 2009. *Social Research Methods: Qualitative and Quantitative Approaches.* 7th ed. Boston, MA: Pearson Education.

WEBSITES OF INTEREST

Macquarie University, Social Science Research Ethics
http://www.mq.edu.au/ethics_training/index.php.

McMaster University, Non-Certificate Version of Tutorial (right column)
http://www.mcmaster.ca/ors/ethics/faculty_tutorial.htm.

---

4. See Dunn (2009, 53–59) for an extended discussion on this subject.

JOURNAL ARTICLE WITH ABSTRACT

Rid, Annette, and Harald Schmidt. 2010. "The 2008 Declaration of Helsinki—First among Equals in Research Ethics?" *The Journal of Law, Medicine & Ethics* 38, no. 1: 143–48. doi: 10.1111/j.1748-720X.2010.00474.x.

The World Medical Association's (WMA) Declaration of Helsinki is one of the most important and influential international research ethics documents. Its most recent 2008 version declares unprecedented universal primacy over all existing national or international ethical, legal, or regulatory requirements. This self-proclaimed status as a set of minimal ethical standards raises important questions about the Declaration's appropriate normative status. The present paper argues that the new claim of ethical primacy is problematic and makes the Declaration unnecessarily vulnerable to criticism. Future revisions of the Declaration should therefore remove this claim and strengthen the document, first, by clarifying its normative status as a set of strong default recommendations, to be followed unless there is compelling ethical reason to do otherwise; and second, by improving the substance of the Declaration through further precision, specification, and argument.

13

VALIDITY AND RELIABILITY

Johan Mostert, DPhil

Christian Smith (2007), professor of sociology at the University of Notre Dame, was the principal investigator of the National Study of Youth and Religion. This massive study investigated the spiritual lives of teenagers in the USA. As one might expect, he was intrigued by an advertisement for a national leadership summit, endorsed by the National Association of Evangelicals. The advertisement stated that "Christianity in America Won't Survive Another Decade Unless We Do Something Now." It was the byline on the advertisement, however, that dumbfounded this highly regarded researcher,

> This generation of teens is the largest in history—and current trends show that only 4 percent will be Evangelical believers by the time they become adults. Compare this with 34 percent of adults today who are Evangelicals. We are on the verge of a catastrophe. (Smith 2007)

Smith decided to investigate these attention-grabbing claims. The statistics were reported by a professor at a major Evangelical seminary, following his "informal survey" of 211 young people in the mid-1990s in three states. This professor reported that only 4 percent of his sample were born-again Christians, yet he provided no information about how the sample was chosen. A similar study, conducted by the same professor (ostensibly using the same procedures), concluded that 34 percent of older Americans were born-again Christians.

Smith concluded that both studies were methodologically flawed and should never have been reported. He also argued that the use of such poorly generated data represents an inexcusable abuse of statistical research.

Missiological research should be characterized by a best-practice commitment to excellence. Establishing the validity and reliability of methods and data-gathering instruments is central to best-practice missiological research.

VALIDITY AS A BEST-PRACTICE BENCHMARK

A study is said to have validity when it actually investigates what it purports to investigate. "Validity refers to the accuracy and trustworthiness of instruments, data, and findings in research. Nothing in research is more important than validity" (Bernard 2011, 41). The study introduced by Smith (above) claimed to analyze the spiritual status of American young people. Yet the sampling was embarrassingly invalid. As a result, the entire study was invalid.

When missiological researchers investigate phenomena, their commitment to the use of valid procedures must be unwavering. How they design their studies, gather and interpret their data, and report their findings can be evaluated for validity. Every aspect of their research must conform to generally accepted scientific procedures and the definition of best-practice.

ESTABLISHING VALIDITY

The technical aspects of establishing the validity of research instruments, especially those that generate quantitative data, is beyond the scope of this chapter. Emphasized here is the importance of ensuring that valid instruments are used. One effective way of establishing validity is to use instruments that have already been validated in previous research. Literally hundreds of validated instruments—scales, questionnaires, and tests—can capture missiologically relevant data: cross-cultural adaptation, cross-cultural leadership styles, ethnocentrism, spirituality, and religious behavior. And many of these may be used without cost.

Researchers must, at times, construct their own questionnaires. When this is necessary, their instruments can, at least, establish adequate "face" validity. This least-sophisticated form of validity can be developed as researchers circulate their new questionnaires among colleagues in the field and social science professionals, soliciting their feedback. Through this process of review and refinement, researchers can be reasonably confident that their questionnaires will measure what they purport to measure.

The need to establish methodological validity also applies to qualitative studies. Qualitative researchers must attempt to protect their data from personal or methodological bias that could skew their results. To illustrate, imagine a veteran Western missionary conducting structured interviews with younger indigenous pastors from a poor central African nation. His or her status in that culture, as both foreign missionary and older person, would likely bias the interview data. Another researcher conducting the same interviews could obtain quite different results. The validity of the qualitative interview data would be increased significantly if the missionary trained one or more local people to conduct the interviews for him.

RELIABILITY

Reliability refers to the extent to which an instrument yields the same results if a researcher re-measures the same people, under the same conditions. If the two sets of data correlate highly,[1] the instrument (and, by implication, the study itself) is said to be reliable.

Differences in the data when measurements are repeated can be evaluated statistically using the standard error of measurement (SEM). When polling organizations report findings on some variable, such as the public's view of a certain politician, they will normally also publish the SEM. This statistically determined measure of variance warns that the sample's opinion may vary from the larger population's opinion by a stated percentage (e.g., plus or minus 3.2%): the lower SEM (this percentage), the greater the poll's reliability.

A variety of psychometric methods have been developed to test the reliability of self-report questionnaires, especially attitude-assessment scales. These include the use of (1) split-half comparison methods, (2) test-retest methods, (2) alternative forms of the same test, and (4) sophisticated statistical procedures, such as the Kuder-Richardson formula.

Establishing the reliability of qualitative studies is more complex because researchers are often intimately involved with those they are studying. One way to establishing reliability in qualitative research is to

---

1. See the chapters 39 and 40 titled, "Statistically Speaking" and "Inferential Statistics," respectively.

use more than one observer, comparing their results; this is labeled inter-rater reliability. When this strategy is not possible, qualitative researchers must be explicit in their research reports about any biasing factors that may have influenced their findings or interpretations.

Babbie (2014) suggests that qualitative researchers must decide whether to observe as outsiders or as participants.[2] This decision influences how the researcher will negotiate his or her relationship with the research participants. The researcher's characteristics and decisions can significantly impact the reliability of their research.

CONCLUSION

Missiological researchers must strive to engage in valid research; affirming that their findings are both reliable and valid. Of the two, validity is primary. Findings from valid studies can be applied with confidence and replicated easily by other researchers, ensuring that missiological knowledge advances for the benefit of the Church.

REFERENCES AND RESOURCES FOR ADDITIONAL READING

Babbie, Earl. 2014. *The Basics of Social Research*. 6th ed. Belmont, CA: Wadsworth Cengage Learning.

Bernard, H. Russell. 2011. *Research Methods for Anthropologists: Qualitative and Quantitative Approaches*. 5th ed. Alta Mira, CA: AltaMira Press.

Kirk, Jerome, and Marc L. Miller (eds.). 1995. *Reliability and Validity in Qualitative Research*. Thousand Oaks, CA: Sage Publications.

Smith, Christian. 2007. "Evangelicals Behaving Badly with Statistics: Mistakes Were Made." *Christianity Today* (January-February). http://www.booksandculture.com/articles/2007/janfeb/5.11.html (accessed October 25, 2011).

---

2. See Babbie's (2014) chapter 10 entitled "Qualitative Field Research" for an excellent discussion on best practices in qualitative investigations.

WEBSITE OF INTEREST

Teaching Resources, Reliability and Validity [gateway website with links
      to seven papers on reliability and validity, plus a number of other
      research links.]
      http://sydney.edu.au/science/uniserve_science/school/addres
      /relval.html

JOURNAL ARTICLE WITH ABSTRACT

Aarons, Gregory A. Elizabeth J. McDonald, and Cynthia D. Connelly. 2007.
      "Assessment of Family Functioning in Caucasian and Hispanic Americans:
      Reliability, Validity, and Factor Structure of the Family Assessment Device."
      Family Process 46:557–69. doi: 10.1111/j.1545-5300.2007.00232.x.

The purpose of this study was to examine the factor structure, reliability, and validity of the Family Assessment Device (FAD) among a national sample of Caucasian and Hispanic American families receiving public sector mental health services. A confirmatory factor analysis conducted to test model fit yielded equivocal findings. With few exceptions, indices of model fit, reliability, and validity were poorer for Hispanic Americans compared with Caucasian Americans. Contrary to our expectation, an exploratory factor analysis did not result in a better fitting model of family functioning. Without stronger evidence supporting a reformulation of the FAD, we recommend against such a course of action. Findings highlight the need for additional research on the role of culture in measurement of family functioning.

UNIT 2
Theological Research in Missiological Inquiry

14
INTRODUCTION TO BIBLICAL AND THEOLOGICAL RESOURCES

Paul W. Lewis, PhD

The procedure for using biblical and theological tools in missions research is somewhat different from that used in the social sciences. Many of the established biblical/theological methodologies that will be introduced in this chapter overlap and are frequently dependent on each other.[1]

AN OVERVIEW OF VARIOUS THEOLOGIES

The Scriptures[2] are foundational to the whole theological (and missiological) enterprise. As such, the role of good biblical hermeneutics is also foundational to the whole process. This does not mean, however, that all research endeavors require the same amount of biblical exegesis. The extent of detailed biblical engagement necessary depends largely on the subject matter. Biblical theology is fully based on the biblical hermeneutics, but it applies that foundation on a larger scale—either in terms of an entire book, a corpus, a testament, or in terms of a theme. All of these applications and engagements with Scripture are predicated on good hermeneutical practices.

Historical theology follows a different trajectory. While the theological issues are biblically derived, the focus in historical theology is on the historical development of issues and formulations over time.

Systematic theology employs a hybrid methodology. In order for systematic theology to be done well, the systematician must have:
- a biblical footing (exegesis and hermeneutics);
- a clear understanding of biblical theology;

---

1. Two helpful guides for Biblical-theological research are Appendix 15, "Guidelines for Biblical-Theological research," and Appendix 16, "Using Indices and Abstracts for Biblical-Theological Research."
2. On differing Bible versions, see Appendix 17, "Bibles and Bible Versions."

- a full awareness of historical theology, including the issues, dynamics, and development of theology and doctrines;
- and the ability to engage the contemporary scene by answering contemporary questions.

Contextual theology should, like systematic theology, be supported by biblical hermeneutics, biblical theology, and historical considerations. The real emphasis, however, lies on the cultural context and cultural engagement in which the theology is constructed. For this reason, contextual theology is frequently constructed by missionary or indigenous personnel.

Narratology and narrative criticism can both function as tools for examining biblical narratives. Narratology and narrative criticism, thereby, have a role in biblical hermeneutics and historical theology. In contrast, narrative theology and narratology are both interested in the story-like expression of life experience. As a result, both have potential influence in historical theology, systematic theology, and contextual theology. Specifically, narratology examines stories in a general way, while narrative theology focuses on the narrative dynamics of theology and the Christian life. The proclamation usage of narrative called "narrative preaching" (or the "new homiletic") highlights the missional homiletic dynamic of telling stories with a spiritual objective. This proclamation could employ all of the theological tools listed above.

The missiological usage of the theological methods identified above must be done in a best-practice manner. Specifically in missiological research, it is important to use these tools appropriately. For example, doing good biblical hermeneutics or developing a solid biblical-theological base must be done while also looking through the lens of cultural context and missions objectives. Missions can, thereby, become a "practical" test as well as a lens by which the applicability and relevance of certain theology can be assessed.

Each following chapter in this unit focuses on an individual element listed above. Narratology, narrative criticism, narrative theology, and narrative proclamation are, however, examined together.

WHERE TO BEGIN?

Your Bible-theology literature review should provide the *biblical foundation* (motivation, basis) for your missiological research. Sometimes it is difficult to know where to begin to achieve that end. The table below will help you begin. Before you delve into the excellent resources available, take time to review the table regarding *steps to take* to begin the biblical-theological literature review of your project. These steps and recommended key texts will help you work from a *broad* topic to a *narrow* one.

NOTE: *The chart below represents going from the *broad* (at the top) to the *specific* (at the bottom) in researching your biblical/theological engagement. You do not need to present *all* your research from each of these steps in your project; rather, your presentation will serve as the "tip of the iceberg" (see below) that synthesizes your findings from these fundamental biblical-theological research resources.[3]

STEP	TYPE OF RESOURCES	SUGGESTED TEXTS
(1) Determine theological or topical themes and key biblical texts that inform the topic of your research.	Biblical/Topical/Theological Dictionaries or Encyclopedias These will give you the nomenclature needed for your subject matter.	*New Dictionary of Biblical Theology*, ed. Rosner, Alexander, Goldsworthy, Carson. *New ISBE* 4 Vols. (1939 edition is free online), ed. Bromiley *NIDB (New Interpreter's Dictionary)* 5 Vols. *Anchor Bible Dictionary (left of Evangelical)* 6 Vols., ed. Freedman *Harper's Bible Dictionary*, ed. Achtemeier SECOND LAYER: IVP Dictionaries (see all at link) OT 4 Vols; *Baker's Dictionary of Practical Theology*

---

3. Note that the sources highlighted in the chart below are found in full citation in Appendix 18, "Selected Bibliography for Biblical and Theological Research."

STEP	TYPE OF RESOURCES	SUGGESTED TEXTS
(2) Address the texts yourself to gain a *panoramic overview*.	Learn Exegetical Methodology: Various Bible translations, concordances, lexicons, word studies, texts to gain the historical/cultural/ literary understanding of the text	Stuart – OT Exegesis Fee – NT Exegesis (includes a resource for pastors) Nancy Vhymeister, *Quality Research Papers: For Students of Religion and Theology*– Chapter 13, on Exegesis *Dictionary of Biblical Imagery (IVP)* *The Oxford Encyclopedia of Archaeology in the Near East* (5 Vols.) HALOT (T*he Hebrew and Aramaic Lexicon of the Old Testament*):– current standard Holladay (*A Concise Hebrew and Aramaic Lexicon of the Old Testament*) NIDOTTE (*New Intl. Dictionary of OT Theology and Exegesis*), ed. Van Gemeren; TWOT (*Theological Wordbook of the Old Testament*) ed. Archer, Harris, Waltke BDB (*Brown-Driver-Briggs Hebrew and English Lexicon*) – old standard; still good NIDNTT (*New Intl. Dictionary of NT Theology*) ed. Brown NIDNTT (*New Intl. Dictionary of NT Theology: Abridged*), ed. Verbrugge BDAG (*A Greek-English Lexicon of the New Testament and Other Early Christian Literature*) ed. (Bauer, Danker, Arndt, Gingrich)

STEP	TYPE OF RESOURCES	SUGGESTED TEXTS
(3) Consult commentaries and monographs to *zoom* in and do more in-depth **analysis**. (Use these to confirm or contrast with your discoveries.)	Commentaries and monographs: Build a bibliography of sources on your texts • Journals • Historical Theology (biblical & ecclesial) *only if necessary*	Longman, *Survey of OT Commentaries* Carson, *Survey of NT Commentaries* NIVAC (*New International Version Application Commentary*) 20 Vols. Indices (HUM & RELG) OT and NT abstracts (tied to text or topic) via ATLA/EBSCO *Dictionary of Biblical Imagery* *Oxford Encyclopedia of Archaeology* Also: essays/chapters in books; monographs (On missiological hermeneutics: Brownson, Redford, R. Daniel Shaw/Charles Van Engen, Christopher Wright), dissertations
(4) **Synthesize** your research.	Write Section(s)	Synthesis Biblical/theological Chapter or sections Research

REFERENCES AND RESOURCES FOR ADDITIONAL READING

For general biblical aids, apart from those listed with the individual chapters, see Bible Apps at www.bible.com/ under YouVersion.

For software, note that Accordance (www.accordancebible.com), Logos Bible Software (www.logos.com), and Bible Works (http://bibleworks.com/) all have available software (for a price) that can help in all exegetical (Greek, Hebrew, Aramaic sources, and historical/archaeological resources), and modern translation endeavors.

15
DOING THEOLOGY MISSIOLOGICALLY

DeLonn L. Rance, PhD

For missiologists, doing theology and engaging in research are both means of spiritual discernment, prayer processes in which the Spirit guides "into all the truth" (John 16:13). Confronted by problems, questions, and opportunities in diverse contexts, missiologists seek the mind of Christ in order to think and act according to the will of God and in the power of the Spirit. They desire to give witness to Christ among all peoples so that they might be reconciled to God and bring glory to his name. Missiologists make assertions and decisions, not on the basis research findings alone, but also on the voice of the Spirit. They believe that the Spirit communicates throughout the research process and the reflection that follows the data gathering. The Spirit is the source of all truth; missiological researchers must connect with, and surrender in obedience to, that divine source.

The Spirit's empowering presence enables the missionary people of God to continue the ministry of Jesus in the world, a ministry of revelation and reconciliation. The Spirit communicates through general revelation; this is why the natural and social sciences are important. He also communicates through the Word of God (the inspired and authorized record of God's words, acts, and Son: the *logos*) and directly to his people (both corporately and individually). Missiologists thus *expect* God to speak and act in the present through the written text, through people (especially the people of God), through the created order, and through supernatural interventions. For those missiologists, doing theology and missiological research are both expressions of worship.

Charles Van Engen identifies several of the unique characteristics of missiological research, particularly theologizing in mission (2011, 116–18). He observes that while validity and reliability are relevant constructs in social science research, the dynamic nature of missiological research[1]

---

1. Doing missiology in context is essentially unrepeatable as each context is unique in time and space.

forces missiologists to grapple with a totally different question: Are the findings and conclusions of the research trustworthy and true? Van Engen identifies five key *trust*-based questions and four *truth*-based questions that characterize best-practice in missiology (2011, 116–17). Van Engen's five key *trust*-based questions are:

1. Did the researcher read the right authors, the accepted sources?
2. Did the researcher read widely enough to gain a breadth of perspectives on the issue?
3. Did the researcher read other viewpoints correctly, fairly, and seriously?
4. Did the researcher understand what was read—and demonstrate a basis for agreeing or disagreeing with what was read?
5. Do internal contradictions exist either in the use (and understanding) of the authors or in their application to the issue at hand? (2011, 116)

Van Engen's four *truth*-based questions that characterize best practice in missiological research are:

1. Is there adequate biblical foundation for the statements being affirmed?
2. Is there an appropriate continuity of the researcher's statements with the theological affirmations made by other thinking, down through the history of the church?
3. What contradictions or qualifications of thought arise? Does the mission theologian's work adequately support the particular theological directions being advocated in the study?
4. Are the dialectical tensions and the seeming contradictions allowed to stand, as they should, given what we know and do not know of the mystery of God's revealed unknown qualities as they impact our understanding of God's mission? (2011, 117)

Van Engen then provides ten criteria for evaluating a biblical theology of mission (2011, 117–18). These criteria relate directly to the truth-trust approach to determining the credibility of missiological research.

1. Revelatory—Acceptable mission theology is grounded in Scripture.
2. Coherent—It holds together and is built around an integrating idea.

3. Consistent—It has no insurmountable glaring contradictions and is consistent with other truths known about God, God's mission and God's revealed will.

4. Simple—It has been reduced to the most basic components of God's mission in terms of the specific issue at hand.

5. Supportable—It is by nature logical, historical, and practical.

6. Externally Confirmable—Other significant thinkers, theological communities, or traditions lend support to the thesis being offered.

7. Contextual—It interfaces appropriately with the context.

8. Doable—Its concepts can be translated into missional action that in turn is consistent with the motivations and goals of the mission theology being developed.

9. Transformational—The carrying out of the proposed missional action would instigate appropriate changes in the status quo that reflect biblical elements of God's mission.

10. Productive or Appropriate Consequences—The results of translating the concepts into missional action would be consistent with the thrust of the concept themselves and with the nature and mission of God as revealed in Scripture.

Van Engen concludes with these important observations:

> One of the most profound differences in the way biblical theology of mission does its research as compared with social science-based research in missiology is *that biblical theology of mission is more intentionally and strongly prescriptive as well as descriptive.* It is synthetic (bringing about synthesis) and integrational (bringing about new conjunctions and inter-relations of ideas). (2011, 118, italics in original)

The critical role of synthesizing and integrating missiological research is addressed by Anita L. Koeshall, Alan R. Johnson, DeLonn L. Rance, Mark A. Hausfeld, and John L. Easter below.[2] While social science and Western theological research is frequently linear, the missiological research process can be described as "looping" as the researcher

---

2. See chapters 48 to 53 in unit 7 titled "Theological and Empirical Integration."

continually moves between (1) the various research disciplines represented in the study,[3] (2) theory and praxis, (3) theology, history, culture, and the practice of ministry,[4] and (4) the description, affective expression, analysis, discernment, and action.[5] Each discipline and each research process are tools that can lead to discernment when yielded to the Spirit.

Missiological research is grounded in the axiom that "all truth is God's truth" (Holmes 1977). However, not all truth is equally significant in any given situation. Only the Spirit can communicate the significance of truth discovered in a given context. Therefore, the critical task of the missiologist is to hear the voice of the Spirit, live in obedience to that voice, and communicate significance in word and deed in contextually appropriate ways.

Does the research discern the stories of individuals and communities of faith as they intersect with God's story in the biblical text, in the church, and in the world? This overarching question uniquely defines missiological research. Missiological researchers, as scholar-practitioners, must ask themselves a number of difficult questions as they engage in the challenging task of best-practice missiological research. Has the researcher:

1. listened to and depended on the Spirit?
2. saturated the entire research process in prayer?
3. analyzed all aspects of the research with the eyes of the Spirit?
4. identified the mind of Christ and communicated concrete actions in such a way as to empower the missionary people of God to respond in obedience to revealed will of God calling the people and peoples of the world to reconciliation with God and each other?

And finally, the missiological researcher must face the most important question: Will this research facilitate obedience in the power of the Spirit for the glory of God?

---

3. In a given study, these disciplines may include theology, biblical studies, anthropology, sociology, psychology, religious studies, and linguistics.

4. See Van Rheenen's "Missional Helix" found in "From Theology to Practice: The Helix Metaphor," (2002).

5. My gratitude goes to Roger Heuser for bringing this to my awareness.

REFERENCES AND RESOURCES FOR ADDITIONAL READING

Elliston, Edgar J. 2011. *Introduction to Missiological Research*. Pasadena, CA: William Carey Library.

Holmes, Arthur F. 1977. *All Truth is God's Truth*. Grand Rapids, MI: Eerdmans Publishing Company

Nussbaum, Stan. 2011. *Breakthrough! Prayerful, Productive Field Research in Your Place of Ministry*. 2nd ed. Colorado Springs, CO: GMI Research Services.

Sögaard, Viggo. 1996. *Research in Church and Mission*. Pasadena, CA: William Carey Library.

Van Engen, Charles. 2011. "Biblical Theology of Mission's Research Method." In *Introduction to Missiological Research*, ed. Edgar J. Elliston, 113–118. Pasadena, CA: William Carey Library.

Van Rheenen, Gailyn. 2002. "From Theology to Practice: The Helix Metaphor." http://www.missiology.org/?p=203 (accessed March 4, 2013).

WEBSITES OF INTEREST

Great Commission Research Journal
    http://journals.biola.edu/gcr/
International Bulletin of Missionary Research
    http://www.internationalbulletin.org/
International Journal of Pentecostal Missiology
    http://www.agts.edu/IJPM/index.html
Missiology
    http://www.missiology.org/

JOURNAL ARTICLE WITH ABSTRACT

Wan, Enoch. 2003. "Rethinking Missiological Research Methodology: Exploring a New Direction." *Global Missiology* (October); Paper presented at the Southeastern Regional [Meeting of the Evangelical Theological Society], Columbia, SC, March 20–21, 1998.

The purpose of this study is to review missiological research methodology diachronically and synchronically and to rethink related issues with an anticipation of exploring a possible new direction for future study.

16
BIBLICAL HERMENEUTICS

Paul W. Lewis, PhD

Biblical hermeneutics is foundational to the whole enterprise of missiological research. To be Bible-based is essential, yet this demands more than an affirmation of Scripture's authority. A Bible-based hermeneutic requires both an appropriate exegesis and a meaningful application of the biblical text to a target culture.

FOUNDATIONAL PRINCIPLES, AFFIRMATIONS, AND PRESUPPOSITIONS

During a preliminary reading of a biblical text,[1] a missiological researcher must focus on key foundational principles. First, the researcher must approach the text with a certain *preunderstanding*,[2] in particular, an understanding of the text starts with one's faith in Christ. Second, what a missiological researcher learns from the biblical text should enhance and encourage obedience to Jesus. Finally, that the researcher is to approach the biblical text with the belief that the Spirit can illumine the text to one's mind and heart.

The interpretation of the Scriptures does not take place in a vacuum. Therefore, a missiological researcher also interprets Scripture within a faith community, which has identified appropriate methods whereby

---

1. On various Bible versions in English see Appendix 17: Bibles and Bible Versions.

2. It is understood that *preunderstanding* incorporates a wide array of elements, but here this aspect of the *preunderstanding* needs to be emphasized. *Preunderstanding* is the sum of those elements (assumptions and attitudinal) that is the background in the interpreter's mind informing the understanding as the interpreter comes to the biblical text. Some cannot be modified (e.g., the cultural-linguistic background of the interpreter), while some may be (e.g., Marxist view can change to a different ideological perspective).

believers do exegesis and hermeneutics. Adopting this communal perspective requires four specific theological affirmations relating to the text:

1. God's universal, timeless truth is found within a cultural/historical context embedded in Scripture.
2. The Bible depicts human dynamics by human authors, yet it also contains divine elements through the processes of inspiration, preservation, canonization, and illumination of the text.
3. The biblical text is clearly meant to be understood; it is also meant to mold the beliefs, actions, and character of the followers of Jesus.
4. Being missional is an attribute of God (e.g., John 3:16; 2 Pet 3:9). Thus, a missional perspective of the biblical text is fundamental to the interpretive process. To illustrate, God's initiative, love, and redemption are embedded and embodied throughout the Scripture, even in texts where these attributes are not clearly apparent.

Key presuppositions relating to the text itself, beyond its affirmed authority, inform the interpretive process. Three such presuppositions include:

1. Scripture is unified (although diversity of genre is noted).
2. Scripture interprets Scripture.
3. Scripture demonstrates the progressive nature of revelation.

Undergirding all of these, the missiological researcher must engage in the interpretive process with a "let-the-text-transform-me" (not a "let-me-transform-the-text") attitude.

THE OBJECTIVES AND PARAMETERS OF INTERPRETATION

The initial objective of interpretation is to determine the plain meaning of the text (what the author intended) within its original context (including its linguistic, cultural, geographical, and historical aspects). The second objective, the application of the text, must always be based on this plain meaning; this restricts the potential abuse of the text. Stated differently, the three-part goal of hermeneutics is to determine (1) what the text meant then and there, (2) what it means now, and (3) what it means in a given contemporary cultural situation. For some authors, hermeneutics can be defined as the interpretive process of understanding the text.

In this chapter, hermeneutics will include the whole process of exegesis within the historical-social and literary settings through the interpretative process (including the *preunderstanding*) into application.

As indicated above, one parameter of context is the grammatical-linguistic structure of the text itself. The historical tradition of interpretation can also clarify what a text has *never meant* throughout church history, and thereby set parameters on what the text cannot mean. When examining a text, however, an interpreter must bear in mind that all compilations, editions, and translations are at least somewhat susceptible to bias.[3] Also note that in many translations, certain theological positions influenced the translators and, concomitantly, their translations.[4]

THREE STAGES OF INTERPRETATION

In the exegetical part of the hermeneutical process, an interpreter studies the text within its original context. He or she must attend to the following issues during the initial interaction with the text:

1. The words themselves,[5] using quality word studies[6] (Old Testament terms: *New International Dictionary of Old Testament Theology and Exegesis, Theological Dictionary of the Old Testament* or *Theological Wordbook of the Old Testament;* New Testament terms: *Exegetical Dictionary of the New Testament*, or *Theological Dictionary of the New Testament*).[7]

---

3. This is true whether in the original languages (Greek, Hebrew and Aramaic—editions have punctuation, emendations, etc. set by the editors), or in a translation (e.g., NIV, NASB, KJV).

4. For example, the respective perspectives of women in ministry are represented differently in various translations of Romans 16:1–2, and other texts.

5. Word studies are helpful, but should not be overused (or abused—on this see D. A. Carson's *Exegetical Fallacies* (Grand Rapids, MI: Baker, 1984)), since frequently social and literary contexts set the parameters on the domain of meaning, and a word may not mean the full possible range of meanings within a specific context.

6. For assistance in good word studies see Appendix 19, "Doing Word Studies in the Bible," and Appendix 20, "How to do a New Testament Word Study."

7. For the bibliographical information on these works, and a listing of other relevant works see Appendix 18, "Selected Bibliography for Biblical and Theological Research."

2. The grammar and syntax as used in the original languages (Duvall and Hays 2001, 28–82; Kaiser 1981).
3. The literary context, using various literary criticism methodologies such as rhetorical and narrative criticism (see Klein, Blomberg, and Hubbard 2004, 63–101).
4. The historical-cultural context, using a variety of tools such as historical, cultural, and sociological studies, including Bible dictionaries, Bible handbooks, and Bible atlases.

The focus throughout the initial stage of interpretation is on what the original text meant to the original audience,[8] given the intention of the author (and editor[9]). Further, the researcher must remain aware that the biblical text contains a variety of literary genres. To understand each genre-laden text, he or she must adopt an appropriate literary method. Clear examples of genre-laden texts include wisdom literature and narrative passages.[10]

The second stage of interpretation involves translating the text from "then" to "now." This process illustrates the fact that hermeneutics is both a science, with clearly defined methodologies, and an art: one that requires a "feel" for how the process works. An interpreter must translate the text from its original context into his or her context, focusing on principles, not practices. Note that principles transfer, practices do not.[11]

In the final stage of hermeneutics, the focus shifts to application. Application, which is of utmost importance, leads the reader from biblical principles to contemporary, culture-specific praxis. Application can take a variety of forms: preaching, teaching, writing, and personal application; the latter demands the cultivation of an ethical life and personal growth. This process of application, in turn, informs (and with the Spirit's enablement, transforms) the interpreter's *preunderstanding*, restarting the

---

8. The audience includes both the actual readers and those who heard the text being read by others.

9. *Editor* insofar as there are several of the biblical books with items inclusions from later editor beyond the original author, or the final form canonized was compiled by an editor or editors.

10. A good basic set of guidelines for exegesis, see Appendix 21, "Basic Exegesis Guidelines."

11. If a practice transfers, it has more to do with an incidental cultural similarity to the biblical text's context, and should not be seen as affirming practice transference.

interpretive cycle as the researcher returns to the text. This is called the "hermeneutical circle." Those emphasizing the progress or growth element in this process prefer the term "hermeneutical spiral" (Klein, Blomberg, and Hubbard 2004, 166; Osborne 2006, 22, 417–420).

INTERPRETATION IN MISSIONAL CONTEXT

The missionary endeavor requires proclamation of the Christian message in a context that is neither biblical nor one's own. This endeavor demands an additional interpretive step, one that builds on the first two described above. Thus, the missionary enterprise requires three rounds of biblical interpretation:

1. the "then and there" interpretation of the message in its original context
2. the "here and now" interpretation in the missionary's own cultural context
3. the "there and now" application in third-cultural context of the recipient culture.

This perspective demands that the missionary has developed the following:

- a solid familiarity with the exegetical tools for biblical interpretation in its *original* context,
- a critical awareness of his or her *own* cultural context,
- and an astute insight into, and awareness of, the *recipient's* context and culture.

Inherent in the three cultures identified above are certain values, assumptions, *and* questions. It is important that the missionary not force his or her own questions onto the recipient culture.[12] In the end one may inadvertently strive to answer questions that the indigenous people are not asking. Ultimately, biblical hermeneutics is incomplete without application, for culturally relevant application is the practical outflow of the interpretive process. Not only should exegetical work be substantive, it should also move toward missional action as part and parcel of the *missio Dei*.

---

12. Dr. Lazarus Chakwera, former General Superintendent of the Malawi Assemblies of God, often advised American lecturers and pastors teaching short-term courses in Africa, "Don't export your doubts."

REFERENCES AND RESOURCES FOR ADDITIONAL READING

Duvall, J. Scott, and J. Daniel Hays. 2001. *Grasping God's Word*. Grand Rapids, MI: Zondervan.

Kaiser, Walter C., Jr. 1981. *Toward an Exegetical Theology*. Grand Rapids, MI: Baker.

Klein, William, Craig Blomberg, and Robert Hubbard, Jr. 2004. *Introduction to Biblical Interpretation*. Rev. ed. Nashville, TN: Thomas Nelson.

Osborne, Grant R. 2006. *The Hermeneutical Spiral: A Comprehensive Introduction to Biblical Interpretation*. 2nd. ed. Downers Grove, IL: InterVarsity Press.

Redford, Shawn Barrett. 2012. *Missiological Hermeneutics: Biblical Interpretation for the Global Church*. American Society of Missiology Monograph Series 11. Eugene, OR: Pickwick Publications.

Shaw, R. Daniel, and Charles E. Van Engen. 2003. *Communicating God's Word in a Complex World: God's Truth or Hocus Pocus?* Lanham, MD: Rowman & Littlefield Publishers.

WEBSITES OF INTEREST

Blue Letter Bible (for the resources of the Blue Letter Bible)
www.blueletterbible.org
Bible.org (for the resources of the NET Bible—New English Translation Bible)
https://bible.org/

JOURNAL ARTICLE WITH ABSTRACT

Keener, Craig. 2005. "'Brood of Vipers' (Matthew 3.7; 12.34; 23.33)." *Journal for the Study of the New Testament* 28, no. 1:3–11.

According to a widespread tradition in the ancient Mediterranean world (attested in Herodotus, Aelian, Pliny and other writers), vipers killed their mother during their birth, hence were associated with parent-murder. Ancient writers sometimes used parent-murder as an example of one of the worst conceivable crimes, one that invited divine vengeance. Whereas Matthew's source may apply the image of vipers' offspring generally to the crowds listening to John the Baptist, Matthew applies it specifically to the Pharisees in all three of the passages where he recounts the image. In two of these instances the Pharisees claim honorable descent; Matthew ironically inverts the value of this claim through this image of vipers' parent-murder. Matthew utilizes the image for his intra-Jewish polemic, contending that his Jewish-Christian hearers are truer heirs of the patriarchs and prophets than the Pharisees are.

17
BIBLICAL THEOLOGY

Paul W. Lewis, PhD

In the development of the biblical-theological foundation of missiological research, an important tool is the usage of biblical theology. Whereas a sound biblical theology is Bible-based, it incorporates a broader and wider perspective than a pure exegetical study, and can aid in one's missiological research.

ASSUMPTIONS AND PERSPECTIVES

Biblical theology is the culmination of thorough, accurate exegesis of the biblical text as a whole. It involves the identification of the themes, theological concepts, and the overall message of the individual writers of Scripture, understood within their own terms and worldview, and these themes and concepts throughout the Old and New Testaments, and finally the Bible as a whole. Conservative biblical theology is based on at least three essential assumptions:

- The biblical text is divinely inspired, meaning that the text is both reliable and authoritative while still being situated in a certain time and place in human history. So while inspired, it was also meant to be understood by humans.
- The whole of the canon is characterized by both unity and diversity. A Bible interpreter should celebrate the latter while striving to maintain the overall unity of Scripture;
- Christ is the center, the ultimate heuristic key to all the Scripture.[1]

Biblical theology is concerned with Scripture's overarching themes[2] such as the people of God, the covenant of God, and God's concern

---

1. A point emphasized by the NT writers as well as the early church fathers.
2. A good general aid on how to study a biblical theology theme, see Appendix 22, "Studying a Theme in Biblical Theology."

for the poor. It begins as a book study (e.g., Numbers, Ephesians), then broadens to examine all of the books within an authored group or cluster of books (e.g., Torah, the Pauline or Johannine corpus). Next, the focus expands to include the whole testament (e.g., an Old Testament Theology or a New Testament theology). Finally, a biblical theology focuses on the whole Bible.

A well-developed biblical theology utilizes a historical progression found in each of these four levels, culminating in a whole "biblical theology." As a result, a fully developed biblical theology is a more conceptual work than an atomistic, individual-text oriented study. It is in this way biblical themes, such as redemption or hospitality, can be seen narrowly in a book or broadly in a testament or the Bible as a whole.

THE NATURE OF BIBLICAL THEOLOGY

Historically, a biblical theology could refer to either a *prescriptive* theology derived from the Bible, or a *descriptive* theology found within the Bible. Since the seventeenth century, biblical theology has been consistently viewed as a descriptive process, one that analyzes the biblical authors, genres, and testaments, and then synthesizes the findings (see Morgan 1990). The text is examined through the lens of its historical, sociological, and literary dimensions only.

As a result, in the modern period, biblical theology for much of the church has not been prescriptive nor has it been tied to the dogmas of the church in the academy. In contrast, both dogmatic theology and recent conservative biblical theology are seen as prescriptive as interpretations of God's Word to His people. For the conservative scholar, salvation history is embedded in real history and real culture. Biblical theology is thus seen as a multidisciplinary endeavor. As a result, a variety of historiographical, sociological, and literary tools must be used to formulate a comprehensive and accurate biblical theology.

COMPARISONS WITH SYSTEMATIC THEOLOGY

Biblical theology differs in important ways from systematic theology, and yet it is complementary to it. For example, biblical theology focuses on the issues of the biblical writers and how they expressed theology in their own context and terms. In contrast, systematic theologians focus on the contemporary issues of their ecclesial communities and their societies while engaging the positions of current theologians.

Biblical theology starts with the biblical formulations and biblical historical progression (i.e., Torah to Prophets to the New Testament); it is, therefore, a *diachronic* exercise. Systematic theology, on the other hand, is a *synchronic* exercise that builds on the findings of biblical and historical theology, philosophical methods and categories, and other contemporary tools. Thus, a biblical theology often highlights the *diversity* in the Bible, whereas a systematic theology delineates the *unity* of its truths.

BIBLICAL THEOLOGY AND MISSIOLOGICAL RESEARCH

Missiological researchers ask questions with a distinct investigative and interpretive lens, a lens that makes use of biblical theology. Biblical theology is important in missiological research for three reasons:

1. It can set parameters for the suggested use of a text to support a given *praxis*. If a verse seems to promote a certain missiological practice or perspective, a fully developed biblical theology would attest if the concept is indeed defensible, according to the original context of the text and in the full context of the Scriptures. Thereby, a well-developed biblical theology can guard against "proof-texting."

2. It can provide practical parallels of how to relate effectively to a particular non-Western culture. For example, the Old Testament concept of hospitality (e.g., Gen 18:2–7, 19:1–3) can possibly relate to many cultures that are hospitality-oriented. Biblical theology can also provide insights into those cultures that are not oriented to hospitality. Doing good biblical theology reaffirms and deepens our understanding of Christian theology, clarifies how to communicate theology to other cultures, and highlights values as extensions of practices (e.g., hospitality).

3. It can assist missional research by providing thematic parameters by which to produce a type of a "litmus" test for the recipient culture. For example, when describing a contextual version of a given concept (e.g., sin, redemption, messiah), a missiological researcher can employ biblical

theology to provide full-orbed parameters of the concept or theme. This unique contribution can empower a missionary to develop a stronger biblical comprehension of the cultural issues he or she encounters daily, facilitating better communication of the biblical message (from a more biblical compared to the researcher's own context), and to separate it from aberrant beliefs.

A strong biblical theology can aid in the missiological task. This is true for both the missiological researcher and to the missionary practitioner.

REFERENCES AND RESOURCES FOR ADDITIONAL READING

Alexander, T. Desmond, and Brian S. Rosner, eds. 2000. *New Dictionary of Biblical Theology: Exploring the Unity & Diversity of Scripture.* Downers Grove, IL: InterVarsity Press.

Barr, James. 1999. *The Concept of Biblical Theology: An Old Testament Perspective.* Minneapolis, MN: Fortress Press.

Childs, Brevard S. 1992. *Biblical Theology of the Old and New Testaments.* Minneapolis, MN: Fortress Press.

Clowney, Edmund P. 1961. *Preaching and Biblical Theology.* Grand Rapids, MI: Eerdmans.

Hafemann, Scott J., and Paul R. House, eds. 2007. *Central Themes in Biblical Theology: Mapping Unity in Diversity.* Grand Rapids, MI: Baker.

Morgan, Robert. 1990. "Biblical Theology." In *A Dictionary of Biblical Interpretation,* edited by R. J. Coggings and J. L. Houlden, 86–89. Philadelphia, PA: SCM Press/Trinity Press International.

WEBSITE OF INTEREST

Tyndale Toolbar
    http://www.tyndale.cam.ac.uk/toolbar

JOURNAL ARTICLE WITH ABSTRACT

Keener, Craig S. 2007. "Why Does Luke Use Tongues as a Sign of the Spirit's Empowerment?" *Journal of Pentecostal Theology* 15, no. 2: 177–184.

Luke does not present tongues as a sign of Spirit baptism merely arbitrarily, but because it is logically connected to the purpose of baptism in the Spirit. Luke emphasizes baptism in the Spirit as power to testify for Christ cross-culturally; what better sign to evidence this particular empowerment of the Spirit than inspiration to speak in the languages of other cultures?

18
HISTORICAL THEOLOGY

Charles E. Self, PhD

Historical theology is a discipline that seeks to discover, evaluate, and synthesize Christian beliefs, doctrines, and practices. It does so with particular regard to their historical contexts. Of unique importance to historical theology is the continuity with previous and successive eras, and the understanding that related cultural and intellectual developments have on theological concepts and formulations.

THREE PRIMARY "LENSES" OF HISTORICAL THEOLOGY[1]

The literature presents historical theology in two main ways. The most common is evaluating developments in Christian thought during various eras. For example, working from a Western perspective, a historical theologian will assess theological ideas within five main eras:

- ancient/classical (33–451 AD),
- medieval (5th to 16th centuries),
- early modern (16th to 18th centuries),
- modern (19th and 20th centuries),
- late-modern/post-modern (late 20th century to the present).

Eastern Orthodox theologians evaluate theology in a similar fashion, with particular focus on developments before the mid-ninth century. The non-Chalcedonian Church theologians of the East focus on key thinkers from the fourth to the twelfth centuries. Many general works take this approach, from the magisterial work of Justo Gonzalez (3 vols., 2009–2010) and Jaroslav Pelikan (5 vols., 1975–1991) to the concise works of Jonathan Hill (2007), Tony Lane (2006), Chad Meister and

---

1. References that are cited in this section are all given in full bibliographical format within the "Historical Theology" section of Appendix 18, "Selected Bibliography for Biblical and Theological Research."

discontinuities of revolutionary events and voices, offers missiological thinkers vital insights for their learning and praxis. It is important that patterns and precedents are not seen as deterministic causes, though they certainly influence or shape events.

Theology may take a variety of forms, from tacit intuitional and liturgical practices to explicit confessions and dogmas. It is an animating force for ministers and monks, lay evangelists and merchants, famous saints, and anonymous workers as they strive to bring the gospel to the world. Preaching content, worship practices, discipleship/ethical expectations, church polity and community rhythms all arise from historical theology. But theology is also shaped by the experiences of mission, as the challenges of contextualization call forth creativity and flexibility. Historical theology helps the church distinguish timely experiences and expressions from timeless truth. The historic creeds were all shaped by encounters with heresies arising from both inside and outside the church.

Finally, historical theology engenders humility in the missiological researcher as he or she discovers that current beliefs, challenges, and practices have precedent and contain resources for the future. When history and hope unite in careful reflection, new insights emerge that propel the *Missio Dei* forward.

REFERENCES AND RESOURCES FOR ADDITIONAL READING

Dryness, William, Veli-Matti Kärkkäinen, Juan F. Martinez, and Simon Chan. 2008. *Global Dictionary of Theology: A Resource for the World-Wide Church*. Downers Grove, IL: IVP Academic.

McCormack, Bruce L., and Kelly M. Kapic, eds. 2012. *Mapping Modern Theology: A Thematic and Historical Introduction*. Grand Rapids, MI: Baker Academic.

McGrath, Alister. 2012. *Historical Theology: An Introduction to the History of Christian Thought*. 2nd ed. London: Wiley-Blackwell.

WEBSITES OF INTEREST

New Advent (A Catholic encyclopedia site with good secondary summaries and references to primary sources)
www.newadvent.org

Orthodox Christian Information Center (A solid resource for Eastern
  Orthodox studies)
  www.orthodoxinfo.com
Pentecostal-Charismatic Theological Inquiry International (An excellent
  contemporary work on 100 years of Pentecostal theology)
  www.pctii.org
Reformation Theology (A starting point for Reformed thinking,
  including the Augustine-Lutheran traditions)
  www.reformationtheology.com
Theology Network (A useful general introduction to the great
  theologians and traditions)
  www.TheologyNetwork.org

JOURNAL ARTICLE WITH ANNOTATION

McGrath, Alister. 1982. "Justification—'Making Just' or 'Declaring Just'? A
  Neglected Aspect of the Ecumenical Discussion on Justification." *Churchman*
  96:44–52. www.biblicalstudies.org.uk/pdf/churchman/096-01_044.pdf (accessed
  April 25, 2014)

This important article corrects Protestant misinterpretations of Catholic
theology at the time of Luther.

19
SYSTEMATIC THEOLOGY

Paul W. Lewis, PhD

The theological foundation for the missiological task is Bible-based and centered, and theologically rooted within a believing community. Given this, the biblical/theological engagement with questions of "why" and "how" (possibly also including "who," "what," and "where") must logically be addressed prior to any missiological study. This should happen even if the biblical/theological foundation is not yet fully developed. The biblical/theological perspective and engagement should inform the study's basic design and research questions, as well as aid in the evaluation of the findings.

FOUNDATIONS, METHODS, AND AUTHORITIES
Inherent in the systematic theological task is the utilization of the following methodologies:
- biblical hermeneutics, which focuses on individual passages of Scripture,
- biblical theology, which focuses on the themes and concepts embedded within books, genre, testaments, and the whole Bible,
- historical theology, which focuses on the historical understanding of the Bible, the theological themes, beliefs, and perceptions that have developed throughout church history and in the church universal.

The complex process required for systematic theology must be Spirit-led, incorporating essential methodologies and authorities in the process of theologizing. The primary authority, not surprisingly, is the biblical text itself. Three secondary sources of authority serve as important tools for developing a systematic theology:

- experience: personal experience is essential, and must be developed through personal engagement with God;
- tradition: this includes the corporate experience of God throughout church history and in the church universal;
- and reason: this source of authority emphasizes coherence in theology within themes and across the whole of theology.

A systematic theologian also utilizes philosophy (including logic and internal coherence), the natural sciences, the social sciences, and ethics. All of these other disciplines assist the theologian to engage effectively a given theological topic. However, the theologian must evaluate the potential contributions of the various tools through the primary lenses of Scripture, and notably biblical and historical theology.

COMPARISONS WITH BIBLICAL THEOLOGY

Systematic theology intentionally systematizes theological reflection in a *synchronic* (or ahistorical) manner, unless the theologian is working in narrative theology. Further, theologians working in systematic theology intentionally try to answer questions of contemporary relevance. Thus, systematic theologians strive to enlighten and guide Christians in the contemporary context and, at times, defend the way of Jesus Christ against opponents.

Systematic theology differs from (and compliments) biblical theology in three important ways. First, biblical theology starts with biblical formulations, and its biblical historical progression is a *diachronic* (or history-laden) exercise. In contrast systematic theology addresses the biblical text through the lenses of major biblical themes and contemporary concerns. For example, a systematic theology may focus on the theme of redemption. This would require the identification of references to redemption throughout the Bible, and the utilization of additional resources in that discussion. Second, biblical theology flows from the various book/authorial occasional themes, highlighting the topic's biblical diversity. In contrast, a systematic theology demonstrates (and presupposes) the unity of Scripture and the pervasiveness of a given theme. Finally, biblical theology is a *descriptive* exercise (although some contemporary conservative biblical theologians view it as a *prescriptive* exercise). In contrast, systematic theology is a *constructive* exercise, especially when addressing contemporary questions.

AFFIRMATIONS FOR A SYSTEMATIC THEOLOGY

A systematic theology developed within a more conservative Christian perspective contains four key theological affirmations:[1]

1. It should be Bible-based (as noted above), Christocentric, embedded within the historical Orthodox church, yet also open to the Spirit's leading.

2. It should be missional. God is missional by nature; mission is based both on His action and His very nature.

3. It should incorporate in its audience the following persons:[2]
   A. the "person in the pew" (believing laity at all levels of spiritual growth and maturity),
   B. the "person in the marketplace" (the average person at work),
   C. and the "person on the street" (the average person who is not a follower of Jesus Christ).

4. It should be comprehensive and inclusive. This fourth affirmation functions as an embedded pragmatic test. Theology informs all aspects of the Christian life: belief, attitudes, character, and behavior.

This inclusiveness should be seen in the integration of *orthodoxy*,[3] *orthopraxy*,[4] and *orthopathy*.[5] Orthodoxy emphasizes the theology, and appropriate formulations and beliefs of a Christian. Orthopraxy highlights the practical or ministerial component of theology, including its ethical dimension. Orthopathy focuses on passion for, and personal experience of, God (Land 1993); it also refers to passion for, and personal experience of, our world—particularly its marginalized peoples (Solivan 1998). An integrated systematic theology should be fundamentally inclusive of beliefs, skills, and attitudes. Further, it should be academically rigorous, spiritually attuned, and tested through the crucible of practicality (including in

---

1. Those affirmations are subject to analysis and critique.

2. This affirmation is reflective of, but not limited to, the Wesleyan strand of theology.

3. Historically, *orthodoxy* meant "right glory;" yet through time, the term has come to mean "right belief."

4. Orthopraxy means "right practice or action."

5. Orthopathy means "right passion or experience."

"fleshing out" the *Missio Dei*). Ultimately, the goal of systematic theology is to provide an orderly and coherent understanding of Christian belief for the contemporary culture and generation.

SYSTEMATIC THEOLOGY AND MISSIOLOGY

Theological and missional engagements mirror each other in that each should examine both the biblical text and the contemporary context. Systematic theology can aid in the missiological endeavor by identifying and distilling the essential components of the faith with clarity. However, it is important to remember that the construction of, and the answers given within, a systematic work may not resonate with the recipient culture. This mandates that a missionary (scholar-practitioner) develop an astute awareness of the recipient culture.

A good understanding of systematic theology can also be used to train nationals in the local context to self-theologize within their respective cultural contexts. Within the context of missiological research, systematic theology should provide clarification concerning (1) the core elements of the faith, (2) awareness and models of internal coherence, (3) the usage and evaluation of the other available tools (e.g., the social sciences), and (4) the parameters of what falls outside the norms of Christian faith, including beliefs, actions, and attitudes.

REFERENCES AND RESOURCES FOR ADDITIONAL READING

Erickson, Millard. 2013. *Christian Theology*. 3rd ed. Grand Rapids, MI: Baker Academic.

Green, Joel, and Max Turner, eds. 1999. *Between Two Horizons: Spanning New Testament Studies and Systematic Theology*. Grand Rapids, MI: Eerdmans.

Grudem, Wayne. 1995. *Systematic Theology: An Introduction to Biblical Doctrine*. Grand Rapids, MI: Zondervan.

Land, Stephen.1993. *Pentecostal Spirituality: A Passion for the Kingdom*. Cleveland, TN: CPT Press.

Lewis, Gordon, and Bruce Demarst. 1996. *Integrative Theology*. 3 volumes in 1 ed. Grand Rapids, MI: Zondervan.

Solivan, Samuel. 1998. *The Spirit, Pathos, and Liberation: Toward an Hispanic Pentecostal Theology.* Sheffield, UK: Sheffield Academic Press.

WEBSITE OF INTEREST

A large number of systematic theological works are available online at:
http://www.religion-online.org/

JOURNAL ARTICLE WITH ABSTRACT

Kärkkäinen, Veli-Matti. 2012. "Epistemology, Ethos, and Environment: In Search of a Theology of Pentecostal Theological Education." *Pneuma* 34: 245–61.

The purpose of this essay is to take a theological look at Pentecostal theological education at the global level. While dialoguing widely with various current and historical discussions of the theology of theological education, particularly with David Kelsey of Yale University, the essay urges Pentecostals to negotiate an epistemology that corrects and goes beyond both modernity and postmodernity. The essay also urges Pentecostals to negotiate several seeming opposites such as "academic" *versus* "spiritual" or "doctrinal" *versus* "critical." The final part of the essay offers Pentecostals some advice and inspiration from the reservoirs of the long history and experience of non-Pentecostal theological institutions.

20
CONTEXTUAL THEOLOGY
Alan R. Johnson, PhD and Paul W. Lewis, PhD, with Warren B. Newberry, DTh

There are three kinds of people who have interests in the production or use of contextual theology: researchers, practitioners, and local theologians and laypersons. This chapter is for those who are normally "outsiders" doing theology "in context." Stephen Bevans reminds us that

> theology must be rooted in a *particular* culture or context. . . . in reality, there is no "theology" as such—no "universal theology"—there are only contextual theologies. "Context". . . is a reality that allows one to see clearly from a particular perspective, is also something that can, if not *blindfold* one, then certainly cause one to wear blinders that severely limit vision. (2009, 3–4; emphasis in original)

This means that the production of a full-orbed local or contextual theology must be done by people in their own sociocultural setting. This chapter focuses on the value of contextual theology to missiological researchers who remain outsiders to the social system they are studying. Because of their etic status, missionaries are not in a position to produce complete local (i.e., contextual) theology. Rather, their focus must be delimited to understanding how contextual theologies can be useful to their ministry.

THE USE OF CONTEXTUAL THEOLOGY IN MISSIOLOGICAL RESEARCH
There are at least three primary ways that missiological researchers can use or interact with contextual theology (remembering that contextual theological work is the domain of local believers; theology should not be imposed on those believers by outsiders):

1. In some situations a researcher might act as a facilitator of the actual development of a contextual theology.
2. In other situations, a researcher will use an existing contextual theology as an interpretive lens for understanding a particular group.
3. Sometimes a researcher would actually do a study on a particular expression of contextual theology.

DEFINITION AND SCOPE

Some missionaries and theologians misunderstand contextual theology, local theology, or self-theologizing. They conclude that such theologizing is situated outside of the Bible, unwisely assuming that their own personal/individual focus is the primary hermeneutical key by which to understand and interpret all of the Bible. They fear that self-theologizing will "result in the proliferation of local theologies and thus the relativizing of theology" (Netlund 2006, 29).

Production of local theology and self-theologizing means that local believers engage the Bible themselves. In so doing, believers bring to that process their own cultural questions, interpretive lenses, and culture-informed values. In short, they grapple theologically with issues in their own culture. Paul Hiebert emphasized that local theologies need to be linked with global theologies in a way that "enables local Christian communities to do theology within their own context but in conversation with other Christians globally" (Netlund 2006, 29). So local believers while theologizing within and to their respective contexts, need to continue to dialogue with the worldwide body of Christ to guard against cultish-heretical beliefs or sectarianism.

The scope of doing local theology in context is as broad as the whole gospel itself. Paul Siu (2010) argues, "True contextualization. . . is primarily concerned with the translation of the *whole* gospel of Jesus Christ into the thought forms and daily lives of the people with whom we communicate in any given culture" (156, emphasis original). This means that as the gospel enters a sociocultural system, everything about it needs to be considered in the local setting; the message must *not* be imported from the outside. Thus, how the good news is shared, disciples are made, churches are planted, leaders are trained, doctrines are developed, and worship is expressed should all be tackled with the local context in mind. Here Siu (2010) offers an appropriate warning: some contextual theologies have become so issue oriented that they "neglect or trivialize the doctrinal content of Christian theology" (155). It is important that within the contextualization process of relating locally, the core of the gospel is not diminished, neglected, or lost.

The book *Global Mission: Reflections and Case Studies in Contextualization for the Whole Church* (2011) provides some helpful examples of contextual theological work. These include how to (1) present the gospel in Muslim, Hindu, and Khmer settings, (2) present the Holy Spirit within the Brazilian culture, (3) conduct memorial services in the Korean setting, (4) engage in worship through song in the Sudan, and (5) develop theology in the Filipino context. In each of these examples, contextual theology means local believers grappling with the Bible and their local culture in order to find biblically sound ways to be God's people. This objective stands in sharp contrast to local believers being presented a response developed outside of their culture.

CORE FACTORS IN THE DEVELOPMENT OF CONTEXTUAL THEOLOGIES

Missionaries often strive to facilitate the production of a local theology, identify a local theology, or fully understand an existing theology in order to better comprehend the worldview of and engage with a particular group. In any expression of contextual theologizing, missionaries and missiological researchers must consider three core factors.

Epistemology and rationality. Within a culture, there is a "rationality" of how people think: how they engage in thought processes. This rationality constitutes the internal logic by which people within a given culture communicate, argue positions, and understand any topic. As a result, their epistemological foundations are culturally determined. For instance, Western cultures are typically strongly impacted by the Enlightenment and, thus, highlight the cognitive aspect of epistemology. In contrast, many non-Western cultures tend to highlight affective or other approaches to epistemology.

Delivery systems. Directly tied to epistemology are the acceptable delivery systems by which communication is transmitted within a culture. The way in which information is communicated and processed is tied to

sample the proposals of two of the most innovative African theological thinkers of our times, Lamin Sanneh and Kwame Bediako. Their views have far-reaching implications for the future of Black and African theologies on the one hand and African Christianity on the other. Secondly I will critically evaluate the thoughts of Sanneh, Bediako and other African theologians whose thinking is close to theirs. In evaluating them, I shall refer specifically, but not exclusively, to the thoughts of Itumeleng Mosala, Simon Maimela, Takatso Mofokeng, Jesse Mugambi and Mercy Oduyoye - all being theologians whose views - like those of Sanneh and Bediako, cannot be ignored in the construction of post-cold war African theologies. Finally I will make a few concluding proposals and projections.

21
NARRATIVES, NARRATIVE, AND NARRATIVE THEOLOGY

Paul W. Lewis, PhD

In theological studies, four overlapping but distinct concepts fall under the broad topic of "narrative": *narratology*, *narrative criticism*, *narrative theology*, and *narrative preaching*. All four concepts note the way that life unfolds in a narrative or "story" manner. These varied theological concepts are all predicated on the narrative structure of experience, but the level of this emphasis and the reasons for these experiences differ.

DEFINITIONS AND EXPLANATIONS

Narrative defined

As a basic definition, a narrative is an account of some event, whether historical or fictional, presented by a narrator in a story format. The story must be characterized by a plot, sequenced action with repetitions and gaps, characterization, location and circumstances, and a flow that leads to some form of resolution.

Narrative is a specific genre found in abundance in the Bible, both in the Old Testament (e.g., Joshua, Judges) and the New Testament (e.g., the Gospels, Acts). For this reason, the study of narratives is important for those engaged in biblical and missiological research. Biblical narratives differ from other narratives in certain key respects; for instance, biblical narratives are classified as inspired by God and have a theological tone.

Narratology

The term *narratology* is frequently used by biblical scholars and theologians (including narrative theologians) as a method for understand narratives in literature, particularly in the biblical text. The art or science of narratology seeks to discover structures for one's perception of the world and culture, including forms, media, and functions. Researchers use narratology to examine the basic forms through which a story is told, the structure by which the story is organized, the way the story functions within a community, and the various media by which the story is communicated. As suggested in the preceding definition, the study of biblical narratives includes the Old Testament historical books, and the New Testament historical books: the four Gospels and the book of Acts. Narratology is also applied to the overarching meta-narrative of the entire biblical story.

Narrative criticism

Narrative criticism is the methodology of choice for examining specific narratives (both ancient and modern). In so doing, narrative critics may or may not employ the commonly discussed historical-critical concerns "behind the text."[1] Rather, these critics will emphasize the literary text itself, grappling with questions about the plot, characterizations, and the like. Embedded in the narratives are gaps, repetitions, and various embedded genre (e.g. parables, proverbs). A narrative critic will also examine the arrangement and duration of events, seeking to highlight and focus upon the elements of the narration in order to create an intertwined narrative "tapestry." Although not limited to biblical texts, narrative criticism is now commonly used in biblical criticism.

Researchers employing narrative criticism in biblical studies should avoid extracting purely theological propositional statements from the biblical narratives; the richly complex text must be allowed to speak for itself. Extracted static propositional statements, although true, may miss important dynamic features of the narrative, such as emotive elements and relationship portrayals.

Narrative theology

A movement within the broad field of theology, narrative theology emphasizes believers' life experiences, with those experiences taking the form of a story or narrative that parallels the biblical narratives. Propositional truths, on the other hand, do not completely cover the ongoing development of believers' individual stories in light of God's unfolding story. Doctrines are important, but they only point to the overarching meta-narrative. What gives meaning to believers' narratives (i.e., testimonies),

---

1. "Behind the text" refers to the historical, cultural, and social occasion for which a given text was written.

especially in regards to the Christian story, is found within a community. Stories are told by communities, not by individuals in isolation.

Members of a local church are people of the Christian story. As such, the local church becomes the fundamental community that safeguards and perpetuates a person's story within the Christian meta-narrative. Furthermore, a narrative theology acknowledges that ethics are embedded in the whole theological process; beliefs and actions are motivated, informed, and undergirded by narratives.

Narrative preaching

Narrative preaching, also called the "new homiletic" or "narrative homiletic," focuses on the use of narrative as a rhetorical style of proclamation. The application of this methodology provides an alternative to the traditional formulistic way of presenting a sermon (e.g., three points and a conclusion). Narrative preaching emphasizes the intertwining oration toward a single objective, employing stories, examples, and other elements in a narrative style to provide a key understanding of the text within the audience's own story (Lowry 2001). The focus of the message is on the plot and the unfolding of that plot from beginning to end, with the appropriate climax provided at the end of the message. Frequently the narrative-based sermon will conclude with a single focus that the listener will take home. The presented message will weave together biblical information, current cultural realities, and the resulting take-home element. The entire message is designed to lead the listener to a clear application of the text within that person's own story.

MISSIOLOGICAL APPLICATION OF NARRATIVES

Various facets of the above overview can inform three vital aspects of missiological research and *praxis*. First, for much of the world, especially in oral cultures, narration and stories are embedded in the culturally defined folkways; these include the discussion of myths (in the sociological sense), morals, identity, and life lessons. Given this fact, an effective understanding of narratives, the biblical usage of narratives, and the connection between narratives and life is very important.

Second, narrative criticism as a way of learning about narratives in general is helpful in both Old Testament and New Testament studies. It is also foundational for biblical hermeneutics, including the application of

Scripture to life, teaching, and preaching. Further, narrative criticism is an effective way to accentuate the use of narrative in the text in order to project God's missional activity.

Third, the narrative form of preaching is an effective way of proclaiming the Christian message, especially in oral (and postmodern) cultures. Narrative preaching is not only readily remembered, the audience will also incorporate their own stories into the sermon (pointing to the meta-narrative). This unique benefit of narrative preaching can foster learning and growth as the audience takes ownership of the message. As such, the study of narrative and the usage of narrative can be invaluable to the missionary enterprise, and yet remained underpinned with the foundation of the universal authority of Scripture as a meta-narrative.

REFERENCES AND RESOURCES FOR ADDITIONAL READING

Abbott, H. Porter. 2008. *The Cambridge Introduction to Narrative.* 2nd ed. New York: Cambridge University Press.

Bal, Mieke. 1997. *Narratology: Introduction to the Theory of Narrative.* 2nd ed. Toronto: University of Toronto Press.

Cobley, Paul. 2001. *Narrative.* London: Routledge.

Fludernik, Monika. 2009. *Introduction to Narratology.* Trans. Patricia Häusler-Greenfield and Monika Fludernik. New York: Routledge.

Frei, Hans. 1980. *The Eclipse of the Biblical Narrative.* New ed. New Haven, CT: Yale University Press.

Green, Joel B., and Michael Pasquarello, III, eds. 2003. *Narrative Reading, Narrative Preaching.* Grand Rapids, MI: Baker Academic.

Grenz, Stanley J., and Roger E. Olson. 1992. "Narrative Theology." In *20th Century Theology: God & the World in a Transitional Age,* 271-85. Downers Grove, IL: InterVarsity Press.

Hauerwas, Stanley, and L. Gregory Jones. 1989. *Why Narrative? Readings in Narrative Theology.* Grand Rapids, MI: Eerdmans.

Lowry, Eugene. 2001. *The Homiletical Plot.* Expanded ed. Louisville, KY: Westminster John Knox Press.

Powell, Mark Allan. 1990. *What Is Narrative Criticism?* Minneapolis, MN: Fortress Press.

WEBSITES OF INTEREST

European Narratology Network
    www.narratology.net.
The Living Handbook of Narratology
    http://wikis.sub.uni-hamburg.de/lhn/index.php/Main_Page

JOURNAL ARTICLE WITH ABSTRACT

Adeney, Frances S. 2009. "Why Biography? Contributions of Narrative Studies to Mission Theology and Mission Theory." *Mission Studies* 26, no. 2: 153–72.

This essay examines ways that narrative studies can influence both mission theologies and mission theories. Narrative studies have historically been a part of mission studies. This analysis goes a step further to show how insights gained from studying the lives of particular missionaries in their contexts leads to new theologies and theories of Christian mission.

UNIT 3
Qualitative Research

22
THE NATURE OF DATA

Marvin Gilbert, EdD

Empirical research generates data: raw bits of information that are systematically analyzed to yield objective conclusions ("findings"). These bits of information vary from one study to another, as do the methods used to analyze them. Personal interviews yield data that differ dramatically from standardized testing in public schools. Yet both types of data are valid; both can resolve research problems.[1] Making sense of this variety can be challenging for the novice researcher. The challenge becomes more manageable if the researcher understands the nature of the data being collected.

ONE CHOICE: TWO BASIC OPTIONS

Data comes in only two basic types: *words* or *numbers*. Despite considerable variety within each type, these terms summarize effectively the two types of data generated by empirical research. As explained in another chapter,[2] studies producing number-type data are labeled "quantitative," while studies producing word-type data are labeled "qualitative." The complexity found in major research methodology texts becomes less daunting when this dichotomy is understood.

Quantitative studies often generate and analyze naturally occurring numbers. If IQ scores are compared for two groups (e.g., males and females), those scores are reported as numbers from the start. However, not all quantitative studies begin with numbers. Studies assessing attitudes and opinions begin with qualitative-type responses—producing

---

1. This statement assumes the data were collected with a commitment by the researcher to best-practice research, using sound methods administered in an unbiased, systematic manner.

2. See chapter 23 titled, "Qualitative and Quantitative Research: Similarities and Distinctions."

answers that are, essentially, words. In such studies, people (respondents) must indicate with which of several written descriptors they identify. Afterward those qualitative-type responses are transformed into numbers by the researchers.

Likert-type scales often ask respondents to their agreement or disagreement with a list of statements or items. The table below illustrates the use of a Likert scale. It is taken from a survey instrument developed for use by a church leader desiring qualitative-type feedback from the pastors in his (denominational) district.

District Meeting	Adds no value to my ministry; and to the church I pastor **Unimportant or Irrelevant**	Adds little value to my ministry; and to the church I pastor **Generally Unimportant**	Adds some value to my ministry; and to the church I pastor **Generally Important**	Adds great value to my ministry and to the church I pastor **Very Important**
Very Important	☐	☐	☐	☐
Spring Convention	☐	☐	☐	☐
District Council	☐	☐	☐	☐
Family Camp Meeting	☐	☐	☐	☐

The four response options for each district meeting are categorically distinct verbal descriptions, and are clearly qualitative in nature. Pastors were asked to select one of the four options; their choice reflected the judged importance of each district meeting listed in the left column. All they needed to do was to tick (P) one of the four response options: from "Unimportant or Irrelevant" to "Very Important", with two "milder" (less extreme) opinions in the middle.

If desired, point values could then be arbitrarily assigned to each column, as pictured in the following table. When all the point values for all items (i.e., all district meetings) are added, a clear *numeric* picture emerges of the pastors' attitudes toward district meetings. The higher the scores, the more positive the district's meetings are perceived to be. These total scores could then be evaluated statistically to determine, for example, (1) the entire group's average, (2) the differences in opinion when comparing age groups, (3) the differences in opinion when comparing those in rural versus urban ministry locations, (4) the correlation (relationship) between pastors' opinions and years in ministry, and so forth. In short, a variety of statistical tests could be applied to those qualitative opinions after they have been converted to quantitative data.

District Meeting	Adds no value to my ministry; and to the church I pastor **Unimportant or Irrelevant**	Adds little value to my ministry; and to the church I pastor **Generally Unimportant**	Adds some value to my ministry; and to the church I pastor **Generally Important**	Adds great value to my ministry and to the church I pastor **Very Important**
Very Important	1	2	3	4
Spring Convention	1	2	3	4
District Council	1	2	3	n
Family Camp Meeting	1	2	3	4

LEVELS AND TYPES OF QUANTITATIVE DATA

One aspect of data analysis that troubles novice researchers is the varied levels and types of numeric data that can be produced by quantitative research designs. The table below summarizes this variety in a manner that students have found helpful.

Essential Nature	**Non-Parametric** Data do not conform to expectations of the normal curve (normal distribution)		**Parametric** Data conform to the expectations of the normal curve	
Category	**Discrete** Data assume the form of independent, unrelated numbers		**Continuous** Data assume the form of continuous measurement units	
Levels of Measurement	**Nominal** names only (the level of all qualitative data)	**Ordinal** + ranking	**Interval** + equal units	**Ratio** + absolute zero

The four levels of measurement, listed in the bottom row in this table, offer the most important classification for those seeking to understand the nature of data. Qualitative studies produce nominal-level data *only*: variables are named and verbal labels are applied (e.g., "Very Important"; "Very Unimportant"). Issues of "greater than" or "lesser than" are functionally irrelevant in qualitative studies. One elder's opinion about his pastor's leadership style cannot be judged to be numerically higher or lower than the opinion of another elder when interview data are analyzed. Any distinction based only on their verbal evaluations (based on an interview) would be, at best, a subjective judgment by the researcher.

In contrast, quantitative data (i.e., numbers) must be at least ordinal in nature. The most useful quantitative data are classified as parametric, continuous, and interval level.[3] Such data can be analyzed by the most powerful statistical techniques.

As stated earlier in this chapter, neither qualitative nor quantitative studies yield superior data. Determining which is best hinges on (1) the nature of the researchable problem, and (2) the research methodology frequently reported in the literature when that type of problem is addressed. Thus, missiological researcher should remain open to the literature's guidance when pursuing both theological and social science data.

REFERENCES AND RESOURCES FOR ADDITIONAL READING

Bernard, H. Russell, and Gery W. Ryan. 2009. *Analyzing Qualitative Data: Systematic Approaches.* Thousand Oaks, CA: Sage Publications.

Franzos, Roberto. 2004. *From Words to Numbers: Narrative, Data, and Social Science.* Cambridge: Cambridge University Press.

Janert, Philipp K. 2010. *Data Analysis with Open Source Tools.* Sebastopol, CA: O'Reilly Media.

Leedy, Paul, and Jeanne E. Ormrod. 2009. *Practical Research: Planning and Design.* 9th ed. Upper Saddle River, NJ: Prentice Hall.

Morgan, Susan E., Thomas Reichert, and Tyler R. Harrison. 2002. *From Numbers to Words: Reporting Statistical Results for the Social Sciences.* Boston: Allyn and Bacon.

---

3. See chapter 40 titled, "Inferential Statistics."

WEBSITES OF INTEREST

Center for Psychology Resources—Research Methods and Statistics
    http://psych.athabascau.ca/html/aupr/tools.shtml
Changing Minds.org—Types of Data
    http://changingminds.org/explanations/research/measurement
    /types_data.htm.
The Nature of Data
    www.bootheway.com/user/1-The%20Nature%20of%20Data.doc.

JOURNAL ARTICLE WITH ABSTRACT

Caelli, Kate, Lynne Ray, and Judy Mill. 2008. "'Clear as Mud': Toward
    Greater Clarity in Generic Qualitative Research." *International
    Journal of Qualitative Methods* 2, no. 2:1–13. http://www.ualberta
    .ca/~iiqm/backissues/2_2/pdf/caellietal.pdf (accessed September 14, 2011).

We have observed a growth in the number of qualitative studies that have
no guiding set of philosophic assumptions in the form of one of the established qualitative methodologies. This lack of allegiance to an established
qualitative approach presents many challenges for "generic qualitative"
studies, one of which is that the literature lacks debate about how to
do a generic study well. We encourage such debate and offer four basic
requirements as a point of departure: noting the researchers' position,
distinguishing method and methodology, making explicit the approach to
rigor, and identifying the researchers' analytic lens.

23
QUALITATIVE AND QUANTITATIVE RESEARCH
Similarities and Distinctions
Marvin Gilbert, EdD

Those engaging in social science research of any type have three methodological-design choices. They may choose a design utilized in a:

1. quantitative study
2. qualitative study
3. mixed-design study: both quantitative and qualitative data-collection methods in one study

This chapter compares and contrasts these three options, identifying their respective strengths and weaknesses.

CHARACTERISTICS OF THE THREE DESIGN CHOICES
The three design choices listed above are summarized in the following table.

Type of Study	Data Produced*	Methods of Analysis
Qualitative	Words[†]	1. Subjective judgment applied holistically to all words, searching for trends, similarities, and differences among various demographic variables of the subjects. 2. Qualitative software used to analyze trends, similarities, and differences among various demographic variables of the subjects (e.g., interview transcripts) utilizing key words flagged by the researcher.[‡]
Quantitative	Numbers	1. Descriptive statistics[§] (e.g., means, standard deviations). 2. Inferential statistics, testing the strength of the relationships among two or more sets of data differences between two or more sets of data

Type of Study	Data Produced*	Methods of Analysis
Mixed design	Words and Numbers	Application of both methods of analysis (above) to distinct data sets (some consisting of words only, some numbers only). The research questions (or hypotheses) determine which design is used for a given phase of the overall study.

* See chapter 22 titled, "The Nature of Data."
† Qualitative data can include pictures, images, and objects: as in the case of many anthropological studies.
‡ Atlas ti, Qualrus, Endnote, etc.
§ See chapters 39 and 40 entitled, "Statistically Speaking" and "Inferential Statistics," respectively.

SIMILARITIES

All research designs, no matter how complex in their data-gathering and data-analysis tasks, are similar in at least five important ways:

1. They are applied systematically to a researchable problem.
2. They conform to the guiding principles of the scientific method.
3. They can fit the definition of best-practice research, depending on the nature of the statement of the problem and the research questions (or hypotheses) that grow out of that problem.
4. They adequately address research questions that, collectively, are capable of resolving the research problem.
5. They attempt to limit the influence of threats to validity, including researcher bias.

STRENGTHS AND WEAKNESSES OF QUALITATIVE RESEARCH DESIGNS

Qualitative studies, long valued by anthropologists and historians, have grown in popularity by other social scientists over the past twenty years. For a given research problem, a qualitative design may be the best option. No conversion to numbers is required when analyzing qualitative-type data.[1]

Qualitative designs vary considerably, but have in common the strengths and weaknesses presented in the following table.

---

1. See chapter 22 titled, "The Nature of Data."

Strengths	Weaknesses
Ideal for phenomena that naturally occur in real life (i.e., in natural settings).	Not capable of establishing cause-and-effect statements.
Excel in complex analysis, resisting the "temptation" to simplify what is observed.	Often begin rather loosely defined, "tightening up" (hopefully) as they progress.
Useful for a basic description of new (previously unstudied) phenomena.	The findings do not generalize well to the broader population, despite their real-world commitment.
Useful for research requiring extensive data interpretation (e.g., historical and exegetical studies).	Susceptible to researcher bias.*
Useful for program and policy evaluations.	Often are time-consuming: typically requiring months or years to complete.

* This is largely due to (1) the subjective nature of data interpretation, and (2) the fact that the researcher often becomes a research "instrument" in the data-gathering phase.

STRENGTHS AND WEAKNESSES OF QUANTITATIVE RESEARCH DESIGNS

Quantitative designs characterize research in the "hard" sciences, noted for their rigorous application of the scientific method and objectivity. When quantitative methodology is applied to social science problems, researchers always encounter greater variability in the data. This variability is due to the challenge of measuring human traits, in contrast to measuring inanimate objects, compounds, and materials. The measurement and analysis precision that characterizes physics and engineering studies cannot be matched in social science research. Even so, scientific knowledge can advance using quantitative methods with human subjects when best-practice instrumentation and controls are utilized.

In general terms, the strengths and weakness of qualitative designs (in the preceding table) are the opposite of those found in quantitative research. What appears in the "Strengths" column for qualitative designs may be found in the "Weaknesses" column in the quantitative table (below).

Strengths	Weaknesses
Ideal for phenomena that occur under highly controlled conditions (e.g., in laboratories).	Cannot always be applied to problems found in the real world.
Permit cause-and-effect statements in many cases.	Often conducted in artificial (e.g., laboratory) environments.
Start "tight," that is, planned in great detail; hopefully they stay that way throughout the study.	Not useful for analyzing complex, multifaceted data.
Objective and executed under highly controlled conditions, minimizing the influence of the researcher on the outcomes.	Not ideally suited to new problems for which no hypotheses can be generated (i.e., when no theory has been developed).
Relatively quick to complete; they often require only days or weeks to finish.	Response categories are structured and inflexible, not allowing for nuances in responses to emerge or questions to be raised by respondents.
Results from randomly generated samples can normally be generalized to larger populations.	Statistical tests normally accept a 5 percent margin of error, resulting in possible false-positive and false-negative results.

MIXED-DESIGN STUDIES

Mixed-design studies can maximize the strengths of both qualitative and quantitative designs. Such studies may begin with a qualitative phase, in which a problem is approached in an inductive and open-ended manner. Once those qualitative data have been analyzed and fresh insights reached, the quantitative phase can begin under more tightly controlled conditions.

The reverse pattern is also commonly employed. A researcher may first administer a quantitative-type questionnaire to capture feedback from a large group. After analyzing those quantitative findings, issues identified by that phase are then explored in qualitative interviews, where elaboration and follow-up questions enable the researcher to explore sensitive areas.

REFERENCES AND RESOURCES FOR ADDITIONAL READING

Creswell, John W. 2008. *Research Design: Qualitative, Quantitative, and Mixed Methods Approaches.* 3rd ed. Thousand Oaks, CA: Sage Publications.

Leedy, Paul, and Jeanne Ormrod. 2009. *Practical Research: Planning and Design.* 9th ed. Upper Saddle River, NJ: Prentice Hall.

Mirriam, Sharon B. 2009. *Qualitative Research: A Guide to Design and Implementation.* San Francisco, CA: Jossey Bass.

Teddlie, Charles B., and Abbas Tashakkori, eds. 2008. *Foundations of Mixed Methods Research: Integrating Quantitative and Qualitative Approaches in the Social and Behavioral Sciences.* Thousand Oaks, CA: Sage Publications.

Wrench, Jason S., Candice Thomas-Maddox, Virginia Peck Richmond, and James C. McCroskey. 2008. *Quantitative Research Methods for Communication: A Hands-on Approach.* Cary, NC: Oxford University Press.

WEBSITE OF INTEREST

Qualitative versus Quantitative Research: Key Points in a Classic Debate
http://www.wilderdom.com/research
/QualitativeVersusQuantitativeResearch.html

JOURNAL ARTICLE WITH ABSTRACT

Lee, Linda Y. K., and Eleanor Holroyd. 2009. "Evaluating the Effect of Childbirth Education Class: A Mixed-method Study." *International Nursing Review* 56: 361–68. doi: 10.1111/j.1466-7657.2008.00701.x.

Methods: This two-phase study adopted a mixed-method design with Donadedian's model as the theoretical framework. In Phase One, a random sample of 40 Chinese women was invited to complete a questionnaire after attending a childbirth education class. The questionnaire was focused on their satisfaction with specific aspects of the class. Descriptive statistics were performed to summarize participants' response. In Phase Two, six of the original forty women were purposively selected for a semi-structured interview pertaining to the perceived effect of the childbirth education class on their labour experience. Thematic analysis was conducted on the interview data.

Findings: The participants expressed overall satisfaction with the class. The area that satisfied them the most was the performance of the midwife. The areas that satisfied them the least were the date, length, size and time of the class. Three themes emerged from the interview data, namely, 'larning about labour,' 'contributing to a smooth labour process,' and 'coping with uncertainty and handling anxiety.'

Conclusion: This study supports using a mixed-method approach to evaluate client education activity, and highlights the importance of cultivating positive coping measures among the Chinese women after attending childbirth education class when facing childbirth-related anxiety.

24
ETHNOGRAPHY
Alan R. Johnson, PhD

Ethnography—literally, writing about people—refers to both a process (doing ethnography; an ethnographic approach) and a product derived from that process (an ethnographic report; an ethnography one reads). This social research methodology specializes in encountering alien worlds and making sense of them, showing how "social action in one world makes sense from the point of view of another" (Agar 1986, 12).

WAYS THE TERM "ETHNOGRAPHY" IS USED

Ellen (1984) identified five major usages for "ethnography" (7):

1. an empirical account of the culture and social organization of a particular human population (as in ethnographic monograph, an ethnography),
2. a completed record, a product,
3. "an ethnographic account" referring to a living people, in contrast to historical and archaeological accounts,
4. a set of research procedures, usually indicating the intensive qualitative study of small groups through participant observation, and
5. an academic subject: the comparative study of ethnic groups.

ELEMENTS IN AN ETHNOGRAPHIC APPROACH

1. **Entering the field.** This element entails finding the gatekeepers, gaining permission to enter, establishing relationships, and being introduced to the right people.
2. **Exploratory open-ended observation.** This element involves several related skills: observing settings, tracking events and event sequences, counting things and people, developing ethnographic maps (to show where things

happen), and seeking indicators of social and economic differences.

3. **Informal interviews.** Some researchers feel that the best place to begin ethnographic research is with informal interviewing, supplemented with observational data. Others posit that the observation work should come first, using informal interviews to follow up lines of interest from that material. This kind of informal work is critical; it enables the researcher to learn key ideas, themes, and terms that will shape lines of further inquiry and question construction.

4. **In-depth, open-ended interviews.** This type of interview is discussed at length in the chapters 29 and 30 entitled, "Foundations of Interviewing" and "Strategies for Effective Interviewing," respectively.

5. **Semi-structured interviews.** Semi-structured interviews make use of preformed questions but the answers given by interviewees are open-ended. Researchers use this type of interview to identify the variables of factors and subfactors. For example, a given study may focus on the domain of family, exploring the factor of discipline in the family. Through semi-structured interviews, a researcher may look for subfactors through semi-structured questions, such as "Tell me how discipline occurs in your home."

6. **Ethnographic surveys.** These surveys select and then test variables that have been discovered during earlier interviews and observations.

7. **Archival and secondary data.** These are qualitative or quantitative data collected for governmental, research, education, or service purposes. They are available to researchers in usable raw data formats.[1]

---

1. LeCompte and Schensul 2010; especially see chapter six on collecting ethnographic data.

SEEKING UNDERSTANDING:
AGAR'S NOTION OF BREAKDOWN/RICH POINTS

The research techniques listed above are encompassed in the broader strategy known as participant observation. Using this approach, ethnographers develop intimate familiarity with particular social segments (a community, village, or some kind of subgroup) over an extended period of time through intensive involvement. This intentional self-positioning places ethnographers in the midst of a different social world which they can observe, but not necessarily understand.

Agar used two terms to describe the experience of not understanding. In his earlier work (1986), he used "breakdowns," later adopting the term "rich points" (1996), hereafter referred to as with the combined term "breakdowns/rich points" (BRPs). These occur where an ethnographer's assumptions and worldview are insufficient to create understanding. An ethnographer can also create BRPs by working with informants on scenarios that, as an outsider, he or she does not understand.

The experience of a BRP starts a resolution process; the goal is coherence. A *coherent* resolution will demonstrate why it is better than other possible resolutions (Agar 1986, 22). "Rich points, the words or actions that signal those gaps, are the raw material of ethnography, for it is this distance between two worlds of experience that is exactly the problem that ethnographic research is designed to locate and resolve" (Agar 1996, 31).

When a BRP occurs, the ethnographer, not the people being studied, must own the incoherence. The people are not irrational or disorganized; a BRP simply indicates that the ethnographer does not yet understand something. "There is, you assume, a point of view, a way of thinking and acting, a context for the action, in terms of which the rich point makes sense" (Agar 1996, 31–32).

KEY TERMS IN BREAKDOWN/RICH POINTS

After experiencing a BRP, the resolution process begins by harnessing a host of ethnographic methods, including those listed above, to develop understanding. This process requires ethnographers to adjust their "frames" (Agar 1996, 32). The following terms will be helpful in comprehending Agar's notion of this resolution process.

Frames. Frames are knowledge structures, schema, or scripts. Frames permit linkage of different kinds of knowledge in different kinds of ways at different levels. An actor develops plans of action based on anticipations and expectations in the stock of knowledge available. This stock of knowledge is primarily organized into "typifications," also called "frames" or (in psychological language) "schemas." In short, frames are knowledge structures that can change with experience and be enlarged and restructured (Agar 1986, 23–25).

Strips. These are ethnographic data or units of experience (such as an interview, sequences of observed behavior, passages in a novel, film, or archival document). When an ethnographer encounters a strip, a BRP results because the frames the ethnographer brought to the encounter do not work. The ethnographer cannot make sense of the experience, but *can* recognize that previously unrecognized frames, or frames another system, are at work.

Schemas. Schemas assume the form of goals, frames, and plans (Agar 1986, 27). When a BRP occurs, a schema problem has become obvious.

Coherence. The goal of the ethnographic process is coherence. This occurs "when an initial breakdown is resolved by changing the knowledge in the ethnographer's tradition so that the breakdown is now reinterpreted as an expression of some part of a plan" (Agar 1986, 25).

RESOLVING BREAKDOWN/RICH POINTS

The recursive process of building ethnographic understanding can be illustrated in the following table. The process moves from left to right:

The ethnographer observes social action through his or her own schemas and frames	Strip: Informant social act	Result: BRP because of ethnographer lack of understanding
1. The ethnographer, through a repetitive process, tries to build new frames/schemas based on	2. Informant perspective and understanding	3. Result: Growing coherence from new or adjusted frames/schemas
1. The ethnographer takes two schemas, "x" and "y," and posits a linking relationship (R), and applies R to	2. A new strip-informant social act	3. If BRP occurs, modify R repetitively until coherence is achieved

REFERENCES AND RESOURCES FOR ADDITIONAL READING

Agar, Michael. 1986. *Speaking of Ethnography*. Vol. 2 of *Qualitative Research Methods*. Thousand Oaks, CA: Sage Publications.

———. 1996. *The Professional Stranger: An Informal Introduction to Ethnography*. San Diego, CA: Academic Press.

Atkinson, Paul, Amanda Coffey, Sara Delamont, John Lofland, and Lyn Lofland, eds. 2001. *Handbook of Ethnography*. Thousand Oaks, CA: Sage Publications.

Ellen, R. F. 1984. Introduction. In *Ethnographic Research: A Guide to General Conduct*, ed. R. F. Ellen, 1–12. London: Academic Press.

Hammersley, Martyn, and Paul Atkinson. 2007. *Ethnography: Principles in Practice*. 3rd ed. London: Routledge.

LeCompte, Margaret D., and Jean J. Schensul. *Designing and Conducting Ethnographic Research: An Introduction*. Book 1 in *Ethnographer's Toolkit*. 2nd ed. Lanham, MD: Altamira Press, 2010.

WEBSITES OF INTEREST

Ethnography.com [blog site; articles written by experienced ethnographers]
http://www.ethnography.com/all-about-ethnographycom/
A Synthesis of Ethnographic Research—Center for Multilingual, Multicultural Research, University of Southern California [online textbook]
http://www-bcf.usc.edu/~genzuk/Ethnographic_Research.html

JOURNAL ARTICLE WITH ABSTRACT

Clarke, Kamari M. 2010. "Toward a Critically Engaged Ethnographic Practice." *Current Anthropology* 51 (S2): S301–S312. doi: 10.1086/653673

This article interrogates what it means for anthropologists as "social critics" to be engaged in documenting efforts that not only have explanatory power but connect that power to praxis. The key here is to recognize how delimiting innocence and guilt in the context of war is clearly a political act that is not without problems. It involves identifying our public spheres and determining what has happened to those publics within which we speak. I suggest we first rethink what it means for ethnography to serve a public domain within which we speak. This involves rethinking what it means for ethnography to serve a public domain as a mechanism of engagement with all types of subjects—victims, warlords, negotiators, intermediaries, child soldiers, and even so-called terrorists. In this regard, I suggest that return to the intentions at the core of the anthropological code of ethics, codes that guide our commitment to our informant publics. By locating the limits of our code of ethics we can rectify the ways that the history of anthropological engagement in the twentieth and twenty-first centuries has been preoccupied with documenting "local" peoples as the "authentic" voices to be protected and understood while it has excluded other interlocutors. By rethinking the ethics of research, we can use the tools of our discipline in principled forms of engagement with a range of publics.

25
RITOLOGY
Daniel E. Albrecht, PhD

RITOLOGY OR RITUAL STUDIES: AN ACADEMIC DISCIPLINE

The field of ritual studies or *ritology*[1] concentrates "on enactment and performance, that is, it gives priority to the acts, the actions and the gestural activities of people," with a secondary focus on the words, [written] text, or objects used in the rituals (Albrecht 1999, 13). Ritual studies incorporate several of the human sciences; consequently scholars from other academic disciplines have become interested in the emerging field.[2] Ronald Grimes (2013, 19–33) noted that the contemporary turn toward the study of ritual is marked by a variety of approaches and methodological perspectives. As a result, the nature of ritual studies has become interdisciplinary, comparative, and cross-cultural.

Hermeneutics, the study of interpretation, is closely tied to ritual studies. Numerous hermeneutic strategies are applied within the study of ritual. In fact, ritology, as of yet, has no single or prescribed method. Ritual studies, then, is better described as an emerging discipline. However, mapping rituals and employing the components of a ritual "map" can be most helpful to cultural field work, the subsequent descriptions, and interpretations. Such a map can serve as a foundation for a method.[3] Employing ritual studies, a researcher can consider, analyze, describe and better understand elements and practices of a social or religious group (e.g., Christian devotion including worship services and other gatherings; a local Buddhist funerary rites).

---

1. In this chapter, *ritology* and *ritual studies,* the more contemporary term, are used interchangeably.

2. Disciplines such as religious studies, liturgiology, missiology, cultural anthropology, sociology, psychology, biology, neuro-biology, and many of the arts, especially the performing arts.

3. Grimes' "mapping" of ritual is discussed below.

DEFINING RITUALS

The term *ritual* has many definitions. Victor Turner (1973, 1100) described it as "a stereotyped sequence of activities involving gestures, words, and objects, performed in a sequestered place." He then added:

> Rituals may be seasonal, hallowing a culturally defined moment of change in the climatic cycle or the inauguration of an activity. . . . Or they may be contingent, held in response to an individual or collective crisis . . . [such as] life-crisis ceremonies, which are performed at birth, puberty, marriage, death, and so on, to demarcate the passage from one phase to another in the individual's life-cycle. (1100)

Ritual designates "those acts, actions, dramas and performances that a community creates, continues, recognizes and sanctions as ways of behaving that express appropriate attitudes, sensibilities, values, and beliefs within a given situation (Albrecht 1999, 22)." Such rites and rituals not only express, they shape, nurture, enliven, transform, and authenticate the community's beliefs, values, self-identity, "story," and spirituality (see Albrecht 1999, 5, 16–17).

At its heart, a ritual is symbolic-expressive behavior. It is more than merely functional, technical, or mundane communication. It expresses, enacts, and communicates symbolically. Its actions also reveal structure, function, and often portions of the group's history, "myth" (story or narrative) and traditions. Various types or genre of rituals are briefly discussed in Appendix 23.

Turner argued that ritual is more than mere symbolic expression. It can possess an efficacious dimension—it can mark, even transform individuals within the group as well as the group itself. This is particularly true in the "liminal period" associated with rites of passage.[4]

The Church's rites and rituals help support the spirituality of the faithful. Further, a vital spirituality enacts and even generates ritual. It ritualizes. In a dynamic corporate Christian spirrualty, the Holy Spirit

---

4. Turner's (1969) concept of liminality (implying transition) as an anti-structural period in rites of passage pervades his work: *The Ritual Process*. According to Turner, rites of passage have three distinct phases: separation, liminal, incorporation.

can breathe through the practices (e.g., rituals) of worshipers, to the glory of God. Ritual and spirituality live hand in hand, or die together.

MAPPING THE DIMENSIONS AND CHIEF COMPONENTS OF THE RITUAL LANDSCAPE

When considering almost any rite or ritual, a "map" of ritual terrain can be helpful. The following list of six mapping elements includes some of the broad, though primary, symbolic categories/components of ritual. These categories will assist those launching into a ritual study; each are a part of the "ritual field."[5] These categories evoke numerous questions as one studies a particular expression of a ritual—question to be pursued in the study.

Ritual actions

These are those behaviors that are a part of a rite. Such behaviors may include sitting, standing, walking/running, dancing, bowing, hand movements and gestures, facial movement, and those unique expressions and actions that are performed with objects.

Ritual roles or identities

A variety of roles/identities are dynamically in play during a particular ritual. These include forms of ritual leadership, elders, musicians, dancers, pastors, teachers, healers, exorcists, congregants, and the audience. Some roles persist beyond the ritual itself, moving into the faith community's life or even the larger society. Roles differ in centrality to the ritual as well as the diversity of actions.

Ritual space and ritual objects in the space

A given ritual is enacted in a particular place; it may be indoors or outdoors. The space itself takes on its own symbolic significance as do the objects that are a part of the place. The space is "shaped" by the ritual, even if it is sometimes used for other purposes. The symbolic reality of the space is also affected by its shape, design, size, color, sounds, and sights. Particular

---

5. "Ritual field" is a conceptualization that includes the contexts, dynamics, and elements of ritual. It is a "physical-social place," "a pattern of interconnecting forces." It is "both the locus of ritual practice and the totality of a ritual's structures and processes" (Grimes 2013, 10), and is also addressed by Turner (1967, 260–78). This section adapts Grimes' (2013, 19–50) categories and field research approach.

quadrants within the whole of the ritual place may be used by participants with particular roles within the ceremony.

Ritual time

Ritual time may include particular times of a day, a day commemorating a historical event, specific seasons of the year, and even lifecycles. It may also include how time is shaped *during* the ritual (e.g., phases, stages, breaks) and how it is contextualized by non-ritual time and societal structures of time.

Ritual language and other sounds

Ritual language may be expressed in written text or oral transmission or a mix. A rite may include one or several genres of language (e.g., systematic, narrative, confessional, expositional, penitential, praise, poetry, dialogue, creeds, and other forms of rhetoric). Genre, tone of voice, sensibility of attitude, spontaneity, and planned language must also be considered when researching ritual language. Sounds, too, may have a role in ritual; musical, instrumental, or vocal sounds including moans, shouts, and ululation. The absence of sound, that is, silence, may also play an important role in ritual.

Modes of ritual sensibilities

While many types of rites and rituals exist in every culture (see Appendix 23), the type, structure, and function are not the end of the story. Ritual sensibilities must also be considered. A ritual sensibility is an embodied attitude that emerges in the midst of an overall ritual. Grimes (2013, 35–50) identified six such sensibilities:

1. A *ceremonial* sensibility shows intentionality with a suspension of individual idiosyncrasies.
2. A *celebratory* sensibility is embodied in highly expressive, even playful attitudes.
3. *Decorum* constitutes a sensibility of propriety.
4. A *liturgical* sensibility is an embodied attitude of sacral worship and meditation, pointing to human interaction with the Ultimate.
5. An *efficacious* sensibility orients to the causal: a rite as a means to an end.
6. *Ritualization* involves actions that might be pre-ritual, proto-rite/ritual, or nascent rites expressed in patterns of behavior,

but are not fully developed as a rite. Ritualization may occur as an innovation or improvisation within an established rite. It may invent and cultivate ritual. Thus this ritual attitude can provide a certain flexibility and newness to a rite.

A final note on the above six modes of sensibility: one or more of these embodied attitudes can animate and orient the overall ritual expression, or micro-rites within the larger ritual. One sensibility may dominate a rite. Alternatively, a variety of attitudes may come into play in a particular ritual event.

The field of ritology is a fertile avenue by which to study a people group. This lens can empower a researcher to understand key aspects of a culture. Ritology can also enable a missionary or missiologist to comprehend a people's rituals within their context. For missiological research, especially research of an ethnographic nature, this methodology can become a valuable tool in the researcher's "tool kit," facilitating the study of a unique aspect of people's lives.

REFERENCES AND RESOURCES FOR ADDITIONAL READING

Albrecht, Daniel E. 1999. *Rites in the Spirit: A Ritual Approach to Pentecostal/ Charismatic Spirituality*. Journal of Pentecostal Theology Supplement Series 17. Sheffield, UK: Sheffield Academic Press.

Bell, Catherine. 2009. *Ritual: Perspectives and Dimensions. Rev ed.* New York: Oxford University Press.

Bradshaw, Paul F., and John Melloh, eds. 2007. *Foundations in Ritual Studies: A Reader for Students of Christian Worship*. Grand Rapids, MI: Baker Publishing.

Grimes, Ronald L. 1995. *Readings in Ritual Studies*. Upper Saddle River, NJ: Prentice Hall.

———. 2013. *Beginnings in Ritual Studies*. 3rd ed. Waterloo, Canada: Ritual Studies International.

Turner, Victor. 1967. *The Forest of Symbols*. Ithaca, NY: Cornell University Press.

———. 1969. *The Ritual Process: Structure and Anti-structure*. Chicago: Aldine Publishing.

———. 1973. Symbols in African Ritual. *Science* 179, no. 4078 (Mar 16): 1100–1105.

WEBSITES OF INTEREST

Center on Myth and Ritual in American Life (MARIAL) Emory
      University: http://www.marial.emory.edu/research/references.html
The Journal of Ritual Studies (University of Pittsburgh): www.pitt
      .edu/~strather/journal.htm

JOURNAL ARTICLE WITH ABSTRACT

Candrett-Leatherman, Craig. 1999. "Ritual and Resistance: Communal
      Connectivity in a Church Retreat." *Missiology: An International Review* 27,
      no. 3: 311–31.

In order to nurture respect for all persons in a racist world, Christian discipleship requires powerful resistance. Drawing on the work of Victor Turner, this paper proposes that the communal connectivity of ritual process enhances hegemonic resistance. Rite of passage provides a three-stage process of separation, marginality, and reincorporation that produces communal connectivity in the margin or liminal stage. Andrew Apter indicates that liminality also produces political dynamism. Muslim pilgrimage and church retreats follow the rite of passage structure. On a Muslim pilgrimage, Malcolm X was connected to pilgrims across racial lines and imagined the reformation of society. The phenomenon and the religious and historical foundation of the Irving Park Free Methodist Church (Chicago, Illinois) retreat is examined beginning with Jesus' dramatic participation in pilgrimage. In the powerful center of ritual liminality, communal connectivity may affect both political reconfiguration and social habit reformation toward resisting hegemonic racism and promoting respect for all persons.

26

CASE STUDIES
Alan R. Johnson, PhD

COMPARING CASE STUDY AND ETHNOGRAPHY

Ethnography, case study, narrative analysis, phenomenology, and action research are all qualitative research frameworks. While sharing common methods of data collection, these five approaches are "distinguishable according to individual characteristics" (Court 2003). In the context of teaching and mentoring graduate students, Deborah Court noted that the most difficult distinction to make among these five methodologies is that between ethnography and case study. This challenge is compounded by the fact that some social science journals use the terms interchangeably (2003).

The following table summarizes important characteristics of both ethnography and case study. Juxtaposed, the information in this table highlights the distinctions between these methodologies.[1]

Ethnography	Case Study
The goal is to obtain all the knowledge necessary for a complete stranger to masquerade as a participant, only on the basis of the information obtained from the ethnographer.	Outward looking and, based on intensive study of a case, aims to contribute to our understanding of a phenomenon.
Ethnography describes the behaviors, values, beliefs, and practices of the participants in a given cultural setting.	Studying a particular case yields a detailed understanding of that one case, shedding light on the wider phenomenon of which that case is an example.
Analyzing a culture means not simply recounting behaviors and events, but inferring the cultural roles that guide behaviors and events.	A case is an intensive study of the "individual": the individual can be defined as a group, a society, an institution, an incident, or even one person.

---

1. Information presented in this table is based on Court (2003).

Ethnography	Case Study
The intention of ethnography is to capture the everyday events, the unwritten laws, and the social conventions and customs that govern the behavior of persons and sub-groups within a culture.	A case is (1) a source of ideas and hypotheses, (2) a resource for new interventions, (3) a way to study rare phenomena or offer a counter-instance to a widely accepted notion, and (4) a mechanism with persuasive and motivational value.
Ethnography seeks to uncover tacit knowl-edge of participants in the specific culture under study, and is most likely to emphasize interpersonal interaction.	The case study examines a limited number of events or conditions and their interrelationships in a shared context.

DEFINING A CASE

As implied in the preceding table, the key to distinguishing between ethnography and case study lies in the definition of a case. The literature consistently identifies a case as one specific entity ("individual") of something or a class of things: an event, an organizational unit, a person, a phenomenon, a site, or a program.[2]

Robert Stake noted that a case should be a specific, complex, functioning thing (1995, 2). He offered some helpful examples of what could be a case and what would never be considered a case. These examples are summarized in the following table.

Could Be Studied as a Case	Would Never Be Labeled a Case
A child	Why children act a certain way
A teacher	A given teacher's teaching (it lacks specificity and boundedness)
An innovative program	The reasons for innovative policies or teaching (these are generalities not specifics)
All the primary schools in a given city	The relationship among schools

SETTING THE CASE BOUNDARIES

Setting the boundaries of a case is a challenging task; it constitutes a key step in case study methodology. The boundaries drawn around a problem,

---

2. E.g., Baxter 2008, 546; Knight 2002, 41; Mill, Durepos, and Wiebe 2010, xxxii.

in order to conceptualize and define it, are fundamental to the findings. As Peter Knight (2004) succinctly observed, "Change the bounds of the case and you are likely to be changing the research findings" (41). Boundaries can be set in one of three ways: by time and place, by time and activity, or by definition and context.[3]

IMPLEMENTING A CASE STUDY

A case study design should be considered for any of four conditions (Baxter 2008, 546):

1. The focus of the study is to answer "how" and "why" questions.
2. The researcher cannot manipulate (empirically) the behavior of those involved in the study.
3. The researcher wants to cover contextual conditions, believing they are relevant to the phenomenon under study.
4. The boundaries between the phenomenon and context are not clear.

After selecting a specific case, the researcher's focus shifts to (1) the interrelationships that constitute the context of a specific entity, and (2) analysis of the relationship between the contextual factors. All of this activity is centered on the goal of generating new theory or contributing to existing theory (Mill, Durepos, and Wiebe 2010).

After determining the case and setting its boundaries, the researcher should choose the type of case study that best fits the research objectives. Writers have used a variety of terms to describe the types of case studies that are possible. These include exploratory, explanatory, descriptive, single-case, multiple-case, holistic, instrumental, intrinsic, and collective. Baxter and Jack summarized well the distinctions between the various types of case studies (2008, 547).

A researcher implements a case study by developing propositions that will focus the data collection. Case study data may be generated from a variety of sources: the literature, personal experience, existing theories, and generalizations based on empirical research (Baxter and Jack 2008, 551). Pamela Baxter and Susan Jack recommended that case-study researchers

---

3. See Baxter (2008, 547) for a discussion of boundary setting.

seek multiple data sources, since the convergence of those sources creates greater understanding of the case.

STRENGTHS AND WEAKNESSES OF CASE STUDIES

The following table is based primarily on material from Phil Hodkinson and Heather Hodkinson (2001) in their conference paper on the strengths and limitations of the case study method.

Strengths	Weaknesses
They help researchers understand complex inter-relationships.	They are inherently subjective.
They are grounded in lived-reality.	Generalization in the conventional sense is limited.
They can facilitate the exploration of the unusual and unexpected.	They have questionable reliability and validity.
Multiple case studies can enable research to focus on the significance of the idiosyncratic.	They do better at description than explanation and establishment of cause-effect relationships.
They can show the processes involved in causal relationships.	They may generate so much data that the researcher may struggle to analyze it all, despite clearly setting the case boundaries.
They can facilitate conceptual and theoretical development.	They are quite costly if attempted on a large scale.
They produce more detailed information than possible through statistical data analysis.	It is hard to represent the complexity of the case in a simple fashion.
They excel in addressing situations that are not homogeneous and routine, but rather involve creativity, innovation, and context.	It is difficult to represent the results numerically.
They allow for greater flexibility in exploring a subject.	They cannot answer a large number of relevant and appropriate research questions.
The emphasis on context places a more human face on research and can serve to bridge the gap between abstract research and concrete practice.	They are easily dismissed by policy-makers or managers because of their small sample size, potential for researcher bias, and lack of connection to many real-life settings.

REFERENCES AND RESOURCES FOR ADDITIONAL READING

Baxter, Pamela, and Susan Jack. 2008. "Qualitative Case Study Methodology: Study Design and Implementation for Novice Researchers." *The Qualitative Report* 13: 544–59.

Court, Deborah. 2003. "Ethnography and Case Study: A Comparative Analysis." *Academic Exchange Quarterly* 7, no. 3. http://www.thefreelibrary.com/Ethnography+and+case+study%3A+a+comparative+analysis.-a0111848865 (accessed November 2, 2011).

Hodkinson, Phil, and Heather Hodkinson. 2001. "The Strengths and Limitations of Case Study Research." In *Learning and Skills Development Agency Conference: Making an Impact on Policy and Practice.* Cambridge, UK. education.exeter.ac.uk/tlc/docs/. . ./LE_PH_PUB_05.12.01.rtf (accessed November 3, 2011).

Knight, Peter T. 2002. *Small-scale Research: Pragmatic Inquiry in Social Science and The Caring Professions.* London: Sage Publications.

Mills, Albert J., Gabrielle Durepos, and Elden Wiebe. 2010. *Encyclopedia of Case Study Research.* Vol. 2. Thousand Oaks, CA: Sage Publications.

Stake, Robert E. 1995. *The Art of Case Study Research.* Thousand Oaks, CA: Sage Publications.

Yin, R. K. 2003. *Case Study Research: Design and Methods.* 3rd ed. Thousand Oaks, CA: Sage Publications.

WEBSITE OF INTEREST

Colorado State University, Writing @CSU. *Case Studies.* http://writing.colostate.edu/guides/research/casestudy/com4a1.cfm

JOURNAL ARTICLE WITH ABSTRACT

Flyvbjerg, Bent. 2006. "Five Misunderstandings about Case-study Research." *Qualitative Inquiry* 12: 219–45. doi: 10.1177/1077800405284363.

This article examines five common misunderstandings about case-study research: (a) theoretical knowledge is more valuable than practical knowledge; (b) one cannot generalize from a single case, therefore, the single-case study cannot contribute to scientific development; (c) the case study is most useful for generating hypotheses, whereas other methods are more suitable for hypotheses testing and theory building; (d) the case study contains a bias toward verification; and (e) it is often difficult to summarize specific case studies. This article explains and corrects these misunderstandings one by one and concludes with the Kuhnian insight that a scientific discipline without a large number of thoroughly executed case studies is a discipline without systematic production of exemplars, and a discipline without exemplars is an ineffective one. Social science may be strengthened by the execution of a greater number of good case studies.

27

HISTORICAL RESEARCH

Charles E. Self, PhD

History both attracts and repels; exasperates and fascinates. Just when a researcher thinks all the facts are accurately assessed and contextualized, new evidence emerges. In addition, the hubris of late- to post-modern Western scholarship questions the validity of any objective knowledge of the past. As a result, historical research has been devalued within the social sciences.

The Internet Age has made enormous amounts of primary and secondary information available,[1] both a boon and a challenge for the serious scholar. The good news is that many data points and academic reflections are available to inform scholars through all stages of their work and make field research more efficient.

The challenge posed by the internet for historical work is that the sheer weight of information can be mistaken for knowledge and wisdom. Further, philosophical and sociopolitical agendas color the evaluation of this material. Many scholars delve into the data with unabashed aims of overturning tradition, subverting academic or social authority, or proving their ideological stances. In light of these challenges, how can missiological scholars maintain intellectual integrity when conducting historical research?

FOUNDATIONAL PRINCIPLES

The following seven statements form an epistemologically sound starting point for historical research and writing:

1. Many past events really "happened" even though they can be viewed through radically different "lenses." For example, the British (both in the eighteenth and twenty-first

---

1. See chapter 8 titled, "Primary and Secondary Sources."

centuries) see the events of the Revolution of 1776 much differently than do most Americans.

2. By definition, "history" is a human record of past events and is, therefore, selective. However, "selective" is not the same as "subjective." We do not know the thoughts of all twelfth-century French peasants, for example, but we can, however, surmise some of their ideas.

3. The "losers" and the marginalized are underrepresented in many historical narratives. Fortunately, this bias has been corrected in recent decades, with new insights enriching our knowledge of the past. Reading Amerindian accounts of the European conquests unveils the complexities of 16th- to 18th-century life in Latin America.

4. Ideological foci are part of life, but they can hinder sound research and color conclusions. For example, Marxist analysis of nineteenth and twentieth century labor history often ignores the religious impulses behind socioeconomic reform movements.

5. Religious concerns profoundly affect historical research and writing. As long as these are acknowledged, good historical work can be done. Neither antipathy nor sympathy for past missionary efforts need necessarily distort objectivity.

6. "Political correctness" can infect historical perceptions and publications; such pressures are more complex than a researcher's ideology. How self-critical can research be when one's livelihood rests on approval from insiders? Recently, a political leader spoke of the many contributions of Muslims to American history and society. This was a benign statement on the surface, but unattested by the weight of history until the last three decades.

7. History is both a subset of social science and an integrative discipline. Historical methodology contextualizes all research with the foci on precedent interpretation and potential applications of findings. When done well, historical research offers the consumer multiple windows into the past, with perspective that may deeply influence the future.

BASIC METHODOLOGY FOR HISTORICAL RESEARCH

The serious scholar is guided by two primary questions when conducting historical research. First, will the efforts yield new information previously unknown to most of the audience? Second, will the research alter current interpretations of the events under study? Generating both new information and new insight are essential to this process. In this regard, a scholar typically completes five steps when conducting historical research.

Step 1: Define the issues, foci, and topics of the research

The basic perspectives of historical understanding fit within this first step: (1) topical historical research, (2) autobiographical and biographical works, (3) chronicles and narratives, and (4) oral history. Stating the issues clearly and establishing the parameters of the work are critical.

Step 2: Review the literature

By evaluating past and current literature on the topic, the researcher can position the new research and writing. This review should include primary and secondary sources,[2] global scholarship, and the notable ideological and philosophical positions.

Step 3: Conduct fresh research

This involves locating and examining historical sources: archaeological findings, artifacts, and archival materials—the primary focus of this chapter. Archival materials must be carefully documented, including location, time of examination, and the precise positioning[3] of the sources. The possible permutations here are endless; the parameters established in steps one and two must be clear. The following table summarizes the type of resources available in step 3:

Archival sources	Public archives (governmental, libraries, the Library of Congress (USA), etc.) Academic and institutional organizations (universities, think tank groups, etc.) Private collections (individuals or smaller groups)
Oral history interviews; "living history" materials	These data sources are invaluable when the facts can be verified—or at least not contradicted—by other reliable sources.

---

2. These are defined and discussed in chapter 8 titled, "Primary and Secondary Sources."

3. Such as in the bin, drawer, shelf and/or other physical referents.

Like a good detective, the diligent researcher will find clues that lead to connections between various resources, and will begin to see the relative importance of the materials in each locale.

Step 4: Evaluating and synthesizing historical data

Not all information is created equal! Apart from unearthing a hitherto unknown piece of data, a historical researcher should assess and rank the sources of information (guided by the literature), including the number of citations, the context of the writing and academic evaluations. Key points to consider include:

- The context (sociocultural location) of the material—when it was written and archived, and its importance.
- The way events and their interpretations compare with other narratives.
- The nature of the evidence: either direct (eyewitness) or indirect (a narrator's synthesis).
- The relationship between primary and secondary sources.

Step 5: Modifying hypotheses and reformulating insights

Thorough historical work unearths more than data. The events and people under study "come to life," making evident the intrinsic value of the knowledge. Research implications are woven into a narrative that informs global academic (and, in some cases, popular) communities for years to come.

CONCLUDING OBSERVATIONS

Excellent historical research on a given subject replies credibly to both unwarranted epistemological absolutism ("Everyone knows that . . .") and complete agnosticism ("It is impossible to say anything conclusive about . . ."). As a part of a larger, multidisciplinary work, historical research contextualizes current thinking and offers avenues for further study. Within the Christian tradition, history offers evidence of the providence of God and the profound sinfulness of human persons and their institutions. Paradoxically, the more historians learn, the less able they are to generalize about some historical topics, even as their knowledge of events grows.

History unveils profound continuities and discontinuities, compelling honest thinkers to reconsider simplistic causal explanations. For example,

28

GROUNDED THEORY METHOD

John L. Easter, PhD

INTRODUCTION TO THE THEORY

Grounded theory method (GTM) has become a commonly used qualitative research approach across the range of academic disciplines. Grounded theory represents a systematic method for constructing a theory *grounded* in data collected and analyzed by GTM principles. In other words, for a researcher using GTM, the objective is two-fold. First, the researcher seeks to discover a major problem in a specific situation from the perceptions of the participants. Second, the researcher then seeks to determine how the study's participants attempt to process the problem. This method provides a pragmatic approach for missiologists to investigate questions of interest, and to discover and conceptualize implicit social patterns and structures at work in a given context through a process of constant comparison.

In grounded theory, the research process begins with data.[1] Using GTM principles, researchers raise questions through a reflective process of collected data which shapes the collection of additional data. The analysis of data induces analytical categories (themes) to emerge that lead to the discovery of patterns constructed in a study. Data are examined through a *constant-comparison* process that enables the researcher to develop hypothesis. Findings are then reported as an explanation of what a researcher believes is at work within a given context of study. A grounded theory study, therefore, is a description of the processes that make up a theory—including a comparison of how an emergent theory and existing theories add to the body of knowledge of a particular subject.

---

1. A basic tenant of grounded theory is that "all is data." In GTM, data form the foundation for theory. How this data is derived is discussed below.

PHILOSOPHICAL CONSIDERATIONS

Grounded theorists assume that a person's communication and activity express meaning; meaning is shared by social groups and viewed as dynamic. In GTM, the emphasis placed on meaning and action helps the researcher to better understand *what is happening* in the experiential world. Leading grounded theorists, like Antony Bryant and Kathy Charmaz (2007), assert this perspective. They assume that society, reality, and self-understanding are formed through this dynamic activity. Thus grounded theory seeks to define fundamental processes of social life. Those processes, in turn, lead to theory development, contingent on specific conditions; the theory, then, is modified as conditions change.

METHODOLOGICAL CONSIDERATIONS

Though GTM represents a systematic qualitative method, it also utilizes contributions of quantitative measures. Unlike the deductive approach that characterizes quantitative research, however, GTM represents an inductive process of moving from particular observations to more general theory.[2]

Methodologically, GTM facilitates a multi-focused approach to data-collection and data-analysis, utilizing varied techniques. This approach encourages the utilization of textual, ethnographical, and phenomenological research techniques. A variety of data sources enable a researcher to identify potential themes and heuristically determined insights. The data reflect clearly a respondent's experiences, feelings, and views, allowing the GTM researcher to explain social behavior.

In GTM, fresh insights and understanding are gained, and themes and concepts emerge by closely examining transcribed texts of verbal interviews. The GTM researcher then links those themes and concepts, creating the substantive components of a theory that emerges from the findings; these components are sometimes labeled "probability statements." This critically important process involves inductive-coding and memoing procedures.[3]

---

2. A deductive approach moves from general theory to specific observations.

3. See chapter 35 titled "Memoing and Coding in Qualitative Field Research" for an introductory description of, and key resources for, these qualitative methodologies.

GTM involves several steps in the analysis and reporting of data. The following list represents some of these steps:

1. Produce transcripts of interactions from observations, interviews, and similar data sources.
2. Evaluate the textual data to identify analytic categories (themes).
3. Compare the textual data from the analytic categories that emerge.
4. Determine how the analytic categories relate to one another.
5. Construct theoretical frameworks and test them against continued emerging data.
6. Write up the findings, utilizing exemplars (e.g., quotes from transcripts) that illustrate the emergent theory.

APPROACH TO THE PRECEDENT LITERATURE

Classic proponents of GTM advocate delaying the literature review until after completing the analysis (e.g., Glaser and Strauss 1967, 35–39). Pre-research literature reviews, they argue, can de-sensitize the researcher to data, hindering efforts to generate new explanations of processes at work within the context of an investigation (Strauss and Corbin 2008).

Other GTM scholars have rejected the classical position of delaying the literature review, referring to it as a *tabula rasa* (or "blank slate") approach to research. Grounded theorists like Charmaz argue that, at times, theoretical sampling is more effective if the researcher has already formed some real categories (2006, 2–10, 163–168).[4] Though a certain level of "theoretical agnosticism" is ideal in GTM, the notion that researchers engage their field studies with a blank slate is unrealistic. Thus, there is growing acceptance of sampling the literature after some initial work in the field has been completed, in order to increase theoretical sensitivity in the later

---

4. Charmaz is one of the world's leading GTM theorists. She identifies herself as an exponent of a "constructivist" approach to GTM; her guidelines have moved GTM away from its positivist origins, allowing for a more nuanced and reflexive practice of GTM. Her text, *Constructing Grounded Theory* (2006), provides a user-friendly guide to newcomers to GTM. The novice GTM researcher should, however, bear in mind that a constructivist approach represents only one stream of thought among grounded theorists.

stages of the study. It is generally recommended, however, that a researcher delay an exhaustive literature review until the data analysis is completed.

The library can help the researcher to discover elements of a concept that will enrich further investigation on the ground. Nonetheless, the wise GTM researcher will take great care while in the library; he or she must not to allow existing theories to distort the field-generated data.

MISSIOLOGICAL IMPLICATIONS

A goal of missiological research is to gain a better understanding of dynamics at work within the physical, socio-cultural, and spiritual environments of a people group. The knowledge acquired equips gospel workers to cross barriers that impede the meaningful communication of Christ. Grounded theory provides a useful method of conducting a missiological study because it enhances a researcher's capacity to draw nearer to a social group's reality, thereby facilitating theory construction about what is happening within the given cultural framework and its consequential implications.

REFERENCES AND RESOURCES FOR ADDITIONAL READING

Bryant, Antony, and Kathy Charmaz. eds. 2007. *The Sage Handbook of Grounded Theory*. Thousand Oaks, CA: Sage Publications.

Charmaz, Kathy. 2006. *Constructing Grounded Theory: A Practical Guide through Qualitative Analysis*. Thousand Oaks, CA: Sage Publications.

Corbin, Juliet, and Anselm Strauss. 2008. *Basics of Qualitative Research: Grounded Theory Procedures and Techniques*. 3rd ed. Thousand Oaks, CA: Sage Publications.

Glaser, Barney, and Anselm Strauss. 1967. *The Discovery of Grounded Theory: Strategies for Qualitative Research*. New York: Aldine Publishers.

WEBSITES OF INTEREST

Grounded Theory Online, Supporting GT Researchers: http://www.groundedtheoryonline.com.

Grounded Theory Institute: http://www.groundedtheory.com.

JOURNAL ARTICLE WITH ABSTRACT

Parry, Ken W. 1998. "Grounded Theory and Social Process: A New Direction for Leadership Research." *The Leadership Quarterly* 9, no. 1: 85–105.

This article examines the use of grounded theory as a valid method for researching the process of leadership. The author contends that leadership is a social influence practice and that conventional leadership research methodologies have been relatively unsuccessful in theorizing about the nature of these processes. Grounded theory, it is argued, helps to overcome the deficiencies in conventional leadership research methodology.

29
FOUNDATIONS FOR INTERVIEWING

Alan R. Johnson, PhD

Interviewing has been described as a conversation with a purpose (Kahn and Cannell 1969, 149). The research interview is most often a two-person conversation[1] initiated by the interviewer for the specific purpose of obtaining information relevant to a given inquiry. It focuses on content specified by the research objectives of systematic description, prediction, explanation (1969, 149). While it is difficult to make hard and fast distinctions between the various methods of inquiry, one helpful way of organizing them is to think in terms of inquiry at a distance or face-to-face (Knight 2002, 49–50, 55). In the former there is a deliberate attempt to reduce the impact of the researcher, while in the latter the researcher is the main "instrument" and can directly impact the participants.

A CONTINUUM OF INTERVIEW TYPES

While all interviews can be classified as a face-to-face research method, interview types differ considerably in reference to the impact of the researcher, and to epistemological[2] position. King labeled interviews as either "depth," "exploratory," "semi-structured," or "unstructured" (King 1994, 14). The useful classification offered by Herbert Rubin and Irene Rubin (2004, 9–11) also includes also four major interview types:

1. Unstructured interviews
2. Semi-structured interviews
3. Cultural interviews, which target shared understandings, roles, and values
4. Topical interviews, which target processes, oral histories, life histories, and evaluation

---

1. With the stipulation that there can be translators, intermediaries, etc.
2. See chapter 2 titled, "Epistemological Frameworks in Qualitative Research."

The Continuum of Interview Types

Broad focus Focus, for instance, on the individual's whole life, classic ethnographic research tends toward this direction	**Narrow focus** Particular topics and how they are perceived and understood by interviewees.
Interviewee as Subject In structured interviewing the concern is accurate information, and the situation is to be untainted by relationship factors with the researcher. Response is passive, to pre-set questions.	**Interviewee as Participant** Associated with open ended, informal interviewing where there is no such thing as a relationship-free process. The interview process is shaped by researcher and interviewee. Response is active and constructing meaning.
High Level of Researcher Control Associated with formal interviewing.	**Low Level of Researcher Control** Associated with informal interviewing. This requires a repertoire of question-asking strategies, and may require the interviewer to be a learner, not an interrogator (Agar 1996, 140).
Structured Interview Closed Questions Highly structured research instruments with fixed-response items; they follow the natural science model and reduce the impact of the researcher by standardizing the interviews, questions and responses. At the highest levels of structure the interviewer follows a script and asks questions in the same sequence. All questions are fixed-response, and the introduction and conclusion are all scripted in advance (Knight 2002, 51). **Strengths/Weaknesses** The strengths are its production of data that are clear and easy to organize/analyze. The weakness is that it constrains the interviewee to a single response per question. "The respondents only get to talk about the things that the researcher thinks are important . . . [with] no scope for them to talk about other things that may be far more significant for them. This is an inescapable feature of highly structured inquiries: they reflect the researcher's theory of what matters" (Knight 2002, 51).	**Unstructured or Lightly Structured** Open questions that invite the interviewee to share as much as they wish to. **Strengths/Weaknesses** For those in the interpretivist tradition the subjectivity of the informal interview is seen as a strength as the researcher and informant create the interview together. The ability to improvise (move away from lines of questioning that are not working, change questions, and allow informants to talk about what is important to them) is key for building understanding and seeking meaning (see Knight 2002, 50–54). However, it is hard to generalize to a larger population with this type of data.

In the table on the previous page, each row represents a continuum of a different issue in research interviewing.[3] When reviewing each continuum, it is important to bear in mind that the type of interview used depends on the research question (King 1994, 15–16).

PREPARING FOR INTERVIEW RESEARCH

Nigel King (1994, 18–21) divides the interview process into four stages: (1) defining the research questions, (2) creating the interview guide, (3) recruiting participants[4] to be interviewed, and (4) conducting the interviews.[5] The creation of the interview guide merits additional discussion.

The interview guide will vary according to the type of interview determined by the research questions defined in the first stage. Highly structured interviews versus unstructured, open-ended interviews require dramatically different interview guides. Every question must be developed in advance for structured interviews. In contrast, the interview guide for unstructured interviews is a list of topics to be covered; pre-written questions are not used. Even so, interviews that are "exploratory, conversational, and free-flowing . . . still need to be carefully planned" (Knight 2002, 62). Without careful planning, informants in unstructured interviews can range off into topics that are far removed from the researcher's interests.

The topics addressed in interviews emerge from three distinct sources: (1) the literature, (2) the researcher's personal knowledge and experience, and (3) information gleaned from earlier phases of the study. In any case, what an interviewer asks, or does not ask, reflects implicit notions about what is, or is not, important. Peter Knight (2002) recommends that when creating an interview agenda (or set of prompts), the researcher should "revisit the literature review and use it to construct a working account of the phenomena in question" (62, 66). The interview guide must be flexible within appropriate parameters; it will change and expand throughout the research process as new areas of interest emerge from the interview process.

---

3. Epistemological frameworks are often tied to some of these extremes.

4. This depends upon the aims of the study, and the amount of time and the resources available. Informed consent must be obtained before interviewing participants. See chapter 12 titled, "Ethical Research with Human Subjects."

5. See chapter 30 titled, "Strategies for Effective Interviewing."

A wise researcher will invite others to critique drafts of the questions and prompts as they are developed. Conducting pilot interviews also allows a researcher to evaluate the questions and prompts, ensuring the questions can be answered and identifying other issues that were not addressed in the literature.

REFERENCES AND RESOURCES FOR ADDITIONAL READING

Agar, Michael. 1996. *The Professional Stranger: An Informal Introduction to Ethnography*. San Diego, CA: Academic Press.

Briggs, Charles L. 1986. *Learning How to Ask: A Sociolinguistic Appraisal of the Role of the Interview in Social Science Research*. Vol. 1 of *Studies in the Social and Cultural Foundations of Language*. Cambridge: Cambridge University Press.

Kahn, David, and Charles F. Cannell. 1968. "Interview." In *International Encyclopedia of the Social Sciences*, ed. David L. Sills, 8: 149–161. New York: MacMillian Co. and Free Press.

King, Nigel. 1994. "The Qualitative Research Interview." In *Qualitative Methods in Organizational Research: A Practical Guide*, ed. Catherine Cassell and Gillian Symon, 14–36. London: Sage Publications.

Knight, Peter T. 2002. *Small-scale Research: Pragmatic Inquiry in Social Science and the Caring Professions*. London: Sage Publications.

Rubin, Herbert J., and Irene S. Rubin. 2005. *Qualitative Interviewing: The Art of Hearing Data*. 2nd ed. Thousand Oaks, CA: Sage Publications.

INTERNET RESOURCES

Doyle, James K. Chapter 11: Introduction to Interviewing Techniques
    http://www.wpi.edu/Academics/GPP/Students/ch11a.html.

Web Center for Social Research Methods. Interviews
    http://www.socialresearchmethods.net/kb/intrview.php.

JOURNAL ARTICLE WITH ABSTRACT

Berry, Rita S. Y. "Collecting Data by in-Depth Interviewing." British Educational Research Association Annual Conference, September 2–5 1999 (accessed November 3, 2011). Available from http://www.leeds.ac.uk/educol/documents/000001172.htm.

Interviews have been used extensively for data collection across all the disciplines of the social sciences & in educational research. There are many types of interviews, as suggested in the literature. However, this paper does not attempt to look at every single type of interview. Instead, it focuses on one particular type—in-depth interviewing. In the presentation, the presenter will briefly explain her interpretation of in-depth interviewing & report on how she used this research method to collect data for her study.

30
STRATEGIES FOR EFFECTIVE INTERVIEWING

Alan R. Johnson, PhD

The first three steps in preparing to do interviews are to define the research questions, develop the interview guide, and recruit participants. This chapter will address the final stages in the interviewing process; conducting the interviews, followed by analyzing the transcript, and finally writing up the research. Beginning by briefly examining some general issues related to the interview process; the rest of the chapter focuses in on question-asking strategies. Appendix 11 enumerates important techniques for conducting interviews.

GENERAL ISSUES RELATING TO THE INTERVIEW PROCESS[1]

Broadly stated, conducting an interview consists of three sequential phases: starting the interview, phrasing the questions and recording them, and concluding the interview (King 1994, 21–22). Before the researcher begins the interview process, Charles Briggs asserts that "adequate applications of interviewing techniques presuppose a basic understanding of the communicative norms of the society in question" (1986, 94). It is important to try to find out the different ways that people communicate, learn the linguistic and socio-cultural knowledge that allows them to do so, and "discern the basic norms that underlie specific communicative patterns" (1986, 94–95). It is obvious these issues require ample time to master when working in an unfamiliar environment.

Setting up the actual interview process requires several related tasks. These include fixing a time, planning how long the interview will last, determining how to record it (handwritten notes, taping, videotaping),

---

1. One of the primary sources for this chapter is a lecture on qualitative research by Steve Woolgar at the Saïid Business School, Oxford University in October-November, 2003.

and preparing the tools to do so in advance (batteries, microphones, video equipment, etc.).

The actual interview starts with an introduction, obtaining permission if the researcher is recording, followed by opening questions to gain background information. Early on, it is best to use questions that can be easily answered, moving to more sensitive and complex questions later (King 1994, 21). The ending of the interview should also be characterized by easier questions, shifting the focus in a positive direction, and leaving a chance for the interviewee to make further comments about the subject (King 1994, 22).

QUESTION-ASKING STRATEGIES

This section consists of twelve question-asking strategies gleaned from the literature[2] and the author's own experience. These strategies can enhance any interview. The author will use his own research work as illustrations for certain points.

1. Avoid ambiguous questions.

Asking questions with two or more propositions may yield ambiguous responses.

2. Avoid biased or leading questions, particularly negative leading questions.

The researcher must avoid rephrasing a statement, providing the answer him or herself, then asking, "That is what you did/said/thought isn't it?" Rather than explaining or clarifying *their* answers, they could easily agree with *the researcher's answer*! It is also easy to take a concept that the researcher is working on and ask a question that would require an answer in those terms, rather than leaving it open enough for them to provide the concept. An example of a negative leading question would be, "You don't find this . . . ?"

3. Use *who, what, where, why, when,* and *how* questions.

These basic questions are essential for setting up the situation and determining the context. Often, when people start talking, they assume the

---

2. Agar 1996, 141–49; Kahn and Cannell 1969; Knight 2002, 139; Silverman 2006; and Spradley 1979.

interviewer knows the background for their responses. Asking these kinds of questions will help the researcher as an outsider to grasp the scenario.

4. Begin with *how*; later ask *why*?

An interviewer can easily cut off conversation by asking about motive, using *why* questions. People cannot always explain why they did something. It is more profitable to ask how they felt, how it happened, and how it was done, gradually teasing out the motive behind an action.

5. Use the baiting strategy.

This involves trying to falsify or contradict what an informant has said to see how they respond. In the author's research on slum leadership, the question, "Must a person have money to become a leader?" was an important one. Non-leaders said leaders needed money, while current position holders said leaders did not need money, adding that they were not people of means. So, when talking about money and leading, if they said they did not have money, the author would then pose the question, "People say you need to have money to lead, so you must have money. Is that right?" This would allow the author to watch their response and, when in a group, the responses of the people who had made that assertion. It would provoke conversation about the role of money and community leadership.

6. Use distribution checks.

Try to find out where particular things happen or are found in the social setting under examination. During the author's fieldwork, he discovered that the slum community was characterized by three geographic divisions, with separate names and different kinds of people in each. Where people were from geographically mattered a great deal in that community.

7. Use contrast and comparison questions.

In the author's research he learned words relating to trustworthiness, respect, and an even higher term beyond that, spending large amounts of time asking for comparisons and contrasts to learn about each of these terms.

8. Depersonalize the question: "Does *someone* do X?" rather than "Do *you* do . . . ?"

Depersonalizing the question is particularly important in societies that value face-saving and indirect communication. Talking about a third party is a great way of letting people share information that they would feel uncomfortable sharing about themselves.

9.   Use semantic relationships to learn cultural details.

J. P. Spradley (1979) called this ethnographic semantics, providing details on the kinds of questions that develop what is known as a cultural grammar. A few examples would be, X is a kind of Y, X is used for Y; A entails B, A is a sufficient condition for B; and looking at agents, instruments, and objects, such as X is done with a Y. For instance, when trying to discern the differences between Thai words for respect, *nabthuu* and *khaorop*, I would suggest a particular action, like obeying someone, and ask my interviewee, "does this happen when we *nabthuu* someone, *khaorop* someone, or in both?" That material would then help me to build the kinds of behaviors that entail from each of these terms.

10.   Use answers to questions to pick up terminologies and concepts that can then be used in asking new questions.

Particularly when working in a second language, a respondent may answer a question and use a word that will help unlock more fruitful answers in the future. In the early stages of the author's research, he was exploring terms for the domain of leading and wielding social influence. One person answered the question with a word that the author had not thought of; translated literally as "touches the heart." Discussing a boss, department lead, or foreman that "touched the heart" turned out to be a very fruitful line of questioning that yielded abundant and rich answers.

11.   Experiment with asking questions using different shades of the same construct.

The researcher may find that one term elicits longer responses in an easier fashion, while another term is more difficult for respondents.

12.   Develop actual scenarios from real-life and have the interviewees respond in terms of what they would do, explaining what is happening, and so on.

This is particularly important in settings where people are more concrete-relational thinkers than abstract thinkers. To ask an informant to "define X concept" may yield very little information. But to create a scenario and then ask how concept X is activated, how it operates, what would facilitate it or block it, and so on can be very fruitful. This is also a very helpful strategy when dealing with sensitive issues that people may not want to discuss. Developing a hypothetical scenario can make it easier to talk because no specific people are involved and it thus avoids potential loss of face.

REFERENCES AND RESOURCES FOR ADDITIONAL READING

Agar, Michael. 1996. *The Professional Stranger: An Informal Introduction to Ethnography*. San Diego, CA: Academic Press.

Briggs, Charles L. 1986. *Learning How to Ask: A Sociolinguistic Appraisal of the Role of the Interview in Social Science Research*. Vol. 1 of *Studies in the Social and Cultural Foundations of Language*. Cambridge: Cambridge University Press.

Kahn, David, and Charles F. Cannell. 1968. "Interview." In *International Encyclopedia of the Social Sciences*, ed. David L. Sills, 8: 149–61. New York: MacMillian Co. and Free Press.

Knight, Peter T. 2002. *Small-scale Research: Pragmatic Inquiry in Social Science and the Caring Professions*. London: Sage Publications.

Silverman, David. 2006. *Interpreting Qualitative Data: Methods for Analysing Talk, Text and Interaction*. 3rd ed. London: Sage Publications

Spradley, J. P. 1979. *The Ethnographic Interview*. New York: Harcourt, Brace Jovanovich College Publishers.

WEBSITE OF INTEREST

Conducting the Information Interview [7 modules]
    http://www.roguecom.com/interview/

JOURNAL ARTICLE WITH ABSTRACT

Opdenakker, Raymond. 2006. "Advantages and Disadvantages of Four Interview
    Techniques in Qualitative Research." *Forum qualitative sozialforschung /
    Forum: Qualitative social research* 7:4 [44 paragraphs]. http://www.qualitative
    -research.net/index.php/fqs/article/view/175/391. Accessed November 8,
    2011.

Face-to-face interviews have long been the dominant interview technique
in the field of qualitative research. In the last two decades, telephone interviewing became more and more common. Due to the explosive growth of
new communication forms, such as computer mediated communication
(for example e-mail and chat boxes), other interview techniques can be
introduced and used within the field of qualitative research.

For a study in the domain of virtual teams, I used various communication possibilities to interview informants as well as face-to-face interviews.
In this article, a comparison will be made concerning the advantages and
disadvantages of face-to-face, telephone, e-mail and MSN messenger
interviews. By including telephone and MSN messenger interviews in
the comparison, the scope of this article is broader than the article of
BAMPTON and COWTON (2002).

31

FOCUS GROUP INTERVIEWS

Anita L. Koeshall, PhD

A focus group interview (FGI) is a qualitative data collection strategy that uses synergistic group interaction to illumine informants' attitudes, values, and assessments of a topic or issue. An expertly facilitated focus group becomes a dynamic social environment characterized by the free expression of personal opinions and contrasting views. Unlike data generated by individual interviews, focus group data also includes observation of emotional reactions, body language, and group relational exchanges.

This interview method can be employed at several junctures in mixed methods research:

1. Early in a study, an FGI can identify variables in exploratory research, contribute to the content of survey items, gain insight into a particular people group, identify local vocabulary, and create a concourse for further research (Côté-Arsenault and Morrison-Beedy 1999).

2. Later in a study, an FGI can be used to verify and explain data collected by other research methods, such as Likert scales or participant observation.

3. As a final step in a mixed-method research design, an FGI can aid in affirming and validating the assumptions and conclusions made by the researcher. In action research, this methodology can be used to present findings from earlier methods to the study population, enabling those participants to determine the appropriate course of action to be taken in response to those findings.

A COMPLEX METHOD

An FGI may appear to be simple to execute, however, a great deal of work must go into its design in order to obtain the desired data and ensure the validity of the results. The eight steps discussed here illustrate how challenging this dynamic research method can be.

Step 1: Defining the data to be collected

A well-designed study may link an FGI to one or more research questions. Focus groups "explore issues of salience for participants rather than rigidly pursuing the researcher's agenda" (Barbour 2008, 110). Even so, the researcher knows precisely what data need to be pursued and how those data will contribute to the resolution of the central research problem.

Step 2: Designing the interview guide

The group moderator (typically the researcher) must develop an interview guide that will stimulate the group's conversation in order to produce the desired data. This interview guide must facilitate the moderator's efforts to move the group through five major phases of an FGI:

1. Ice-breaker: Identify characteristics the participants have in common in order to build trust among them; this is especially important if the group members do not know each other.

2. Introduction: Place the topic in a context that would be familiar to all.

3. Major transition: Guide the discussion to the broader scope of the topic. The moderator can facilitate this transition by relating a typical case or story, or using a cartoon, a pamphlet, a movie clip, or other form of stimulus that will encourage conversation (Barbour 2008, 84).

4. Discussion: Provoke and guide the discussion through the varying aspects of the topic with two to five well-designed questions.

5. Closure: Summarize and bring closure to the discussion by giving opportunity for participants to make final statements. The moderator should end the FGI by asking two key questions: "Is this an adequate summary?" and "Have we missed anything?"

Step 3: Selecting and soliciting the desired participants[1]

Participants should possess shared knowledge or experience that connects them with the discussion topic. Thus, purposive sampling is typically used when soliciting group members.[2] Participants should also be sufficiently homogenous in order to discuss the topic freely. Differences in attitudes and experience—when expressed freely—add depth and "spice" to the dialogue, exposing the reasoning behind opinions. While some diversity of opinion is helpful, a wise researcher will not intentionally mix "together people who are known to have violently differing perspectives on emotive issues" (Barbour 2008, 59).

Commonly, multiple focus groups are formed in a single study, each containing a relatively homogeneous segment of the total research population. For example, Bible school teachers may compose one group and students another. Alternatively, church elders might be selected for one group, and younger lay members for another.

Focus groups should include no more than twelve members. However, a smaller group of five to six members may be more useful when a topic has strong emotional overtones and each participant has a story to tell in relationship to the topic. Thus, the group size must be controlled to ensure that sufficient time is available for all members (particularly the less expressive ones) to have a voice and contribute to the interview (Denscombe 2010, 354–55).

Step 4: Planning and preparing the venue

The space dedicated to the FGI should be welcoming, comfortable, and quiet.[3] Participants should sit around tables or on comfortable couches;

---

1. Informed consent (IC) protocols must be used in focus group research; each participant must sign an IC form.

2. In some cases, snowball sampling is needed to locate people with a common interest in the topic. In snowball sampling, the researcher asks the participants to recommend others in their networks who have the same expertise and or experience. The required participants in the sample must have shared experiences or knowledge (for instance, experts in a field, Bible School presidents, or mothers who have homosexual children), snowball sampling often is one of the best methods of finding more participants.

3. Quiet is especially needed for the post-session transcribing of the FGI when ongoing or sporadic background noise besides potentially distracting the session can also make it hard to hear for transcribing.

a high-quality digital recording device should be placed in the center of the room. Many researchers also video tape their interviews to capture both verbal and non-verbal data.[4] The moderator may distribute nametags in order to track with the recording who is speaking.[5] The moderator should sit in the circle, but the assistant should sit to the side.

Step 5: Executing the focus group

An FGI normally lasts from one and a half to two hours. The moderator plays a vital role in the focus group by focusing on several essential activities (Schensul, et al. 1999):

- quickly building trust and a sense of confidentiality within the group;
- stimulating debate, ensuring that the conversation addresses the guide's questions;
- interjecting appropriate probes to clarify comments and ensure understanding;
- and encouraging reticent participants to share in the conversation while restraining group members who would dominate the conversation.

The moderator must constantly remember that he or she is not the focus of the FGI, the *topic* is. The data generated by the dialogue among the participants is of primary importance. The moderator must be a good listener, avoiding the temptation to reveal his or her own biases!

A research assistant plays a vital, complex role during the FGI. He or she must be a skilled observer of group dynamics: (1) identifying the speakers, (2) memoing observations about emotions and body language, (3) noting the flow of the dialogue, and (4) capturing other vital observations required by the researcher. The assistant must also operate the recording device(s).

---

4. The video recording can also help in the transcription in distinguishing between voices.

5. Numbers or pseudonyms should be used if the participants are strangers, to ensure anonymity for the participants. In such cases only the researcher should know the identity of the participants.

Step 6: Debriefing immediately after the participants have departed

The moderator and the assistant should debrief immediately after the participants depart. They should first make a diagram of the seating arrangements, noting the divergent viewpoints within the group. They should then (1) make a list of significant themes and ideas, especially those that were surprising or unexpected, (2) compare the data revealed in this focus group with others in the project (if relevant), (3) evaluate the usefulness of the questions, and (4) make sure all recordings are correctly labeled and saved.

Step 7: Transcribing the recordings, integrating the assistant's observations, and coding

The researcher and his or her assistant must transcribe and integrate both the verbal and non-verbal data from the audio or video recordings and the assistant's notations. In some situations, however, a full transcription may not be required[6] in order to code the interview data: coding directly from the audio or visual recordings may be possible (Schensul 1999, 24).

Step 8: Analyzing and comparing data

The researcher must then analyze the transcribed information using recognized best-practice coding methods used in analyzing any textual source. Richard Krueger and Mary Ann Casey (2014) suggest that the following categories be considered in this analysis:

- key words
- context
- internal consistency
- frequency or extensiveness of comments
- intensity
- specificity
- big ideas

The researcher must carefully compare the differing opinions and values expressed *within* each focus group. This analysis is important in its own right and may directly answer a research question or sub-question.

---

6. Although it would be preferable should the information be used later, and previous insignificant details are found in the transcripts. Transcripts allow for later re-evaluation.

Careful, detailed analysis also will facilitate comparison *between* focus groups in those studies utilizing more than one FGI.

CONCLUSION

Excellent resources abound that clearly outline the steps that must be taken in order to conduct a successful FGI. However, nothing can replace the contribution of an experienced moderator who is equipped with excellent focus group interview guide. Before starting an actual study group, therefore, a wise researcher will conduct several groups in order to gain competency in this complex and demanding interview method.

REFERENCES AND RESOURCES FOR ADDITIONAL READING

Barbour, Rosaline. 2008. *Doing Focus Groups.* Thousand Oaks, CA, Sage Publications.

Côté-Arsenault, Denise, and Dianne Morrison-Beedy. 1999. "Practical Advice for Planning and Conducting Focus Groups."*Nursing Research* 48, no. 5: 280-283. http://libres.uncg.edu/ir/uncg/f/D _CoteArsenault_PracticalAdvice_1999.pdf.

Denscombe, Martyn. 2010. *The Good Research Guide for Small-Scale Social Research Projects.* New York: McGraw-Hill.

Krueger, Richard A., and Mary Ann Casey. 2014. *Focus Groups: A Practical Guide for Applied Research.* Thousand Oaks, CA, Sage Publications.

Schensul, Jean J., et al. 1999. *Enhanced Ethnographic Methods: Audiovisual Techniques, Focused Group Interviews, and Elicitation Techniques.* Lanham, MD: AltaMira Press.

WEBSITE OF INTEREST

Fieldwork

   http://www.fieldwork.com/join

JOURNAL ARTICLE WITH ABSTRACT

Iversen, Maria Helen, Astrid Kilvik, and Wenche Malmedal. 2015. "Sexual Abuse of Older Residents in Nursing Homes: A Focus Group Interview of Nursing Home Staff." *Nursing Research and Practice*, 2015: article ID 716407, 6 pages. doi:10.1155/2015/716407.

The objective of this study was to increase knowledge of sexual abuse against older residents in nursing homes. A qualitative approach was used. Through a focus group interview with staff in nursing homes, the aim was to reveal employees' thoughts, experiences, and attitudes. Findings from the focus group interview show that sexual abuse of older residents is a taboo topic among health professionals. Acts of sexual abuse are difficult to imagine; it is hard to believe that it occurs. The fact that staff are not aware that it could happen, or have a hard time believing that it actually happens, can amplify the residents' vulnerable position as potential victims of abuse, and it makes it even more challenging to report or uncover such acts. The study highlights the need for education of all health care workers in Norway as well as more research on sexual abuse against older residents in nursing homes. Furthermore, there is a need for good policies and reporting systems, as an important step towards addressing sexual abuse of the aged in a more appropriate way. Further research must aim to reveal more about this taboo area.

32
QUALITATIVE DATA ANALYSIS

John L. Easter, PhD and Alan R. Johnson, PhD

This chapter focuses broadly on data analysis in qualitative research. Its characteristics and basic strategies are overviewed as a foundation for more detailed data-analysis discussions. Two issues that are critical to qualitative analysis, coding, and memoing, will be dealt with in chapters 34 and 35, respectively.

CHARACTERISTICS OF QUALITATIVE RESEARCH

The pursuit of making sense of real-world phenomena generates data that can be captured in two forms: number-type data, or word-type data.[1] Both approaches have their strengths and weaknesses, both are tied to certain epistemological commitments, and both address empirically relevant research questions. However, in this chapter the focus is on qualitative data which is word-type data.

Qualitative methods allow participants to respond to questions in their own words; these methods also rely on the researcher's direct observation and participation in a given social setting. Thus, qualitative research is especially helpful for developing explanations of social and cultural reality, and when existing theory is not available to guide interpretation of observed phenomena.

Missiological researchers often focus on phenomena not adequately addressed by current theory: where little empirical understanding exists concerning worldviews, lifestyles, spirituality, cultural patterns and configurations, social perceptions and attitudes, and the dynamics of interpersonal interactions in various social settings. For these reasons, qualitative methodology is ideally suited for many missiological studies.

---

1. For details see chapters 22 and 23 titled "The Nature of Data," and "Qualitative and Quantitative Research: Similarities and Distinctions," respectively.

The three most common qualitative research categories are participant observation, in-depth interviews, and focus groups. Each method facilitates the collection of specific kinds of data; these may be captured in field notes, audio and video recordings, or transcribed textual documents. By using multiple research procedures, a researcher can "triangulate" the study's findings (Bernard 2011). Triangulation helps a researcher verify whether findings are reliable by cross checking the results.

These collection methods can generate copious amounts of data. It is not uncommon for people to feel overwhelmed with the mass of material and the challenge of a systematic and methodical analysis of it. This is not reason for discouragement, but is where the excitement and serendipity of research journey begins as you apply basic strategies for qualitative analysis to your data set.

BASIC STRATEGIES OF QUALITATIVE DATA ANALYSIS

While qualitative data-collection methods produce large amounts of data, Peter Knight reminds us that methods do not generate understanding (2002, 18); only careful, thoughtful data analysis does this. Missiological researchers must seek explanation—the "why" and the "how" of phenomena, not just their description. In this context, Keith Punch argues that explanation:

> Involves finding the reasons for things, events and situations, showing why and how they have come to be what they are. . . . We can describe without explaining, but we can't really explain without describing. Therefore explanation goes further than description. . . . It is description plus something else. (1998, 15)

The basic strategies proposed for qualitative data analysis, in broad terms, consist of two dynamic, interactive phases (Knight 2002, 182).

1. Coding or indexing the data consists of tagging or marking units of coding so that similar themes, ideas, examples, or

cases are put in the same categories. Counter-examples are also identified and indexed for later attention.[2]

2. Developing and reflecting on interpretations of the data, looking for the simplest stories, hypotheses, or judgments that makes defensible sense of the whole. Veteran researchers call attention to the fact that there is no set formula here, there are things that one does, but ultimately one must build one's own trail in making sense of the subject of one's investigation.[3]

While there is not a single fixed set of procedures for making sense of qualitative data, within these two interactive phases are several key steps that will help researchers move from data, through sensemaking, to theory development (for a more descriptive treatment of these steps refer to Appendix 14, and also refer to chapters 34, and 35).

1. Prepare and organize transcribed texts, all interview and observational data, and documents involved with the research site or research questions.
2. Identify analytical categories (themes) and concepts that emerge from the texts.
3. Compare the data from each of the categories identified.
4. Examine how the categories are connected to each other.
5. Build a theoretical model in light of relational dynamics between the major themes.

These steps are broadly taken from Bernard (2011), and supplemented by ideas, tips, and rules of thumb from Knight (2002, 182–90), who drew upon Miles and Huberman (1994). Steps two through four must be worked through recursively. Often the researcher will find that the emerging themes and categories will lead them to go back to collect more data for further clarification and expansion of previous rounds of analysis.

---

2. See chapters 34 and 35 entitled, "Coding in Qualitative Field Research" and "Memoing in Qualitative Field Research," respectively.

3. See Appendix 14, "Steps in Qualitative Data Analysis."

THE ONGOING NATURE OF DATA ANALYSIS

Veteran researchers suggest that the analysis of qualitative data actually begins with the data-gathering process. This means that the two interactive phases of data analysis (see above) continuously engage with the emerging data and findings throughout the course of the study.

Analysis must be an ongoing process of reflection, refining, and shifting the lines of questioning as new categories emerge. A missiological researcher cannot wait until he or she has amassed all relevant data to sit down and work through it; doing so will allow many intriguing data "trails" to go cold. While you cannot address every possible data trail that emerges, the researcher needs to carefully evaluate which of these themes relate to the current investigation and which ones should be noted for future research in the conclusion of the final presentation of your results. Researchers who are conscientious and disciplined to carry out analysis throughout the data-collection process will position themselves to discover richer data to inform their study.

REFERENCES AND RESOURCES FOR ADDITIONAL READING

Bernard, H. Russell. 2011. *Research Methods in Anthropology: Qualitative and Quantitative Approaches.* 5th ed. Lanham, MD: AltaMira Press.

Knight, Peter T. 2002. *Small-scale Research: Pragmatic Inquiry in Social Science and the Caring Professions.* London: Sage Publications.

Kolb, William L. 1964. "Science." In *A Dictionary of the Social Sciences*, ed. Julius Gould and William L. Kolb, 620–22. New York: Free Press of Glencoe.

Miles, Matthew, and A. Michael Huberman. 1994. *Qualitative Data Analysis.* 2nd ed. Thousand Oaks, CA: Sage Publications.

Punch, Keith F. 1998. *Introduction to Social Research: Quantitative and Qualitative Approaches.* London: Sage Publications.

Silverman, David. 2006. *Interpreting Qualitative Data: Methods for Analysing Talk, Text and Interaction.* 3rd ed. London: Sage Publications

WEBSITE OF INTEREST

Online QDA—What is Qualitative Data Analysis (QDA)?
    http://onlineqda.hud.ac.uk/Intro_QDA/what_is_qda.php

JOURNAL ARTICLE WITH ABSTRACT

Ratcliff, Donald. 2008. "Qualitative Data Analysis and the Transforming
    Moment." *Transformation* 25, no. 2 & 3: 116–33.

Insight is an important and repeated component of most qualitative research studies. Yet insight is often a vague concept that is not well articulated in textbooks and research reports. The late James Loder of Princeton University posited a theologically-based process he termed 'the transforming moment' that identifies predictable phases in a wide variety of transformations, including those of a psychological, scientific, and spiritual nature. This process corresponds at many levels with the role of insight in qualitative research. As a result, careful examination of Loder's outline of the transformative process can help clarify what is meant by insight and how it informs research activities.

33
FIELD WORK AND FIELD NOTES
Building an Ethnographic Database
Alan R. Johnson, PhD

In qualitative research, the researcher becomes the instrument for data collection and analysis. Peter Knight (2002) explains that those who participate in a social setting and immerse themselves in culture typically keep journals because "their fieldnotes usually *are* their research evidence" (2). This immersion is known also as field work, with field notes being the product and record of that work.

The term "field notes"[1] means different things to different researchers. Narrowly defined, these are the notes taken while actually interviewing and observing. In this chapter, this term is used in reference to the whole enterprise of taking notes. This obviously includes capturing what the researcher is seeing and hearing; it also encompasses the researcher's (1) reflections on those notes, (2) plans for future research—things to pursue, and (3) ongoing coding and analytical work. Taken as a whole, these notes become the "ethnographic database" that includes both raw material and the researcher's reflections upon it as he or she constructs her understanding and interpretation.

FIELD WORK AND THE ACT OF GATHERING DATA[2]

Observation is at the core of most social science research, particularly ethnographic work. Given this, what the researcher observes and how he or she observes (captures) it are both important. Veteran researchers assert that a one-to-one correspondence between what the researcher observes and the text he or she writes does not exist. The act of writing up accounts

---

1. The term "field notes" has the common alternative spelling of "fieldnotes;" either spelling is acceptable if used consistently.

2. These guidelines and ideas for building the ethnographic database presented in this section reflect the contribution of other researchers and the author's own experience.

of one's experiences and observations is neither straightforward nor transparent (Emerson, Fretz, and Shaw 1995, 5).

Emerson, Fretz, and Shaw offer useful suggestions for capturing data in the field (1995, 5–10):

1. It is not possible to catch everything; reduction and selective attention are inevitable. The researcher frames objects and events in particular ways. These choices reflect both the theoretical underpinnings of the research and the researcher's assumptions about social life and how to understand it.
2. The researcher must be mindful that recordings are not a mirror, but a construct that involves the researcher's perceptions and interpretations.
3. The researcher is not just passively copying facts, but is actively interpreting and making sense of the social life and discourse she is studying.

Steve Woolgar[3] also notes that what the researcher observes is everything that relates to the research questions; this is done by watching, listening, asking questions, and even making mistakes.

These suggestions indicate that qualitative data collection and data analysis are closely linked. They are examined separately when discussing qualitative research; the reality is that they happen simultaneously.

TAKING NOTES IN THE FIELD

As mentioned above, the term "field notes" is used in a broad sense, covering the whole enterprise connected with immersion into, and observation of, a social setting. The following two sections will first discuss activities done in the field while immersed in social life, followed by those that are typically completed later with the captured material.

The researcher records observations in three major ways. The researcher may take notes—either with paper and pen or using a computer—completing this task either off site or as close and as soon as possible to the actual interactions. The second and third ways to record observations are audio and visual recordings made at the research site. After digitally

---

3. Steve Woolgar, "Lecture #5: Qualitative Research Methods: Field Work, Field Notes and Data Collection," presented at the Saïd Business School, Oxford University, UK, in 2003.

capturing the data, the researcher works through the data at a later time. At this point the creative/interpretive process occurs, as the raw observations are transformed into reflective written summaries.

When writing down notes while in the field and interacting with people, the following ten suggestions can make the process less daunting:

1. Describe the observation itself, avoiding a low-level inferences about what is happening. Do not interpret at this point; only record in as much detail as possible as it is happening.

2. Make notes during or immediately following interactions, if possible.

3. Make additional notes at the end of the day after observations are complete.

4. Record separately inferences, personal observations, hunches, and emotional reactions.

5. How the researcher "records" the material will vary, depending on the circumstances. One may use pen and paper during conversations. At other times, it is better to talk naturally, and then stop to record observations soon thereafter.

6. Develop an interview guide with suggested themes to investigate. This document should be internalized to the extent that one need not reference it during a conversation or interview.

7. Take notes on conversations, stories, anecdotes, interviews, feelings and things observed during participation of events.

8. Take notes on official descriptions regarding the research site; this includes official documents, reports, articles, and books. Remember to document the how, where, what, and when of their production.

9. Get graphic: make diagrams, take pictures, and sketch the scenes observed.

10. Take notes to eventually develop characterizations of the major players in the research effort; collect "asides" that can be used to clarify, explain, interpret, or revise questions in the field notes (Emerson, Fretz, and Shaw 1995, 81, 101).

SUMMARIZING, JOURNALING, AND RECORDING AFTER FIELD WORK

On leaving the research site, the researcher will have amassed raw data that must be organized, interpreted and analyzed. Much of this analysis will involve coding and producing memos on these raw data.[4] Six points of practical advice for organizing an ethnographic database merit discussion:

1. The researcher must develop her own system for recording and organizing information and use it consistently, constantly refining it. The key to success in ethnographic research is being able to retrieve information once it is captured. This involves taking field notes—quick jottings, brief sketches, and abbreviated thoughts—and filing them so they can be quickly recovered and analyzed.

2. Keep a research journal containing notes about what has been done (Knight 2002, 2). This creates the researcher's "paper trail" of how she achieved her results.

3. Keep copies of all instruments used such as interview guides, recordings made, exercises done such as pile sorts and so on (Knight 2002, 2).

4. Organize jottings by themes, and then file these in folders. Include relevant items from newspapers, references read or needing to be read, and so on (Knight 2002, 3). Utilize, as needed, both hardcopy and digital (computer) folders.

5. As soon as possible after making observations in the field, develop a summary of thoughts and note any special ideas. This material could initially be captured in a research journal chronicling what the researcher has done. It can also take the form of separate memos.[4]

6. R. Emerson, R. Fretz and L. Shaw recommended writing "commentaries" (1995, 102); commentaries are more elaborate reflections of what the researcher has done, her experiences, and her reactions.

Diligently following these steps and being careful to keep and document all of one's actions in research provides and ethnographic database that helps to show your readers how it was that you arrived at the end of the day at the conclusions you make.

---

4. See chapters 34 and 35.

REFERENCES AND RESOURCES FOR ADDITIONAL READING

Emerson, R., R. Fretz, and L. Shaw. 1995. *Writing Ethnographic Fieldnotes*. Chicago: University of Chicago Press.

King, Nigel. 1994. "The Qualitative Research Interview." In *Qualitative Methods in Organizational Research: A Practical Guide*, ed. Catherine Cassell and Gillian Symon, 14–36. Thousand Oaks, CA: Sage Publications.

Knight, Peter T. 2002. *Small-scale Research: Pragmatic Inquiry in Social Science and the Caring Professions*. London: Sage Publications.

Sanjek, Roger, ed. 1990. *Fieldnotes: The Makings of Anthropology*. Ithaca, NY: Cornell University Press.

Silverman, David. 2006. *Interpreting Qualitative Data: Methods for Analysing Talk, Text and Interaction*. 3rd ed. London: Sage Publications.

Spradley, James P. 1980. *Participant Observation*. Ft. Worth, TX: Harcourt College Publishers.

WEBSITES OF INTEREST

American Anthropology Association, Statement on the Confidentiality of Field Notes
http://www.aaanet.org/stmts/fieldnotes.htm
Writing Ethnographic Fieldnotes [full pdf textbook]
http://www.pacificdiscovery.org/credit/SEAreadings /Robert%20et.al.%20-%20Writing%20Ethnographic %20Fieldnotes.pdf

JOURNAL ARTICLE WITH ABSTRACT

Walford, Geoffrey. 2009. "The Practice of Writing Ethnographic Fieldnotes." *Ethnography and Education* 4: 117–30. doi: 10.1080/17457820902972713

Fieldnotes are central to ethnographic practice, yet there is surprisingly little written about how fieldnotes are constructed. This article reports the results of some interviews with four well-known ethnographers of education who were questioned about their practice. It is designed to be a resource for those new (and, maybe not so new) to ethnography.

34
CODING IN QUALITATIVE FIELD RESEARCH

John L. Easter, PhD and Alan R. Johnson, PhD

Qualitative social science inquiry produces a large volume of material; this material becomes the database of information a researcher seeks to understand through careful analysis and interpretation. When this interpretive work is completed, the researcher can begin to develop theory that models interrelationships and explains how things work.

Chapter 33 titled "Field Work and Field Notes: Building an Ethnographic Database" is predicated on the principle that walls separating data collection and data analysis are artificial in qualitative research. The qualitative researcher is actively and continuously involved in constructing meaning and selectively choosing what to record and focus upon.

Certain activities are specifically designed to analyze the mass of data generated in qualitative research. These activities are labeled differently by researchers in different research traditions. In general, however, the notion of *coding* and *memoing* as interconnected and related activities is central to analyzing qualitative materials. Qualitative coding refers to the process a researcher uses to classify data: a short label summarizes and accounts for each piece of data. Memos are running records of insights, hunches, hypotheses, discussions, implications of codes, and additional thoughts (Strauss 1987, 110). This chapter focuses on coding; the next chapter discusses memoing. Though they are presented in separate chapters, coding and memoing are closely related activities.

DEFINING CODING

How do researchers make sense of the data generated by interviews and observations? A major assumption in social research is that discernible patterns and configurations exist in social life. It is not simply disconnected and random activity. The process of qualitative coding is the core activity in discerning patterns and configurations in the data. In turn, these codes help the researcher to retrieve, categorize, and organize this material. These processes facilitate the accounting of codified segments of rich data, a process analogous to the construction of an analytic framework upon which to hang interpretations. Finally, theory is then developed from the insights and interpretations generated from this process.

In essence, coding represents an interpretive rendering of qualitative data. Coding reflects the process of studying and defining what a researcher believes is happening in the empirical world of the informants. The practice of coding forces the researcher to ask systematic questions of data sources, which include observations, interviews, field notes, surveys, film, historical records, and other textual documents. Carefully chosen words, phrases, or sentences help define analytic categories (themes) and set the trajectory for a study. Each code is assigned a unit of meaning. A researcher then clusters chunks of data together that relate to specific research questions.

Researchers use a variety of approaches for codifying material. Matthew Miles and A. Michael Huberman designate three types of codes: (1) descriptive codes, (2) interpretive codes, and (3) pattern codes (1994, 57–58). Descriptive codes require little interpretation, typically attributing a class of phenomena to a piece of data. Interpretive codes become useful as a researcher learns more about local dynamics and implicit layers of social motivations. Pattern codes are much more inferential and explanatory, and are particularly useful when a researcher discerns a pattern at work in local events and relationships. Pattern codes typically come into play in the latter part of a study as patterns become clearer.

In addition, three methods are commonly recommended for coding data: (1) line-by-line, (2) incident-to-incident, and (3) *in vivo*. Using line-by-line coding, a researcher labels each line of written data (e.g., interview transcripts). Incident-to-incident coding allows a researcher to codify data based on a comparative study of incidents germane to a study's focus. *In vivo* coding refers to codes that use participants' special terms; it allows a researcher to preserve participants' meaning of their views and actions.

OVERVIEW OF CODING PRACTICE

How do researchers actually do coding? While differences based on theoretical orientation and researcher style exist, the coding process moves from initial labeling to building categories to increasingly abstract categorization that encompasses more data to defining core categories that are central to the research questions. Thus rounds of coding characterize qualitative analysis, starting broadly and becoming more selective as categories emerge.

OPEN CODING: BREAKING THE DATA DOWN

The first step in coding involves seeing the data through the lens of a coding paradigm. Anselm Strauss suggested that the material be examined for conditions, interaction among the actors, strategies and tactics, and consequences (1987, 27–28). Labels can then be assigned to the data; these labels are, in fact, codes (also called categories). An important point here is that assigning a category is not just summarizing the field notes. Instead, the researcher strives to develop a concept that is based on empirical indicators, such as actions, events, and things described in the words of informants. Thus, the researcher must (1) examine the data, working from specific indicators, and (2) give those data a name as a class of events or behavioral actions. The name is a coded category (Strauss 1987, 25). Strauss observed that coding is not simply applying shorthand to the data at a totally descriptive level. It is, rather, seeking to render *explicit* the conditions, interactions, tactics, and consequences that are *implicit* in the respondent's words (1987, 29, 58).

Words and phrases like "unrestricted," "open," "cracking the data," and "microscopic approach" are common when describing this first round of coding work—when a researcher asks specific questions about words, phrases, and sentences, line by line. Every researcher develops a personal style in doing this. It can be helpful to conceive a name for a code provisionally (something that is under constant review and revision), placing next to it or under it a note, question, or idea about the data.

The mental processes happening at this phase of analysis include (1) seeing categories and subcategories, (2) looking for connections, (3) itemizing category properties, (4) examining conditions, strategies, tactics, and consequences, and (5) starting to hypothesize about what is happening in the data (Strauss 1987, 62–63). The researcher moves past the level of the thematic analysis of journalism to begin breaking things down analytically at the word and sentence level.

AXIAL AND SELECTIVE CODING

After the initial round of coding and continued data collection on emerging categories of importance, the researcher begins seeking linkages in a more concerted fashion. Axial coding involves choosing one category (phenomenon) and coding it again, looking for dimensions along the lines of the coding paradigm that are the components that comprise it. For instance, in my research a major code was built on the Thai word *samakhii* which has a range of meanings around harmony, unity, and accord. Axial coding this material meant taking a piece of material that I had coded as *samakhii* and coding it in order to understand the dimensions, component parts, conditions and so on of how *samakhii* works. At the same time, the researcher begins building hypotheses about a variety of conditions, consequences, strategies, and interactions that are part of that phenomenon (Strauss 1987, 64).

Selective coding involves re-analyzing a core category identified in earlier coding. The researcher limits this analysis to the codes that relate to that core category, with a particular focus on linkages between the codes. In so doing, "all other subordinate categories and subcategories become systematically linked with the core" (Strauss 1987, 69).

Coding is labor-intensive work, but is essential to moving past superficial analysis and mere descriptions of the data to abstract levels of theory. The next chapter addresses memoing and shows how this activity is closely connected with coding. Both are essential to advancing the analysis of qualitative data and developing new theory.

REFERENCES AND RESOURCES FOR ADDITIONAL READING

Charmaz, Kathy. 2006. *Constructing Grounded Theory: A Practical Guide through Qualitative Analysis*. Thousand Oaks, CA: Sage Publications.

Corbin, Juliet, and Anselm Strauss. 2008. *Basics of Qualitative Research: Grounded Theory Procedures and Techniques*. 3rd ed. Thousand Oaks, CA: Sage Publications.

Miles, Matthew, and A. Michael Huberman. 1994. *Qualitative Data Analysis.*2nd ed. Thousand Oaks, CA: Sage Publications.

Saldaña, Johnny. 2009. *The Coding Manual for Qualitative Researchers*. Thousand Oaks, CA: Sage Publications.

Strauss, Anselm. 1987. *Qualitative Analysis for Social Scientists*. Cambridge: Cambridge University Press.

WEBSITE OF INTEREST

Qualitative Research Guidelines Project
    http://www.qualres.org/index.html

JOURNAL ARTICLE WITH ABSTRACT

Birks, Melanie, Ysanne Chapman, and Karen Francis. 2008. "Memoing in Qualitative Research: Probing Data and Processes." *Journal of Research in Nursing* 13: 68–75.

This paper explores the practice of memoing in relation to qualitative research methodologies. The functions of memos in the research process are discussed and a number of techniques for employing memo writing to enhance the research experience and outcomes are examined. Memoing is often discussed in the literature as a technique employed in grounded theory research, yet there is limited exploration of the value of memo writing in qualitative methodologies generally. While guidelines exist to aid in the production and use of memos, memoing remains a flexible strategy wherein the process of construction and nature of content is determined by the preferences and abilities of the researcher and the aims and focus of the specific research study.

35

MEMOING IN QUALITATIVE FIELD RESEARCH

John L. Easter, PhD and Alan R. Johnson PhD

The previous chapter introduced coding and memoing as connected activities in analyzing qualitative data. While some researchers use the term memoing in their actual fieldwork, here memoing is defined as something done away from the research site and informant interactions. Memoing is based on one's fieldnotes and coding work, but is not synonymous with them.

The kind of memos discussed here is specifically focused on qualitative data analysis. Memos are not generic notes to oneself about which research tasks need attention. As illustrated in this chapter, many types of memos have been developed. The core notion of memoing, however, is interacting with coding work in order to explore what is happening and facilitate theoretical development.

In essence, the practice of memo writing provides a systematic way for a researcher to keep track of critical thoughts related to one's study. Memo writing represents an intermediate step in qualitative research analysis. Through memoing, a researcher can record his or her thoughts while approaching the data, making comparisons, and questioning which "trails" to pursue during the course of a study. Memoing in the early stages of the research, in particular, helps a researcher to explore relationships relevant to the focus of the investigation.

HOW TO WRITE MEMOS

Memo writing should begin early in the research process and continue throughout the study. Anselm Strauss advised researchers to frequently interrupt coding to write theoretical memos, advice that illustrates the close relationship between coding and memoing (1987, 31). When coding, a researcher is building categories. In the midst of that process, however, the researcher should also think theoretically about the categories that are emerging. Coding allows a researcher to note questions and thoughts, potential links, and so forth. Memos allow him or her to explore those issues more thoroughly. While coding work is done inside the data, memoing must be kept separate from the data.

Memos can be developed in several ways, including informal free-hand writing and/or typed-written memos. They can be developed towards achieving several functions, such as key insights, definitions, causal relationships, and categories. A memo can be a short, to-the-point statement, a lengthier sentence, a paragraph, or several pages of text. Memo writing serves to probe one's thinking regarding the underlying, unstated, implicit assumptions embedded in categories that emerge over the course of a study.[1] This analytical skill helps to identify codes and tie various pieces of data together, in order to move towards a general theory.

TYPES OF MEMOS AND RULES OF THUMB[2]

The use of memos helps a researcher to "connect the dots" by explicating and filling out categories. In that context, the following memo-writing categories may be helpful:

1. Theoretical memos identify existing theories in the literature, questions about theories, and thoughts on connecting theories.
2. Methodological memos reflect thoughts on the methodology chosen, why it was selected, and any changes to the methodological approach that may be required in the middle of the study.
3. Analytical memos capture thoughts during data analysis.
4. Implicational memos record thoughts on major connections and results that prove useful in the introduction and theoretical development chapters.

---

1. Those utilizing grounded theory find that memo-writing plays a critical role in forming the nucleus of a "grounded" theory; see chapter 28 on "Grounded Theory." Miles and Huberman (1994) provide a helpful description on issues pertaining to definitions, structure, and levels of detail.

2. Most of the material for this section and on rules-of-thumb for memoing is taken from Strauss (1987). We have also inserted relevant suggestions for developing field notes from Knight (2002); some of these fit Strauss' notion of memoing, even though Knight does not use that term.

5. Structural writing memos track ideas related to the writing of the thesis/dissertation, overlaps, developmental thoughts, and so forth.

Other types of memos are available to the qualitative researcher. Memos can relate directly to analysis of data, annotate emerging major categories or new categories, explore the relationships of categories, capture integrative summaries, and map key ideas and themes. Memoing can also include more "nuts-and-bolts" content that relates in some way to data analysis. There are to-do memos, new-ideas memos, preliminary and initial orienting memos, and tentative memos that explore potential claims that can be made by the research.

The plethora of types of memos are also indicative of the flexible nature of qualitative research. Every researcher must find their own "recipe" for effective analysis. However, it is good to bear in mind that memos and data need to be separated. A researcher should write only one memo per idea, and interrupt both writing field notes or transcribing interviews and coding to memo an idea when it occurs, so it is not lost. A wise researcher will also keep a list of emergent codes handy, and continually modify existing memos as the research develops.

MOVING TOWARDS THEORY AND TEXT: SORTING, DIAGRAMMING, AND INTEGRATING PRACTICE

Before writing a report on qualitative findings, a researcher must invest time in sorting memos. This process enables the researcher to begin diagramming and integrating the major themes in a study, as well as iden-tifying and connecting the theoretical links. Sorting, diagramming and integrating memos are essential, interrelated tasks because they produce an analytic frame for the researcher (Charmaz 2006, 115, 121).

Charmaz identified six areas of consideration when a researcher begins to sort, compare, and integrate his or her memos (2006, 117):
1. Sort the memos by the title of each category.
2. Compare the categories.
3. Use the categories in analysis.
4. Consider how the order of the categories reflects the studied experience.

5. Consider how the order of the memos fits the logic of the categories.

6. Create the best possible balance between the studied experience, the categories that have emerged, and the burgeoning theoretical statements about them.

The key to successfully engaging in this sorting and integrating process is efficiently organizing the material—both coded notes and memos—using a method that facilitates easy retrieval. One such method is to place all raw material from one's hand-written field notes and transcriptions of interviews into a set of files (either hard copy or digital), and code it there. Keep the memos separate from this now coded material, and develop a system of linking them to specific codes and textual material for easy retrieval. Forgetting to create this linking system will result in working with memos without their supportive documentation.

Working digitally offers significant advantages. For example, capturing everything relative to the study in one computer document allows the researcher to find key words easily. Some researchers prefer to enter data, codes and memos directly into a bibliographic database (e.g., Endnote, Zotero, ProCite). Use of such a database also allows researchers to code and memo directly into the file where the raw data were first logged and stored. As is true of word-processing software, the entire database is searchable.

As the analysis progresses, a researcher can then link or organize material into new files around codes or categories, and recode that material. This information can then be printed and used in writing drafts; material from informants and the researcher's analysis of it can be blocked and copied into draft documents.

REFERENCES AND RESOURCES FOR ADDITIONAL READING

Charmaz, Kathy. 2006. *Constructing Grounded Theory: A Practical Guide through Qualitative Analysis.* Thousand Oaks, CA: Sage Publications.

Corbin, Juliet, and Anselm Strauss. 2008. *Basics of Qualitative Research: Grounded Theory Procedures and Techniques.* 3rd ed. Thousand Oaks, CA: Sage Publications.

Knight, Peter T. 2002. *Small-scale Research: Pragmatic Inquiry in Social Science and the Caring Professions.* London: Sage Publications.

Miles, Matthew, and A. Michael Huberman. 1994. *Qualitative Data Analysis.*2nd ed. Thousand Oaks, CA: Sage Publications.

Strauss, Anselm. 1987. *Qualitative Analysis for Social Scientists.* Cambridge: Cambridge University Press.

RESEARCH SYMPOSIUM PAPER WITH ABSTRACT

Birks, Melanie. 2008. "Memoing in Grounded Theory Research." Sigma Theta Tau International Conference. http://vhl.openrepository .com/vhl/handle/10755/153234. Accessed November 4, 2011.

Memoing is an important strategy in all approaches to research and is most often associated with grounded theory. This paper will discuss the significance of memoing in health research generally and grounded theory specifically. The use of memoing to enhance methodological, analytical and procedural processes will be discussed. Practical issues in relation to memo writing will also be explored. The value of memoing as a critical element of the research process will be demonstrated through the use of exemplars drawn from one particular research study into the impact of post-registration studies on nurses in Malaysian Borneo.

UNIT 4
Quantitative and Mixed Methods Research

36
SAMPLING FROM A POPULATION
Marvin Gilbert, EdD

Researchers select the people ("subjects") they study in a variety of ways. Often the total number of people who might be surveyed, interviewed, or tested in some way is larger than the number that can measured practically. If a national church has 632 credentialed ministers, attempting to interview each one for an hour is unrealistic. A smaller number needs to be selected. If that selection process is systematic and objective, the results from a few can be generalized—with some caution—to the entire group of 632. Such is the power of sampling when done correctly.

TWO MAJOR CATEGORIES OF SAMPLES

Not all samples are created equal. Some are relatively clear images of the entire groups from which the samples are drawn: the "sampling frame" (Bernard 2011a; 2011b). Other samples are unfaithful reflections of their parent "populations" because those in the samples are selected out of convenience or their availability. Thus all samples can be placed into one of two categories:

Non-probability samples

In such samples, those in the total group (population) do not have an equal chance of being selected. Often labeled "convenience sampling," samples are generated using people to whom the researcher has convenient access. Expanding on the example above, if only 55 percent of the 632 credentialed ministers attend a national meeting, those 348 ministers in attendance could be surveyed. While this may seem unscientific, it is a common strategy in "real world" applied research. Findings can still be reported and recommendations can still be made to the national church leadership, even though the researcher must exercise caution when generalizing (applying) the results to all 632 ministers.

Probability samples

Probability samples are ideal statistically, in that everyone in a defined "population" has an equal chance of being selected for the sample. A sample of 63 ministers could be selected for interviews by taking every 10th name from a roster of all of the ministers. If no bias or systematic error was at work in the selection process, results from those 63 interviews could be generalized to all 632 with considerable confidence.

KEY DEFINITIONS

Bias

Bias distorts the findings (the data) from a sample when it does not represent or mirror well the population from which it was selected. This distortion is a result of the uncontrolled manner in which the sample is selected. Note in Appendix 12 the bias in sample selection when the *Literary Digest* polled voters prior to the 1936 presidential election.

Chance fluctuations

Whenever a sample is drawn from a population, no matter how large the sample may be, chance fluctuations will distort to some extent the data generated by those in the sample. Their performance will never be identical to that of the population. But if the sample is randomly selected, the influence of chance will be minimal. The purpose of random selection, then, is to permit blind chance—not selection bias—to determine the outcomes of the selection process to as great a degree as possible.

Generalization

This is the process of applying the findings from the sample to the population from which the sample is drawn. Again referencing Appendix 12, note how George Gallup effectively generalized from a relatively small sample of voters to the entire voting population prior to the 1936 election.

Random sampling

As stated above, a sample is representative of the population to the extent it has been randomly selected. Essentially identical to probability sampling, random sampling is a sample-selection procedure in which each individual in the population has an equal chance of being selected for the sample. Only random sampling can ensure that bias does not distort the sample.

Random assignment to research groups

An extension of random sampling, this procedure assigns[1] randomly selected individuals to one of two (or more) groups. The groups are then compared or manipulated in some way. In medical research, one group may receive an experimental drug while another group receives only a placebo: a drug look-alike containing no active ingredients. Because of random assignment to research groups, the researcher can safely assume that the two groups in the study are essentially identical.

DETERMINING THE SAMPLE SIZE

The researcher must determine how many subjects to select for the sample in order for it to effectively represent the population. One of three possible strategies is normally selected, depending in part on how well funded the study is.

The "quick and dirty" approach

In this least-sophisticated selection process, the researcher concludes, essentially, that "the more the better." Funds (and time) may be available to survey a sample of 300 Bible school graduates. By spending just a bit more, however, the researcher may be able to expand the sample to 400; if that is a viable option, it should be taken.

The statistical-test approach

A researcher may compare the performance of two (or more) groups quantitatively, approaching the sample-size question from a statistical perspective. Statistical tests work most effectively when the minimum number of values in each comparative group is thirty. Thus, in a two-group study, at least sixty subjects would be needed.

The minimum-sample-error approach

Statisticians have calculated the minimum sample size for known populations. Appendix 13 presents in tabular format the minimum sample needed for a known population size. Note that samples of only 1,500 can accurately reflect the characteristics of extremely large populations.

---

1. Again, by random-assignment procedures.

GUIDELINES FOR GENERALIZING RESEARCH FINDINGS

Generalizing from the sample back to the population, a common practice in research, is valid if the sample is generated by random selection. The following guidelines, apply to the generalization process:

1. Always generalize from the small (sample) to the large (population).
2. The small can reflect well the characteristics of the large.
3. The small should be selected fairly (with no sampling bias) from the large.
4. Generalizing from small to large is never error-free; chance fluctuations may somewhat distort the findings generated by a sample.

REFERENCES AND RESOURCES FOR ADDITIONAL READING

Bernard, H. Russell. 2011a. "Sampling I: The Basics." In *Research Methods in Anthropology: Qualitative and Quantitative Approaches*. 5th ed., 113–129. Lanham, MD: AltaMira Press.

———. 2011b. "Sampling II: Theory." In *Research Methods in Anthropology: Qualitative and Quantitative Approaches*. 5th ed., 130–42. Lanham, MD: AltaMira Press.

Daniel, Johnnie. 2011. *Sampling Essentials: Practical Guidelines for Making Sampling Choices*. Thousand Oaks, CA: Sage Publications.

White, Paul. 2010. *Basic Sampling*. Kindle ed. Oxford, UK: STM.

WEBSITE OF INTEREST

Experiment-Resources.com: Sampling links
http://www.experiment-resources.com/?cx=partner-pub
-3761557560104333%3A1sv0ac-d7sv&cof=FORID%3A10&ie
=ISO-8859-1&q=Sampling&sa=Search#1031

JOURNAL ARTICLE WITH ABSTRACT

Lloyd-Richardson, Elizabeth E., Nicholas Perrinea, Lisa Dierkera, and Mary L. Kelley. 2007. "Characteristics and Functions of Non-Suicidal Self-Injury in a Community Sample of Adolescents." *Psychological Medicine* 37: 1183–1192. doi: 10.1017/S003329170700027X.

Background. Few studies have investigated non-suicidal self-injury (NSSI), or the deliberate, direct destruction of body tissue without conscious suicidal intent, and the motivations for engaging in NSSI among adolescents. This study assessed the prevalence, associated clinical characteristics, and functions of NSSI in a community sample of adolescents.

Method. A total of 633 adolescents completed anonymous surveys. NSSI was assessed with the Functional Assessment of Self-Mutilation (FASM).

Results. Some form of NSSI was endorsed by 46·5% (*n*=293) of the adolescents within the past year, most frequently biting self, cutting/carving skin, hitting self on purpose, and burning skin. Sixty per cent of these, or 28 percent of the overall sample, endorsed moderate/severe forms of NSSI. Self-injurers reported an average of 12·9 (sd=29·4) incidents in the past 12 months, with an average of 2·4 (sd=1·7) types of NSSI used. Moderate/severe self-injurers were more likely than minor self-injurers, who in turn were more likely than non-injurers, to have a history of psychiatric treatment, hospitalization and suicide attempt, as well as current suicide ideation. . . . The most common reasons for NSSI were 'to try to get a reaction from someone', 'to get control of a situation', and 'to stop bad feelings'.

Conclusions. Community adolescents reported high rates of NSSI, engaged in to influence behaviors of others and to manage internal emotions. Intervention efforts should be tailored to reducing individual issues that contribute to NSSI and building alternative skills for positive coping, communication, stress management, and strong social support.

37
SURVEY RESEARCH

Johan Mostert, DPhil

Survey research, a method of obtaining data about people, has been a part of our history for a long time (see Num 26:1–2). Today it is the most widely used data-gathering technique in the social sciences. Survey research is used in a variety of contexts:

- when businesses ask customers about their service
- when the Census Bureau conducts population research every ten years
- when reading the results of a Gallop poll or a Barna Group[1] report on some trend
- when news organizations provide political poll results as elections approach.

Missiologists will often utilize survey research when discovering what the Church thinks about certain issues, or investigate behaviors that are theologically or missiologically significant. The Barna Group is probably the most well-known marketing research corporation in the evangelical world. Using survey methodology, they publish regular reports on faith and spirituality, culture, media and family issues. Another relevant example of survey research is the work of The Pew Forum on Religion and Public Life[2] (a project of the Pew Research Center). For example, the Forum's interest in Pentecostalism has been most useful for Pentecostal missiologists. Their report, "Spirit and Power: A 10-Nation Survey of Pentecostals" is both insightful and of significant research interest.[3]

---

1. http://www.barna.org/.

2. http://pewforum.org/Christian/Evangelical-Protestant-Churches /Pentecostal-Resource-Page.aspx.

3. See http://www.pewforum.org/2006/10/05/spirit-and-power/.

POSSIBLE USES OF SURVEY RESEARCH

The following examples show the types of questions best investigated using survey research. Missiological researchers should use survey research when they are:

- Investigating the behaviors of their research participants (*How much did you contribute financially to global missions last year? $_____; "How does the missionary's training affect your willingness to contribute to their ministry?"*)
- Trying to discern attitudes, beliefs or opinions (*All missionaries should have formal theological training.*[4])
- Attempting to define characteristics or constructs of their participants (*How many times did you attend a religious gathering last month? ____ times*)
- Clarifying expectations that people might have (*Foreign missionaries should lead the food-distribution program in your nation.*3)
- Measuring levels of knowledge that their participants would have of a construct (*Name as many of the missionaries supported by your church as you can. _____* [multiple lines provided])
- Attempting to discern how their participants self-classify themselves (*I consider myself "Pentecostal."*[5])

As suggested in the preceding list, survey research has been widely used in the field of missiology. Just a cursory glance at recently published studies from an EBSCO host search revealed studies that would use this approach: (1) surveying indigenous church leaders on their attitudes to the church's response to sexual slavery in their nation, and (2) polling US pastors on their attitude to financial support of missionaries involved in social justice activities.

LIMITATIONS INHERENT IN THE USE OF SURVEY RESEARCH

Survey designs contain inherent limitations. For example, it is not useful to ask "why" questions on surveys because people are generally not aware

---

4. Assumes a 1-to-5 Likert scaling (e.g., strongly agree to strongly disagree).
5. Assumes a 1-to -5 Likert scaling (e.g., strongly agree to strongly disagree).

of the causal factors that shape their beliefs or behaviors. If a researcher needs to explore such factors, he or she should choose another research design, such as semi-structured interviews or focus groups.

William Neuman (2009) reported that research participants find some types of questions threatening or sensitive; their inclusion in a survey instrument is generally not appropriate. For example, explicit questions about sexual habits, the use of alcohol or other substances, and even level of income may result in skewed (less than truthful) responses.

Because of the limitations identified above, some topics of missiological interest could not be investigated effectively using survey research. The researcher's relationship with indigenous pastors or local church members might skew the responses to difficult or awkward questions, as respondents try not to offend or create a negative impression. Special strategies to distance the researcher from the research participants would need to be employed in such cases.

Each type of survey method has unique advantages and disadvantages.[6] These are presented in the following table.

Survey Method	Primary Advantages	Primary Disadvantages
Mailed questionnaire	Relatively inexpensive	Response rate is typically low
Telephone interview	Fast	Limited number of questions
Web-based survey	Fast and inexpensive	Inappropriate in many missiological contexts
Face-to-face interviews	High response rate	Expensive and bias-prone

STEPS IN COMPLETING A CREDIBLE SURVEY

Implementing a survey research design typically requires five steps; each step involves a variety of specialized knowledge components that the researcher must master.

---

6. For expanded discussions of the relative advantage and disadvantage of each survey method, see Adler and Clark (2007, 232–239), Babbie (2014, 259–301), and Neuman (2009, 299–304).

Step 1: Planning

Planning is an ongoing process because some of the subsequent steps will require a decision that will necessitates fresh planning. For instance, a researcher may decide to expand his or her sample, or may be forced by unforeseen circumstances to change the way the data are collected. The planning step must be revisited in such cases. Still, sound decisions can be made in the initial planning phase. In every phase of planning, the researcher must determine (1) what information needs to be gathered, and (2) whether the data can be obtained through a self-administered instrument (a mailed questionnaire or an internet program like SurveyMonkey.com), or through interviews (either telephonically or personally).[7] And at the conclusion of the planning phase, the final instrument should be tested in a limited context (i.e., in a pilot test) to ensure that it works as intended.

Step 2: Determining the target population

One of the critical elements of survey research is accurately choosing a sample.[8] This must be done strategically and intentionally.

Step 3: Conducting the survey

This implementation phase requires a decision on an issue addressed earlier. The presence of a missionary or other religious leader during the administration of the survey instrument may skew the results.[9]

Step 4: Processing the data

Analysis of the data can be as simple as tallying the number of responses to each answer option, then calculating the percentages. When a researcher has access to a statistician, survey data can be processed by sophisticated statistical procedures. These include factor analysis (to discover a common component among a number of variables) and regression analysis (analyzing the relationship between a dependent variable and one or more independent variables).

---

7. See chapter 29 titled, "Foundations of Interviewing."
8. See chapter 36 titled, "Sampling from a Population."
9. Mertens (2010, 246–47) has a helpful section on this subject ("Should the Interviewer and Interviewee Be Friends or Strangers?"). Bernard also has a useful section on using and training interviewers (2011, 197–99).

Step 5: Reporting the findings

Finally, the data and related findings and recommendations must be presented to the academy. The medium and format for this presentation will initially be determined by the policies of the institution or organization that approved the study (through its institutional review board). The rights to publish the findings elsewhere are normally negotiated with the approving institution or organization.

REFERENCES AND RESOURCES FOR ADDITIONAL READING

Adler, Emily Stier, and Roger Clark. 2007. *An Invitation to Social Research: How It's Done.* 3rd ed. Belmont, CA: Thomson Wadsworth.

Babbie, Earl. 2014. *The Basics of Social Research.* 6th ed. Belmont, CA: Wadsworth Cengage Learning.

Bernard, H. Russell. 2011. *Research Methods in Anthropology: Qualitative and Quantitative Approaches.* 5th ed. Lanham, MD: AltaMira Press.

Mertens, Donna M. 2010. *Research and Evaluation in Education and Psychology: Integrating Diversity with Quantitative, Qualitative and Mixed Methods.* 3rd ed. Thousand Oaks, CA: Sage Publications.

Neuman, William L. 2009. *Social Research Methods: Qualitative and Quantitative Approaches* 7th ed. Boston, MA: Pearson Education.

WEBSITES OF INTEREST

Association for Information Systems, Tutorial on Survey Instruments
http://home.aisnet.org/displaycommon.cfm?an=1&subarticlenbr=677
Barna Group
http://www.barna.org/
Pew Forum
http://pewforum.org/Christian/Evangelical-Protestant
-Churches/Pentecostal-Resource-Page.aspx

JOURNAL ARTICLE WITH ABSTRACT

Fagan, Donna, and Alice Kiger. 2010. "A Survey of Faith Leaders Concerning Health Promotion and the Level of Healthy Living Activities Occurring in Faith Communities in Scotland." *Global Health Promotion* 17, no. 4: 15–23. doi: 10.1177/1757975910383927.

Faith groups constitute a growing health promotion partner in North America where they help increase community capacity. However, in the United Kingdom this collaboration is seemingly far less developed. This study sought to find evidence of health promotion in faith communities and examine perceptions and attitudes concerning health promotion among faith leaders. It also sought to establish the level to which health-promoting activities currently occur in, and are organized by, places of worship in one Scottish city, Dundee. The authors distributed a self-administered questionnaire to representatives of all faith communities in Dundee (response rate 71 percent, *n* = 50). The survey identified existing, well-formed community groups, some of whom already engaged in health-promoting activities, and shared similar interests with health promotion professionals. Generally, faith leaders were positive towards the concept of health promotion and many considered health promotion to be compatible with their mission. Not all denominations were equally involved in health promotion activities. . . . These results also indicate that faith groups may constitute untapped resources, poised to contribute to local health promotion efforts. The article concludes that as the National Health Service (NHS) invests in community-based health initiatives that can have long-term sustainability, it is reasonable to make links between what is happening in North America, the interest in health promotion reported by faith leaders in this study and the possibilities for their participation in voluntary sector community health partnerships.

38

QUESTIONNAIRE CONSTRUCTION

Johan Mostert, DPhil

The basic tool used in survey research is the questionnaire. Questionnaires vary in their design and level of complexity. Qualitative researchers may use only a basic guide containing open-ended questions designed to capture the type of information they are seeking. In contrast, quantitative researchers will typically utilize close-ended questions in a conventional self-report questionnaire; all the questions and answer categories are exactly the same for all research participants. This chapter explores this latter type of questionnaire, providing guidance to researchers endeavoring to obtain valid and reliable data.

It is not always necessary to create a unique questionnaire in a project or dissertation. Many standardized, well-researched questionnaires have been developed by researchers in the fields of missiology, practical theology, management sciences, psychology, and related social sciences.[1] Some of these research instruments are available without fee and can be used effectively in missiological projects and dissertations. When an existing questionnaire is used, students need to ensure that the wording is appropriate for their audience (that it matches the reading level of their subjects or that questions are culturally appropriate, etc.). Finally, it must be remembered that questionnaires are only appropriate if the researcher already understands the concepts that are being researched and is investigating the salience of these concepts. When little is known about the subject at hand the researcher would be at a loss to construct a questionnaire that would adequately reveal meanings, attitudes, or interpretations. Under such circumstances it would be preferable to use one of the subjective

---

1. In this essay, it is also assumed that surveys used in missiological contexts are adapted for cultural sensitivity, and when they are then encountered in the peer-reviewed literature, they should be usable as is.

methodologies such as structured interviews, sentence-completions, or participant observation.

This chapter summarizes some of the pitfalls that may occur when researchers compose their own questions (Neuman 2009). Relatively simple steps can be taken to avoid most of these pitfalls. The chapter also presents general guidelines for the construction of a good questionnaire.

VALIDITY AND RELIABILITY

Before proceeding further, a word about validity and reliability will be helpful. Researchers design their survey questions to address the research problem posed in their study. When these questions accurately measure the study's central construct or focus, the questionnaire is labeled valid: a valid questionnaire accurately measures the construct that it purports to measure. For example, when the author recently examined a questionnaire purporting to measure a "Christian worldview," upon closer analysis it was discovered that it was actually designed to measure a Republican Party worldview. Therefore, the instrument lacked validity as a measure of a Christian worldview.

A well-designed questionnaire will often be administered repeatedly, assessing the perspective of a variety of research participants. If it consistently measures the same construct, producing similar results with each administration of it, the questionnaire is said to have reliability. Good questionnaires will have both validity and reliability.

NEUMAN'S QUESTION-WRITING PITFALLS

William Neuman (2009) identified ten pithy examples of how NOT to write research questions. Some of his original examples are used here; others have been modified to reflect potential pitfalls for missiological researchers. Suggestions are then presented for improving invalid questions.

1. "Did you get saved when you went to the revival last night?"

It is inappropriate to use slang, technical or religious jargon, or abbreviations. A respondent may not be familiar with terms such as "saved" or "revival" and should try to use commonly understood terms.

2. "Do you eat out often?"

This is a problem of vaguely worded questions. Such questions can confuse the most willing participant. In this case, how often is "often"? Does buying hamburgers and bringing them home to eat qualify as "eating out"?

3. "The respected Grace Commission documents that a staggering $350 BILLION of our tax dollars are being completely wasted through poor procurement practices, bad management, sloppy bookkeeping, 'defective' contract management, personnel abuses and other wasteful practices. Is cutting pork barrel spending and eliminating government waste a top priority for you?"

A question such as this includes biasing and emotive language that already reveals the type of answer that the questioner is trying to obtain. This example of emotional language and prestige bias was actually contained in a real questionnaire sent to voters by a political party during a recent election.

4. "How much time do you spend in prayer and fasting every month?"

This is an example of a double-barreled question. When one question attempts to cover two topics, confusion is unavoidable. The question assumes that the answer for both questions (in this case, time in prayer and time in fasting) is the same. The respondent who has different answers to these two questions would have no way of accurately answering this question and would be forced to provide the researcher with an invalid answer.

5. "Did you do your Christian duty and pay your tithes last month?"

This is an example of a leading questions. Such questions hinder the respondent from answering in the negative.

6. "Two years ago, how many hours did you spend in Bible reading every week?"

This is an example of an impossibly complex or detailed question. A researcher must avoid asking questions that are beyond the capabilities of the respondent to answer. Very few people would have an accurate memory of behaviors two years prior.

7. "When did you stop cheating on your wife?"

This is an example of a leading questions. Unless the questionnaire has established that marital infidelity exists, this question is based on a false premise. A researcher must not assume that the respondent is engaging in a behavior and then ask questions about that behavior.

8. "After you graduate from Bible College, accept a call to a church, and are settled in, will you appoint a youth pastor to deal with children's ministry?"

This is an example of a hypothetical question. Surveying a person's future intentions based on hypothetical situations consistently provides inaccurate information. For example, more people tell pollsters they are going to vote (future intention) than actually end up voting (past behavior).

9. "Do you disagree with those who do not want to build a new youth hall for the church?"

This is an example of a confusing double-negative question. Such questions are extraordinarily difficult to unravel by respondents. Question 9 could just as easily have been posed positively: "Do you agree with those who want to build a new youth hall?"

10. "Did you find the service at our hotel to be: Outstanding, Excellent, Superior, or Good?"

This is an example of a question with unbalanced response options. Such biased, unbalanced response categories will result in invalid feedback. Note that none of the options above are worded negatively.

CHARACTERISTICS OF GOOD QUESTIONNAIRES

Many questions of a demographic nature can be answered using nominal-level response categories (e.g., male/female). Others require the respondent to choose from a list of ordinal-level categories (e.g., age categories, or income and educational levels).

The introduction of the Likert-type scale in the 1930s revolutionized social research. Likert scaling made possible the quantification of respondents' answers about their attitudes and beliefs. It is "the most common and useful numerical scale" in use today (Dunn 2009, 162). Likert scales are based on the twin assumptions that (1) attitudes or beliefs fall on a continuum, and (2) if the researcher can define the two extremes of the continuum, respondents would be able to rate themselves somewhere on that continuum. These continuums typically are numbered (most often on a 5-point scale), and provide descriptions for the respondent to respond to (e.g., from "strongly agree" to "strongly disagree").

Questionnaires can be made more user-friendly by utilizing contingency questions. Some questions can be skipped over when they do not apply to someone. Asking someone about how often they fast ("one day a week, one day a month, two days a month, more often") can be preceded by a question about whether they fast. If they do not fast, they can skip the follow-up question about fasting; respondents can be directed to a later question.

The order of questions is also important. Easier questions should be placed in the beginning of the questionnaire. Questions requiring more thought or self-disclosure should be placed toward the end. Response directions should also be varied. When respondents with a certain perspective discover that all their answers are on the one side of a scale, they may stop reading questions and simply continue marking the answers on that side. This will diminish a questionnaire's validity.

Questionnaires often include some open-ended items, inviting a written response. These questions should be limited in number, and should be used to solicit information that may not fit well into pre-determined categories. For example, workshop evaluation forms often end with open-ended evaluative questions, such as (1) "What was the best thing about this workshop?", and (2) "What would have made this workshop a more productive experience for you?" The responses that are generated must be evaluated as qualitative data, using either manual or computer-based coding to extract meaningful information.[2]

REFERENCES AND RESOURCES FOR ADDITIONAL READING[3]

Babbie, Earl. 2014. *The Basics of Social Research*. 6th ed. Belmont, CA: Wadsworth Cengage Learning.

Dunn, Dana S. 2009. *Research Methods for Social Psychology*. West Sussex, UK: Wiley-Blackwell.

Mertens, Donna M. 2010. *Research and Evaluation in Education and Psychology: Integrating Diversity with Quantitative, Qualitative and Mixed Methods*. 3rd ed. Thousand Oaks, CA: Sage Publications.

---

2. See the chapters describing qualitative data analysis, chapters 22–35.

3. Many recently published research textbooks have helpful sections on questionnaire construction. Particularly noteworthy are Babbie's (2014) chapter 9, Dunn's (2009) chapter 6, Merten's (2010) chapter 6, and Neuman's (2009) chapter 10.

Neuman, William L. 2009. *Social Research Methods: Qualitative and Quantitative Approaches* 7th ed. Boston, MA: Pearson Education.

WEBSITES OF INTEREST

Creative Research Systems
      http://www.surveysystem.com/sdesign.htm
StatPac Survey Design Tutorial
      http://www.statpac.com/surveys/
Survey Monkey (free and user-friendly)
      http://www.surveymonkey.com/

JOURNAL ARTICLE WITH ABSTRACT

Moksnes, Unni K., Don G. Byrne, Jason Mazanov, and Geir A. Espnes. 2010. "Adolescent Stress: Evaluation of the Factor Structure of the Adolescent Stress Questionnaire (ASQ-N)." *Scandinavian Journal of Psychology 51:* 203–09.

The present study reports an evaluation of the factor structure of the Norwegian version of the Adolescent Stress Questionnaire (ASQ-N) among 723 students. Principal components analysis (PCA) revealed nine internally consistent dimensions of adolescent stress. Scales constructed from this PCA correlated positively with measures of depression and anxiety and negatively with self-esteem. Girls reported higher stress levels than boys in seven of the nine scales and age was also positively correlated with the scale scores of adolescent stress. The results revealed that the instrument has potential for measuring adolescent stress. The stability of the ASQ-N needs to be tested repeatedly, across cohorts and over time, to establish the adequacy for use in Norwegian adolescent studies.

39

STATISTICALLY SPEAKING

Marvin Gilbert, EdD

This chapter title may trigger a sense of dread in some readers. Many initially perceive statistics to be a mathematics-intense "never-never land"—one totally unconnected to real life. The truth is the world is filled with important numbers, with frequent reports regarding:

Unemployment (percentages)	Standardized-test percentiles (rank comparisons)
Average income levels (means & medians)	Property values (comparisons for several years)
Life-expectancy data (regression projections)	Drug-safety tests (contrasting a new drug vs. placebo)
Church growth (basic numeric descriptors)	Correlations for smoking and heart disease

All of the above are statistics. All are important. None merit fear or dread!

WHAT STATISTICS CAN DO

Recall from an earlier chapter[1] that all data consist of either words or numbers. In order to be analyzed effectively, numbers must be manipulated.[2] The manipulation of numbers, whether descriptively or inferentially,[3] is common to all quantitative methodologies.

Statistics can accomplish *only three tasks*:

1. They can *describe* one or more sets of data.
2. They can measure the *relationships* between two or more sets of data.
3. They can measure the *differences* between two or more sets of data.

---

1. See chapter 22 entitled, "The Nature of Data."
2. Numeric manipulation is a positive thing in research. Raw untreated data are of no value for resolving research questions or testing empirical hypotheses.
3. See chapter 40 entitled, "Inferential Statistics."

All statistical techniques, no matter how complex, fall into one of these three categories. The table on the next page summarizes these three statistical objectives. Listed within each category are some (not all) of the statistical tests available to researchers.

STATISTICAL TESTS AND LEVELS OF MEASUREMENT

A variety of statistical descriptors and tests are available to allow researchers to manipulate and analyze quantitative data. Quantitative data can be *described* using a variety of statistical formulas: (1) the mean, median, and mode, and (2) the variance and standard deviation can all be calculated for parametric[4] data. In contrast, only the median and mode can be described statistically for ordinal-level data.

Measures of relationships and differences can be calculated for both ordinal-level (non-parametric) data and parametric data. However, the level of measurement (nominal, ordinal, interval/ratio) determines which statistical test—*only one*—can be calculated for a given objective. If a researcher knows the level of measurement(s), the choice of which statistical test to employ is actually an easy one. For example, choosing the correct statistical test to find the relationship between test scores from two separate groups of students is relatively straightforward. If the test scores are at least interval level, the Pearson Product Moment correlation coefficient (for independent sample means) would be the right choice.

---

4. Interval-level and ratio-level data are characterized by the use of equal units of measurement (e.g., IQ scores). The same statistical tests are used for both levels. The higher ratio-level data also has an absolute zero starting point (e.g., height). Generally, parametric statistics are more "powerful" than non-parametric statistics— they are able to detect a true relationship or difference in the data sets (variables) if one actually exists.

The Three Functions of Statistics

Objective	Method of Accomplishing the Objective
Describe Variables (sets of data)	**Measures of Central Tendency** Mode: the most frequently occurring number in the data set. Median: the mid-point of an array of numbers: the median is not impacted by extreme scores. (ORDINAL-level data). Mean*: the mathematical average: the mean is impacted by extreme values (high or low). (INTERVAL- or RATIO-level data) **Measures of Dispersion** Range: the highest number in the data set minus (–) the lowest number, plus 1. Percentile: a comparative ranking, ranging from the 1st percentile (low) to the 99th percentile (high). (ORDINAL-level or INTERVAL/RATIO-level data) Variance (symbol: s): a measure of how disbursed the scores are in a data set—varying around the mean. (INTERVAL/RATIO-level) Standard Deviation (symbol: $\sqrt{s}$): the square root of the variance (above). Like s, $\sqrt{s}$ also measures of how disbursed (spread out) the scores are in a data set—but does so in the same scale values as the mean. (INTERVAL/RATIO-level)
Measure Relationships among Variables	**Correlational Techniques†** Phi coefficient: a measure of correlation between two groups of scores—one at the NOMINAL level and the other at INTERVAL/RATIO level. Spearman Rank Order coefficient: a measure of correlation between two groups of ORDINAL-level scores. Pearson Product Moment (symbol: r): a measure of correlation between two groups of interval (or ratio) level scores. (INTERVAL/RATIO-level) Multiple correlation (symbol: R^2): a complex measure of correlation used to predict values on one variable from two or more predictors. (INTERVAL/RATIO-level)
Measure Differences between Variables	**Analysis of Variance Techniques‡** Mann-Witney U: a test of difference between two group medians when the groups produce non-parametric data. (ORDINAL-level) Chi-Square test (symbol: x^2): a test of difference in frequencies (counts) in two or more groups. (NOMINAL-level) t-Test for Sample Means (symbol: t): a test of difference between two group means when both groups produce parametric data. (INTERVAL/RATIO-level) Analysis of Variance (ANOVA; and its variations): a complex test of differences (variance) *between* two or more means, corrected for the variance *within* each of the groups. (INTERVAL/RATIO-level)

* Statistical tests in SMALL CAPS indicate the more powerful parametric choices.

† The correlation technique of choice depends on the level of measurement of the variables (data sets) being measured, and how many variables are involved: two for basic correlation; three or more for multiple correlation.

‡ The analysis-of-variance technique of choice depends on the level of measurement of the variables (data sets) being measured, and how many variables are involved. One-way ANOVA (and its variations) can analyze differences between multiple groups simultaneously.

MISSIOLOGICAL APPLICATION OF STATISTICS

Statistics can be used to great advantage by missiological researchers in a wide variety of applications. The following list hints at how useful a basic knowledge of statistics can be:

1. Describing the average number of years a large group of pastors have been in ministry.
2. Determining if a Bible knowledge test completed by Bible school applicants predicts grades earned in students' first semester Bible subjects.
3. Discovering if a positive relationship exists between perceptions of leadership skills, when comparing elders' view of their pastor and the pastor's view of himself.
4. Knowing if a workshop on Muslim outreach significantly changed attitudes and behaviors of those attending, when attitudes and behaviors are quantified by self-report survey instruments.
5. Tracking for two years weekly church attendance and income from offerings at two new church plants—one urban and one rural, graphing the results for a report to the national church.

REFERENCES AND RESOURCES FOR ADDITIONAL READING

Coolidge, Frederick. 2012. *Statistics: A Gentle Introduction.* 3rd ed. Thousand Oaks, CA: Sage Publications.

Fox, John. 2008. *A Mathematical Primer for Social Statistics.* Thousand Oaks, CA: Sage Publications.

Hand, David. 2008. *Statistics: A Very Short Introduction.* Oxford: Oxford University Press.

Rowntree, Derek. 2003. *Statistics Without Tears: A Primer for Non-Mathematicians.* Classics ed. Boston, MA: Allyn & Bacon.

WEBSITES OF INTEREST

Experiment-Resources.com. Statistical Tutorial
    http://www.experiment-resources.com/statistics-tutorial.html

Stat-Trek—Statistics and Probability Tutorial: Introduction
http://stattrek.com/lesson1/statistics-intro.aspx

JOURNAL ARTICLE WITH ABSTRACT

Tekinarslan, Erkan. 2008. "Computer Anxiety: A Cross-cultural Comparative Study of Dutch and Turkish University Students." *Computers in Human Behavio*r 24: 1572–1584. doi:10.1016/j .chb.2007.05.011.

The purpose of this study is to determine Dutch and Turkish university students' computer anxiety levels and to find out whether their computer anxiety levels differ according to their culture, gender and computer experience (i.e., personal computer (PC) ownership, computer usage frequency, computer usage level). A total of 106 university students (30 Dutch female, 22 Dutch male, 26 Turkish female, 28 Turkish male) participated in this research. The data were collected through computer anxiety rating scale (CARS). . . . The data were analyzed by t-test and one-way-analysis of variance (ANOVA). The results indicated that the Turkish students have significantly higher computer anxiety levels than the Dutch students. The students' computer anxiety levels do not differ depending on gender. However, post-hoc analysis revealed that the Turkish female students have significantly higher computer anxiety levels than the Dutch female and Dutch male students. Also, results indicated that while the students' computer experience increase their computer anxiety levels decrease significantly.

40
INFERENTIAL STATISTICS
Marvin Gilbert, EdD

Inferential[1] statistics, including many correlation and analysis of variance techniques, are used to empirically test research hypotheses.[2] They are termed "inferential" because social science researchers often strive to infer characteristics of an *un-measurable* population[3] from characteristics of a *measurable* sample[4] selected out of that population. Inferential statistics are essential to such efforts.

CORRELATION: EXAMINING RELATIONSHIPS

Correlation is a measure of relationship; correlational tests reveal the *strength* and *direction* of the relationship between two (or more) groups of scores or values. Correlational values vary in *strength* from no relationship whatsoever (a value of 0.00) to a "perfect" correlation (a value of 1.00). The *direction* of a correlational value is indicated by a plus (+) or negative (–) sign. Negative correlation values range *downward* from –0.01 to –1.00. Similarly, positive correlation values range *upward* from +0.01 to +1.00.

Concerning negative correlations, as values[5] in one data set *increase*, they tend to *decrease* in the second data set. For example, those who carry excess weight (measured in pounds or kilograms) tend to die at earlier ages (measured in years or months). As weight *increases*, age at death *decreases*. This negative correlation is not perfect; some obese people live to be 90

---

1. Essentially the same as "parametric"; see chapter 22 titled, "The Nature of Data."
2. See chapter 41 titled, "Hypothesis Testing."
3. A population may be un-measurable for a variety of reasons, including limited time, money, personnel, etc.
4. See chapter 36 titled, "Sampling from a Population."
5. Scores or other quantitative measurement.

years old or older. And some underweight people die early in life. But these cases would be rare exceptions to the negative correlation trend.

With positive correlations, values in the two groups tend to vary together: high values associated (paired) with high, and low values paired with low. For example, IQ scores are positively correlated, though not perfectly, with level of education.

Perfect correlation values of –1.00 and +1.00 are *never* reported in large-group, real-world research. Correlation values rarely exceed .80 (+ or –); in fact, statistically significant correlations[6] can be as low as .20 (+ or –) for large samples or populations. As correlational values approach 0.00 (no correlation), the relationship between the data sets becomes less meaningful.

CAUTION REGARDING CORRELATION

Warnings are frequently found in the research literature regarding how to interpret correlational values. For example,

> Science is ultimately concerned with identifying cause-and-effect relationships. Since such relationships are always correlated, there is a strong tendency to reverse the process and infer cause-and effect status between two or more variables based on an established correlation coefficient. The danger is clear: correlation does not necessarily imply causation. (Isaac and Michael 1971, 150)

Correlational findings tempt researchers to ascribe *causation* (i.e., cause-and-effect) to outcomes where only relationship exists:

1. Water temperatures and the number of deaths by drowning at California's beaches are positively correlated. But warmer ocean water is *not* more lethal than colder water; more swimmers are in the water when it is warmer.

2. Most weight-reduction meals are consumed by obese people. Yet weight-reduction meals do *not* cause people to become overweight.

---

6. See chapter 41 titled, "Hypothesis Testing."

As stated earlier, a causal relationship will *always* be highly correlated. Cigarette smoking is causally[7] related to several diseases, including heart disease and lung cancer. The reverse possibility—that those with these diseases start smoking cigarettes in large numbers—is both illogical and rejected by empirical evidence.

ANALYSIS OF VARIANCE: DETERMINING DIFFERENCES

Researchers often compare two or more groups on various performance measures. Comparisons are especially common before and after the groups have been "treated" differently by an experimental condition or stimulus. A variety of analysis of variance statistical tests have been developed to compare group performance. These tests analyze the variability (variance) of numeric values and frequency counts to determine if the observed differences are statistically significant. Their usefulness is illustrated in the following hypothetical example.

Do attitudes toward unreached peoples change after attending a workshop that identifies their spiritual needs? Would attitudes, as measured by the Attitudes toward the Unreached[8] (ATU) survey instrument, differ significantly when comparing pre-workshop and post-workshop scores? Those planning the workshop need to know if it actually facilitates attitude transformation. This experimental "treatment" could be evaluated by administering the ATU before and after the workshop, comparing the two sets of scores statistically. The *t*-test for repeated measures analyzes the difference in scores produced by the same people at two times—one before and one after the treatment (the workshop).[9]

Let us assume that the post-workshop ATU scores were significantly higher than the pre-workshop scores. The presenters would rejoice: the workshop was effective in changing attitudes. However, the attitude-assessment literature suggests that such a shift in attitudes may not be permanent. Pursuing this possibility, a researcher could track down in September all who attended the workshop in March, re-administering

---

7. A causal relationship need not be a perfect (1.00) one.

8. A hypothetical instrument.

9. It also takes into account how varied the scores are *within* the pre-workshop and the post-workshop data sets.

the ATU to them. This would produce a third data set, complicating the analysis procedure.

A *t*-test would not be appropriate for this more complex analysis; it can compare only two data sets at a time. A "one-way"[10] analysis of variance (ANOVA) could, however, determine if the attitude changes observed at post-workshop that previous March were indeed lasting ones:

Pre-Workshop Scores	Post-Workshop Scores	Six-Month Follow-Up Scores
(data set listed here)	(data set listed here)	(data set listed here)

Increasingly complex experimental designs are possible. For example, the researcher could subdivide those being studied. The scores of pastors and laymen could be compared using a "two-way"[11] ANOVA:

Gender Group	Pre-Workshop Scores	Post-Workshop Scores	Six-Month Follow Up Scores
Pastors	(data set listed here)	(data set listed here)	(data set listed here)
Laymen	(data set listed here)	(data set listed here)	(data set listed here)

The possibilities of multi-group comparisons using ANOVA are almost endless.

REFERENCES AND RESOURCES FOR ADDITIONAL READING

Asadoorian, Malcolm O., and Demetri Kantarelis. 2008. *Essentials of Inferential Statistics.* 5th ed. Lanham, ME: University Press of America.

Bernard, Russell. 2011. "Multivariate analysis." In *Research Methods in Anthropology: Qualitative and Quantitative Approaches.* 5th ed. 533–58. Lanham, MD: AltaMira Press.

10. Only one row of data is involved, across two or more columns (treatment conditions).

11. Two or more rows of data are involved, across two or more columns (treatment conditions).

Campbell, Donald T., and Julian C. Stanley. 1963. *Experimental and Quasi-Experimental Designs for Research*. Belmont, CA: Wadsworth Cengage Learning.

Isaac, William B., and Stephen Michael. 1971. *Handbook in Research and Evaluation*. 2nd ed. San Diego, CA: R. R. Knapp.

WEBSITES OF INTEREST

Inferential Statistics Tutorial, Introduction
http://www.edurite.com/kbase/inferential-statistics-tutorial
University of Purdue, OWL
http://owl.english.purdue.edu/owl/resource/672/05/

JOURNAL ARTICLE WITH ABSTRACT

Fienup, Daniel M., and Thomas S. Critchfield. 2010. "Efficiently Establishing Concepts of Inferential Statistics and Hypothesis Decision Making through Contextually Controlled Equivalence Classes." *Journal of Applied Behavioral Analysis* 43:437–62. doi: 10.1901/jaba.2010.43-437.

Computerized lessons that reflect stimulus equivalence principles were used to teach college students concepts related to inferential statistics and hypothesis decision making. Lesson 1 taught participants concepts related to inferential statistics, and Lesson 2 taught them to base hypothesis decisions on a scientific hypothesis and the direction of an effect. Lesson 3 taught the conditional influence of inferential statistics over decisions regarding the scientific and null hypotheses. Participants entered the study with low scores on the targeted skills and left the study demonstrating a high level of accuracy on these skills, which involved mastering more relations than were taught formally. This study illustrates the efficiency of equivalence-based instruction in establishing academic skills in sophisticated learners.

41

HYPOTHESIS TESTING
Marvin Gilbert, EdD

Social scientists often measure attitudes, performance, knowledge, and other quantitative factors, capturing those data from one or more groups. If the measurements are valid and reliable, using best-practice methodology, researchers confidently assert that what they measured represents reality. Yet the measurement process or simply chance variability in sampling has likely distorted the outcomes—at least to some extent. *Some* degree of error is thus *always* present when sampling[1] is involved. This is of particular concern when generalizing findings to the population from which a sample was drawn.

The influence of chance can never be eliminated from sample-generated data; it can, however, be managed. In managing the influence of chance, researchers always face a choice. The results generated by a given sample are due either to (1) chance sampling error (and its related threats to the data's validity), or (2) some influence *in addition* to inescapable chance influences. Researchers choosing the latter option assert that this other influence was their experimental treatment administered during the study. In effect, they conclude that their treatment "worked" as hypothesized.

This important choice hinges entirely on whether the numeric outcomes are "statistically significant," which is determined by evaluating the raw data using appropriate statistical tests.[2]

THE STATISTICAL DECISION PROCESS
A theological educator might suspect that intensive short-term ("block") courses are more effective for training missionaries than conventional

---

1. See chapter 36 entitled, "Sampling from a Population."
2. See the table titled, "Three Functions of Statistics" and chapter 39 entitled, "Statistically Speaking."

full-semester courses. Student performance in two sections of a missions course could be evaluated: one section offered in a two-week block, the other section offered during a full-semester. If the class average for the block-course section was significantly[3] higher, the researcher could conclude, with some confidence, that the intensive two-week approach was superior for training missionaries. The course format and schedule would constitute that "influence other than chance" as indicated in choice 2 in the second paragraph (above).

In the hypothetical example above, the conclusion is justified based on the statistical outcome. It assumes that some influence of chance is unavoidable in statistical findings. Chance fluctuations may occur in (1) student selection, (2) student performance, and (3) other difficult-to-control factors. Such chance fluctuations may have resulted in the block-course section performing better than a similar group would in the future. Alternatively, chance factors may have resulted in the full-semester group performing more poorly than a similar group would in the future. The following, therefore, can be concluded:

1. Chance factors are *always* present in sample-generated data.
2. Statistical tests allow researchers to manage—or at least estimate—the impact of those chance factors.
3. Humility is *always* warranted when evaluating the results of statistical tests. Speaking *confidently* about the findings is not the same as speaking with absolute *certainty*.

THE NULL HYPOTHESIS

Researchers test the probability that their results are due to chance, trying to eliminate (as much as possible) chance as the probable cause of their results. If successful, they can then reasonably embrace other

---

3. Statistical significance is mathematically determined through a two-step process. First, a researcher generates a numeric value using an appropriate statistical test. In the example presented above, the correct test would be a *t*-test for independent sample means. After calculating the statistical value, the researcher compares the resultant *t*-value to the "table" value for critical values of "*t*" (such tables are appendices in most statistics textbooks). If the *t*-value value is higher than the table value, the researcher asserts that the relationship or difference being examined is statistically significant.

probable causes—like the treatment or condition they were administering to the sample(s). Researchers do this by testing their data against the *null* ("empty") hypothesis (H_0). Generally, the H_0 proposes that the experimental treatment will *not* be effective enough to yield statistically significant correlations or differences.

TWO CHOICES WITH THE NULL HYPOTHESIS

When the appropriate statistical test is calculated, the value obtained will allow the researcher to make one of two choices:

1. *Reject* the H_0, concluding that *something other than chance* was at work in generating that result. An outcome *that* different from chance—predicted by H_0—could occur by chance factors alone only a few times out of 100.[4]
2. *Retain* the H_0 (literally, fail to reject it), concluding that chance is operating in an important way. An outcome of that magnitude could occur by chance factors alone more than 5 times out of 100.[5]

	(reality) Fact	
Possible Decisions	Results are really due to chance **plus** something else (i.e., the treatment).	Results are really due only to chance fluctuations alone.
Reject the null hypothesis	This is good science.	Type I or alpha **error**
Retain (literally, fail to reject) the null hypothesis	Type II or beta **error**	Try another study.

These two choices are summarized in the 2 x 2 matrix above. Notice that error is possible with either choice. Without replicating the entire study, a researcher will never be *absolutely* certain he or she made the right decision. When testing hypotheses statistically, being *relatively* certain is the best a researcher can ever hope to achieve.

Type I and Type II errors in the table above are caused by one or more uncontrolled factors. These factors impact the magnitude of the observed

---

4. Often 5 times (or less) out of 100; 5 out of 100 is an acceptable decision-making number in social-science research, and is expressed as $p < .05$ (where p = probability).
5. Often more than 5 times out of 100.

statistical outcome. In either case, the study is said to be "confounded," as uncontrolled factors are labeled "confounds" (Bernard 2011). Researchers work hard to eliminate or control every conceivable influence (variable) in their studies because a confounded study is worthless.

Hypothesis testing characterizes quantitative research. Often, theory-informed hypotheses, not research questions, guide the researcher to the resolution of the research problem. And the rejection or retention of the H_0 determines the validity of the theory-informed hypotheses.

REFERENCES AND RESOURCES FOR ADDITIONAL READING

Bernard, Russell. 2011. "Research Design: Experiments and Experimental Thinking." In *Research Methods in Anthropology: Qualitative and Quantitative Approaches*. 5th ed. 82–112. Lanham, MD: AltaMira Press.

Campbell, Donald T., and Julian C. Stanley. 1963. *Experimental and Quasi-Experimental Designs for Research*. Belmont, CA: Wadsworth Cengage Learning.

Lehmann, Erich L., and Joseph P. Romano. 2010. *Testing Statistical Hypotheses*. Springer Texts in Statistics. 3rd ed. New York: Springer Publishing.

Shi, Ning-zhong, and Jian Tao. 2008. *Statistical Hypothesis Testing: Theory and Methods*. Hackensack, NJ: World Scientific Publishing.

WEBSITES OF INTEREST

StatTrek—Statistics Tutorial: Hypothesis Tests
http://stattrek.com/lesson5/hypothesistesting.aspx
Voelz, Vincent A—Hypothesis Testing
http://www.stanford.edu/~vvoelz/lectures/hypotesting.pdf
Weaver, B.—Hypothesis Testing Using z- and t-tests
http://www.angelfire.com/wv/bwhomedir/notes/z_and_t_tests.pdf

JOURNAL ARTICLE WITH ABSTRACT

Levine, Timothy R., René Weber, Craig Hullett, Hee Sun Park, and Lisa L. Massi Lindsey. 2008. "A Critical Assessment of Null Hypothesis Significance Testing in Quantitative Communication Research." *Human Communication Research* 2: 171–87.

Null hypothesis significance testing (NHST) is the most widely accepted and frequently used approach to statistical inference in quantitative communication research. NHST, however, is highly controversial, and several serious problems with the approach have been identified. This paper reviews NHST and the controversy surrounding it. Commonly recognized problems include a sensitivity to sample size, the null is usually literally false, unacceptable Type II error rates, and misunderstanding and abuse. Problems associated with the conditional nature of NHST and the failure to distinguish statistical hypotheses from substantive hypotheses are emphasized. Recommended solutions and alternatives are addressed in a companion article.

42

EDUCATIONAL RESEARCH

Beth Grant, PhD

Education is a domain that has historically been the focus of rich and varied scientific research. The respected American Educational Research Association (AERA) includes twelve major divisions, including administration, organization and leadership, curriculum studies, social context of education, and teaching and teaching education. Illustrating the broad scope of educational research occurring within that one organization, the AERA has over 170 special interest groups, addressing specific areas of educational research (Johnson and Christensen 2012, 6–7).

Organizations like AERA and others promote high-quality educational research, resulting in a vast body of literature. Why, then, should researchers engage in more educational research? Consider the following reasons:

1. Educational research leads to the development of new knowledge about teaching, learning, and educational administration; this ideally leads to improvements in educatiovnal practice. Educational research contributes to four kinds of knowledge: description, prediction, improvement, and explanation (Gall, Borg, and Gall 1996, 4).

2. Researchers approach educational research with varying philosophical positions and worldviews. This variety naturally leads to differing lines of investigation and ultimately diverse theories to explain educational phenomena. Integrating the results of past research with newly emerging inquiry leads to fresh insights into education theory and practice. These insights would not be possible without the richness of different perspectives.

3. As socio-economic, political, cultural and religious changes occur, the contexts of education change. New challenges are constantly emerging for educators and all involved in educative processes. The need for inquiry to acquire new insights

and theory for understanding education phenomena has therefore not diminished; rather, it has intensified.

4. As changes occur in the secular world, educational phenomena reflect those changes. Theologians and missiologists face new questions that beg the integration of truth with ongoing challenging educational issues. The changing contexts of twenty-first century missions provide fertile strategic ground for educational research that will lead to greater understanding, insights and new knowledge for missional education in context.

WHAT DOES EDUCATIONAL RESEARCH LOOK LIKE?

In the twentieth century, three major research traditions characterized educational research: quantitative, qualitative, and mixed-design research. Johnson and Christensen summarized the research methods associated with two of those traditions in educational research: (1) quantitative (experimental, quasi-experimental, and non-experimental), and (2) qualitative (phenomenology, ethnography, case study, grounded theory, and historical) (2012, 52–53).

In recent years, qualitative research methods have become increasingly important to educational research. This is due, in part, to the increasing complexity associated with the contexts of educational phenomena (Smeyers 2010). Qualitative research, with its unique approach and diverse methodologies, is now favored by many twenty-first century educational researchers.

Educational researchers investigate amazingly diverse issues and phenomena associated with the education process. The following list of possible research topics illustrates this diversity. They all have implications for missiological research focused on training concerns.

1. Classrooms:
   - Physical design of the rooms
   - Arrangement of the furniture
   - Acceptable behaviors for teachers, students (i.e., who may talk to whom and when)
   - As a reinforcer and reflector of cultural values
2. Schools or informal education environment:
   - Physical design and location in local community

- Rules of appropriate behavior
- Social and professional relationships of students, teachers, staff, and others.
- Networks of relationships
- Gender issues
3. Libraries:
   - Text books: disciplines, place of publication, transmission of cultural values
   - Digital catalogues
   - Physical design
   - Languages represented
   - Rules for use
   - Access to online resources
4. Artifacts:
   - Historical documents (e.g., constitution and bylaws, Board of Directors meeting minutes)
   - Class syllabi
   - School promotional material
   - Media
5. Curriculum: both explicit (formal) and implicit (informal, unspoken)
6. Historical data: for example, minutes of school board meetings, agendas and minutes from various committees
7. Demographics of student body, teachers, and administrators
8. Values reflected and reinforced through education processes
9. Student extra-curricular activities
10. The education context as community
11. Informal and non-formal education
12. Funding and meanings attached to the funds
13. External influences on the education context which shape outcomes

EDUCATIONAL RESEARCH AS A CHANGING FIELD

Some educational researchers have noted a growing tension within this field regarding what educational research actually is (especially in traditional Western arenas). According to Lee (2010), education itself is undergoing "decentering" (1). Referencing the work of Ferguson and Seddon,[1] Lee noted that the twentieth century perception of education being centered in physical schools with physical parameters no longer accurately reflect the reality of disbursed learning spaces. In short, education is no longer limited to what happens in red brick buildings. Instead, it occurs through networks in the community, sometimes connected to traditional schools or universities, but not in terms of spatial boundaries. This emerging decentered concept of education requires a different perspective and re-evaluation of educational research. Future researchers, including missiological educators, must take these new education realities into account.

While Lee's observations are legitimate as to the actual re-defining and practice of educational research, they are perhaps not as earth-shaking to missiologists engaging in cross-cultural educational research. From a global missiological perspective, education has often had to be decentered by necessity. Economic, political and social realities for theological education students and schools have always required education models that are somewhat decentered and fluid. Rather than being a deterrent to educational research, these challenging realities have often become the focus, context and motivation for it.

REFERENCES AND RESOURCES FOR ADDITIONAL READING

Frank, Carolyn. 1999. *Ethnographic Eyes: A Teacher's Guide to Classroom Observation*. Portsmouth, NH: Heinemann.

Gall, Meredith D., Walter R. Borg, and Joyce P. Gall. 1996. *Educational Research: An Introduction*. 6th ed. White Plains, NY: Longman Publishers.

Johnson, Burke, and Larry Christensen. 2012. *Educational Research: Quantitative, Qualitative, and Mixed Approaches*. 4th ed. Thousand Oaks, CA: Sage Publications.

Lee, Alison. 2010. "What Counts as Educational Research? Spaces, Boundaries, and Alliances." *Australian Educational Researcher* 37, no. 4: 63–78. doi: 10.1007/BF03216937.

---

1. Kathleen Ferguson, and Terri Seddon. 2007. Decentered Education: Suggestions for Framing a Socio-spatial Research Agend" *Critical Studies in Education* 48, no.1: 111–29". doi:10.1080/17508480601120947.

Smeyers, Paul. 2008. "Qualitative and Quantitative Research Methods: Old Wine in New Bottles? On Understanding and Interpreting Educational Phenomena." *Paedagogica Historica* 44:691–705. doi: 10.1080/00309230802486168.

WEBSITES OF INTEREST

The American Educational Research Association (AERA is the largest, most respected educational research association in the USA.) http://www.aera.net

A number of regional associations promote educational research within their geographic regions of the US: See, for example, http://www.nera-education.org/ http://www.mwera.org/ http://msera.org/

JOURNAL ARTICLE WITH ABSTRACT

Freathy, Rob, and Stephen Parker. 2010. "The Necessity of Historical Inquiry in Educational Research: The Case of Religious Education." *British Journal of Religious Education* 32: 229–43. doi: 10.1080/01416200.2010.498612.

This article explores the mixed fortunes of historical inquiry as a method in educational studies and exposes evidence for the neglect of this method in religious educational research in particular. It argues that historical inquiry, as a counterpart to other research methods, can add depth and range to our understanding of education, including religious education, and can illuminate important longer-term, broader and philosophical issues. The article also argues that many historical voices have remained silent in the existing historiography of religious education because such historiography is too generalised and too biased towards the development of national policy and curriculum and pedagogical theory. To address this limitation in educational research, this article promotes rigorous historical studies that are more substantially grounded in the appropriate historio-graphical literature and utilise a wide range of original primary sources. Finally, the article explores a specific example of the way in which a historical approach may be fruitfully applied to a particular contemporary debate concerning the nature and purpose of religious education.

43

ACTION RESEARCH

Beth Grant, PhD

Understanding action research (AR) is facilitated by contrasting it with traditional applied and academic research. Basic research is generally conducted by scholars for the purpose of developing or refining theories and insights within their academic disciplines; those theories and insights, ideally, lead to new practices. AR, in contrast, is conducted by practitioners who focus on local practices to arrive at specific local solutions (Johnson and Christensen 2012, 11).

Proponents of AR challenge traditional social science's claim of neutrality and objectivity, proposing instead a "collaborative inquiry by all participants, often to engage in sustained change in organizations, communities, or institutions" (Marshall and Rossman 2006, 6–7). In the process, the researcher and the participants become co-inquirers in the solution-focused investigative process. The end result, as implied in the AR name, is the development of a strategy for specific action to address a specific diagnosed problem in a defined location.

Approximately a dozen different forms of AR have been developed, each having its own assumptions, methodologies, structures, and goals (Davison, Martinsons, and Kock 2004). Some of these may be particularly well suited to missiological research, for example: Canonical Action Research (CAR), Information Systems Prototyping, Action Science, Participant Observation, Clinical Field Work, and Process Consultation.

Davison, Martinsons, and Kock developed the following five principles for CAR in an effort to improve the quality of CAR studies (2004, 69):

1. principle of the Researcher-client Agreement;
2. principle of the Cyclical Process Model;
3. principle of Theory;
4. principle of Change through Action;
5. and principle of Learning through Reflection.

This is one example of action researchers who are engaged in bringing more standard methodology to AR in order to increase its legitimacy and credibility.

ASSESSING ACTION RESEARCH

AR proponent Ernest Stringer (2007) acknowledges that AR may not meet the stringent criteria and rigor for scholarly scientific research, however, he contends that its strengths commend it nonetheless. Stringer proposes that AR is more democratic, empowering, and humanizing than traditional scientific research. Community-based AR is focused on resulting action leading to equity, social justice, life enhancement, and freedom from oppression (2007, xiii).

The following chart summarizes some of the documented strengths and weaknesses of AR, in comparison with traditional scientific research.

Strengths of Action Research	Weaknesses of Action Research
Focuses on a recognized immediate problem to be solved	Lacks academic research rigor
Research is participatory with those in a local community, school or other organization	Lacks clearly defined recognized methodology (processes)
Results in problem-solving action	Neutrality and objectivity are not guiding principles, terms that characterize academic disciplinary research
Relevant to specific issues that need to be addressed by gaining wisdom and knowledge from community participants	Validity of research is questioned because of the collaborative nature of researcher's relationship with "clients" in local setting
Perceived as democratic and empowering for people who have been marginalized, oppressed, and victimized	Viewed as weak in procedure, reporting of results, and reviewing
Practical in engaging organization problems through intervention: practitioner-oriented	Often lacks triangulation with literature or theoretical models
Researcher is a research-facilitator of participants in local context to investigate and find solutions	Generalization of the findings is not attempted

STEPS IN ACTION RESEARCH

Stringer (2007) proposed a "Basic Action Research Routine" in which he summarized the phases of the inquiry process using the words: look, think, act (8). The "look" phase includes the steps of gathering data, and defining and describing the situation. The "think" phase focuses on asking and analyzing what is happening in the local setting being investigated, followed by theorizing why things are as they are. Lastly, in the "Act" phase, the practitioner-researcher engages in reporting, implementing, and evaluating.

AR proponents view these phases as cyclical, not linear. This quality refers specifically to the Principle of Cyclical Process Model (CPR) discussed by Davison, Martinson, and Kock (2004, 72). The basic CPR process model moves cyclically from (1) diagnosis of the problem to (2) action planning to (3) intervention (action taking) to (4) evaluation (assessment) and finally to (5) reflection (learning). The cycle resumes with an adapted diagnosis of the problem step, informed by the assessment of data from the research and action in the first cycle (2004, 72).[1]

Action researchers offer variations on how to design and implement the cyclical principle in AR studies. These include (1) a spiral model, in which the intervention stage moves closer and closer to the organizational model (Kemmis and Wilkinson, 1998), and (2) the two-simultaneous-cycles model, with one cycle focused on the client's problem solving and the other focused on the researcher's scholarship (McKay and Marshall, 2001).

IMPLICATIONS FOR THEOLOGICAL AND MISSIOLOGICAL RESEARCH

Missiological researchers must work across disciplines, often using multiple traditional, discipline-specific approaches to scientific inquiry. Nonetheless, AR does offer some intriguing non-traditional strengths for investigating missiological issues:

1. The AR focus on local issues and challenges in cultural context is consistent with desired outcomes in many missiological research projects. Researchers move from larger theological and missiological concepts to their implications for the church and missions in local settings.

---

1. Educators familiar with David Kolb's experiential learning cycle (1984) may note similarities between Kolb's cycle and the CAR model. See David A. Kolb. 1984. *Experiential Learning: Experience as the Source of Learning and Development.* Englewood Cliffs, NJ: Prentice Hall.

2. Engaging local participants in an organizational setting as co-inquirers in the research process provides a vehicle for missiologists to engage national churches, ministers, and other stakeholders in their research project. Such broad engagement ensures greater interest and ownership of outcomes of the project and recommended next steps for action.

3. An AR-type missiological research project may ultimately lead to problem-solving action in a local setting while simultaneously drawing tentative conclusions about the generalizability of findings beyond the immediate context. Such conclusions could be evaluated in more conventional research designs.

4. The action-centered-practitioner approach to AR is compatible with the approach of missiologists who tend to be engaged in local contexts as "doers" rather than arm chair "reflectors." However, this approach must intentionally be integrated with the academic research rigor of traditional missiological/theological research in order to maintain the integrity of results and contribute to the larger academy.

Theological and missiological researchers conduct credible research that expands knowledge and insights. When utilizing AR methodology, their research can also facilitate local problem solving and inform specific issues, provided researchers exercise diligence to maintain the rigor of respected scholarship.

REFERENCES AND RESOURCES FOR ADDITIONAL READING

Davison, Robert M., Maris G. Martinsons, and Ned Kock. 2004. "Principles of canonical action research." *Information Systems Journal* 14: 65–86.doi: 10.1111/j.1365-2575.2004.00162.x

Johnson, Burke, and Larry Christensen. 2012. *Educational Research: Quantitative, Qualitative, and Mixed Approaches.* 4th ed. Thousand Oaks, CA: Sage Publications.

Kemmis, Stephen, and Mervyn Wilkinson. 1998. "Participatory Action Research and the Study of Practice." In *Action Research in Practice: Partnerships for Social Justice in Education,* edited by Bill

Atweh, Stephen Kemmis, and Patricia Weeks, 21–36. New York: Routledge.

Marshall, Catherine, and Gretchen B. Rossman. 2006. *Designing Qualitative Research*. 4th ed. Thousand Oaks, CA: Sage Publications.

McKay, Judy, and Peter Marshall. 2001. "The Dual Imperatives of Action Research." *Information Technology & People* 14, no. 1: 46–59. doi: 10.1108/09593840110384771.

O'Grady, Kevin. 2011. "Is Action Research a Contradiction in Terms? Do Communities of Practice Mean the End of Educational Research as We Know It? Some Remarks Based on One Recent Example of Religious Education Research." *Educational Action Research* 19: 189–99. doi: 10.1080/09650792.2011.569205.

Stringer, Ernest T. 2007. *Action Research*. 3rd ed. Thousand Oaks, CA: Sage Publications.

WEBSITES OF INTEREST

Action Research Special Interest Group of the American Educational Research Association
http://coe.westga.edu/arsig/

The Northeast Florida Science, Technology, and Mathematics Center for Education
http://www.nefstem.org/action_research_journals.htm

JOURNAL ARTICLE WITH ABSTRACT

Davison, Robert M., Maris G. Martinsons, and Ned Kock. 2004. "Principles of Canonical Action Research." *Information Systems Journal* 14: 65–86.doi: 10.1111/j.1365-2575.2004.00162.x

Despite the growing prominence of canonical action research (CAR) in the information systems discipline, a paucity of methodological guidance continues to hamper those conducting and evaluating such studies. This article elicits a set of five principles and associated criteria to help assure both the rigor and the relevance of CAR in information systems. The first principle relates to the development of an agreement that facilitates collaboration between the action researcher and the client. The second principle is based upon a cyclical process model for action research that consists of five stages: diagnosis, planning, intervention, evaluation and reflection. Additional principles highlight the critical roles of theory, change through action, and the specification of learning in terms of implications for both research and practice. The five principles are illustrated through the analysis of one recently published CAR study.

44

PROGRAM EVALUATION

Johan Mostert, DPhil

Evaluation research (ER) is one of the fastest growing applications of social research (Babbie 2014, 371–401). As the term "evaluation" implies, this form of applied research is used to evaluate the impact of social intervention programs. After such a program has been implemented, the sponsoring agency may commission research to determine if the program is actually successful. A causal hypothesis (program X is having a positive result on social problem Y) is then tested. The program itself becomes the independent variable and the program's impact is the dependent variable.

A BRIEF OVERVIEW OF ER

ER is often referred to as *program evaluation* or *outcome assessment*. Over the years, this emerging field has grown into a respected discipline. It is now implemented within varied perspectives: economics, education, social policy, community health, and community development. Practitioners from diverse academic and professional backgrounds engage in ER, including psychology, sociology, economics, management sciences, social work, as well as non-profit organizations.

Babbie (2014, Chapter 12 "Evaluation Research") listed a host of recent public policy initiatives that have been subjected to ER. The scope of questions that have been addressed by ER studies is impressive:

- Do no-fault divorce reforms increase the number of divorces?
- Has no-fault automobile insurance really brought down insurance policy premiums?
- Has the "No Child Left Behind" program improved the quality of education?
- Have "Just Say No" abstinence programs reduced rates of sexual activity?

ER IN MISSIOLOGICAL CONTEXT

A plethora of missiologically oriented research questions could be effectively addressed by ER. The following questions indicate how useful this research approach could be:

- Does the establishment of Christian schools contribute to church growth in local Latin American communities?
- Is the rising popularity of social justice initiatives in missionary movements diminishing the evangelistic and church-planting roles of Western missionaries?
- Does the acceptance of the Business as Mission (BAM) model as legitimate missionary activity by national churches decrease the effectiveness of traditional missionary activity?
- Do missionaries involved in social justice ministries enjoy greater financial support from American donors?
- What impact does the bi-vocational status of a missionary or pastor have on his or her effectiveness as a minister of the Gospel?
- How cost-effective is the traditional Western missionary in the context of the global financial crisis?

THE EVALUATION RESEARCH PROCESS

Researchers use a variety of quantitative and qualitative methodologies to determine if social interventions are producing the intended results. These methodologies include experimental designs, surveys, and interviews. Most credible ER studies utilize a mixed-method approach.[1]

Various stages in the evaluation research process have been suggested in the literature. The three-step model proposed by Donna Mertens (2010, Chapter 2 "Evaluation") is a useful example:

Step 1: Focusing the evaluation. In this step, the researcher develops a detailed description of *what* is to be evaluated (the program) and *why* it is to be evaluated (the motivation). The student should also include a relevant literature review (see Machi and McEvoy, 2016). The researcher identifies the stakeholders and solicits their help for the study. The most

---

1. See chapter 23 titled, "Qualitative and Quantitative Research: Similarities and Distinctions."

critical (and difficult) task in the entire endeavor is identifying the criteria needed to determine the program's success or failure. The criteria inform the development of the study's research questions and methods of inquiry. Conflicting opinions are common during this process; the definition of success is often hotly debated.[2]

Step 2: Planning the evaluation. During this step, the researcher makes the critical decision regarding who best can gather the required information. A researcher already inside the organization (an employee) can access information easily without needing to build credibility with internal stakeholders. The ER process could, however, create a conflict of interest; an employee may feel pressure, either overtly or covertly, to produce results that do not harm the prestige or status of the organization. In contrast, a researcher hired from outside an organization may feel little organizational pressure, but may struggle to access information and gain the trust of those inside. This dilemma notwithstanding, an ER may never be conducted at all if the anticipated results would conflict with the organization's perspectives and beliefs (Babbie 2014, 392).

Step 3: Implementing the evaluation. Finally, gathering credible information and processing it accurately and ethically form the final step. A researcher must report conclusions to the stakeholders about a program's effectiveness, supporting that conclusion from the study's evidence.

THE POLITICAL REALITIES OF EVALUATION RESEARCH

Without questions, ER overlaps with the wider field of social research. However, one factor clearly distinguishes ER from other forms of social inquiry: ER is inherently and unavoidably intertwined with politics (Mertens 2010, 49). Evaluations are conducted on policies, programs, products, and personnel. And all of these exist within a political context. ER is typically conducted far from the relative safety of the academic ivory tower.

Only a naïve researcher engages in ER thinking he or she is immune to the influence of stakeholders who have vested interests in an existing program or policy. The desire to build an orphanage in Africa may not be driven by best-practice models; it may, instead, be driven by Western

---

2. For a discussion and guidelines on the definition on "success" see the chapter in Mertens (2010).

concepts of child care—and the power of donor dollars (Mostert 2011, 47–48). Similarly, a Bible college's curriculum in Latin America may have been created by educators with Western conceptions of (1) family life, (2) how a local church should function, and (3) how pastors ought to communicate with their flocks.

Policies, programs, and products are seldom subject to rigorous research precisely because of the risky political implications attending such research. And the Church is poorer because of it. Courageous researchers are needed, capable of engaging in best-practice, Kingdom-relevant ER, gently changing their political reality in the process.

REFERENCES AND RESOURCES FOR ADDITIONAL READING

Adler, Emily S., and Roger R. Clark. 2015. *An Invitation to Social Research: How it's Done.* 5th ed. Stamford, CT: Cengage Learning.

Babbie, Earl. 2014. *The Basics of Social Research.* 6th ed. Belmont, CA: Wadsworth Cengage Learning.

Bernard, H. Russell. 2011. *Research Methods in Anthropology: Qualitative and Quantitative Approaches.* 5th ed. Lanham, MD: AltaMira Press.

Machi, L. A., and B. T. McEvoy. 2016. *The Literature Review: Six Steps to Success.* 3rd ed. Thousand Oaks, CA: Sage Publications.

Mertens, Donna M. 2010. *Research and Evaluation in Education and Psychology: Integrating Diversity with Quantitative, Qualitative and Mixed Methods.* 3rd ed. Thousand Oaks, CA: Sage Publications.

Mostert, Johan H. 2011. *How to Become HIV+: Guidelines for the Local Church.* Harrisonburg, VA: Kerus Global Education.

WEBSITES OF INTEREST

The Centers for Disease Control—Framework for Program Evaluation in Public Health
    http://www.cdc.gov/mmwr/preview/mmwrhtml/rr4811a1.htm

Community Toolbox—Part J (How-to Guide: chapters 36 to 39)
    www.ctb.ku.edu

W. K. Kellogg Foundation—Evaluation Handbook
http://www.wkkf.org/knowledge-center/resources/2010/W-K
-Kellogg-Foundation-Evaluation-Handbook.aspx

JOURNAL ARTICLE WITH ABSTRACT

Chouinard, Jill Anne, and J. Bradley Cousins. 2009. "A Review and Synthesis
of Current Research on Cross-Cultural Evaluation." *American Journal of
Evaluation* 30: 457–494. doi: 10.1177/1098214009349865.

As a fairly new and emergent construct, there remain many gaps in our
knowledge about how to integrate notions of culture and cultural context
into evaluation theory and practice, as well as gaps in our knowledge
about how to conduct and implement evaluations in immigrant and indigenous communities. In this article, the authors provide a comprehensive
review of the empirical literature on evaluations conducted in cultural
communities, with an emphasis on the relationship between evaluators
and stakeholders in the cross-cultural program context. The analysis of
the literature selected for review leads to the development of a theoretical framework describing the inter-related and multi-textual dimensions
(relational, ecological, methodological, organizational and personal) that
interweave throughout the evaluation, and that ultimately inform the
relationship between evaluators and stakeholders in the cross-cultural
program context. The article concludes with an agenda for future research.

45
CONTENT ANALYSIS
Robert Bartels, JD

Within the broad categories of content analysis and historiography,[1] researchers can employ a number of specific methodologies to reconstruct the past, fill in data gaps, and capture a fuller understanding of the history being explored. Six of these research methods are discussed in this chapter: interpretive analysis, narrative analysis, performance analysis, discourse analysis, conversation analysis, and the somewhat-broader qualitative data analysis. Each method of analysis has its own corpus of methodological literature, and each has its own indicators of best-practice research.

Using one or more of these data-collection and data-analysis methods, researchers can search for connections between words and those cultural actions that add meaning to those words. These connections are rarely obvious; content-analysis researchers must search for the evidence hidden within those qualitative data.

INTERPRETIVE ANALYSIS

Interpretive analysis enables researchers to examine the connection between spoken words, their meanings, and the speakers' culture. This method requires a rather thorough understanding of the research participants' language and culture. With that understanding, missiological researchers, for example, can make the connections necessary to appropriately interpret the spoken words of those they are called to serve. For example, in some cultures an affirmative answer implies agreement to a question asked. Those *same words*, spoken within a different culture, carry the meaning of "saving face"; the speaker does not want to embarrass an acquaintance with a negative response. Culture is clearly the key to understanding meaning, as illustrated by this example.

---

1. See chapter 28 titled, "Historical Research" and chapter 8 titled, "Primary and Secondary Sources."

REFERENCES AND RESOURCES FOR ADDITIONAL READING

Bernard, H. Russell. 2011. *Research Methods in Anthropology: Qualitative and Quantitative Approaches*. 5th ed. Lanham, MD: AltaMira Press.

Denscombe, Martyn. 2010. *The Good Research Guide: For Small-Scale Social Research Projects*. 4th ed. Berkshire, UK: Open University Press.

Gilderhus, Mark T. 2009. *History and Historians: A Historiographical Introduction*. 7th ed. Upper Saddle River, NJ: Pearson Education.

Scott, Gregory M., and Stephen M. Garrison. 2008. *The Political Science Student Writer's Manual*. Upper Saddle River, NJ: Pearson Education.

WEBSITES OF INTEREST

Methodology and Content Analysis (a PowerPoint presentation)
http://www.slideshare.net/fpaisey/methodology-content-analysis

Writing@CSU—Content Analysis
http://writing.colostate.edu/guides/guide.cfm?guideid=61

JOURNAL ARTICLE WITH ABSTRACT

Hsieh, Hsiu-Fang, and Sarah E. Shannon. 2005. "Three Approaches to Qualitative Content Analysis." *Qualitative Health Research* 15, no. 9: 1277–1288. doi: 10.1177/1049732305276687

Content analysis is a widely used qualitative research technique. Rather than being a single method, current applications of content analysis show three distinct approaches: conventional, directed, or summative. All three approaches are used to interpret meaning from the content of text data and, hence, adhere to the naturalistic paradigm. The major differences among the approaches are coding schemes, origins of codes, and threats to trustworthiness. In conventional content analysis, coding categories are derived directly from the text data. With a directed approach, analysis starts with a theory or relevant research findings as guidance for initial codes. A summative content analysis involves counting and comparisons, usually of keywords or content, followed by the interpretation of the underlying context. The authors delineate analytic procedures specific to each approach and techniques addressing trustworthiness with hypothetical examples drawn from the area of end-of-life care.

46
Q METHODOLOGY

Robert D. Braswell, PhD

Understanding peoples' subjective views of something can be as important as understanding the thing itself. A rigorous methodology, Q makes shared perceptions observable, measurable, understandable, and communicable. Q methodology is a quantitative (correlation-based) approach to what is normally viewed as the domain of qualitative research. Thus, Q is an exception to most generalizations about quantitative and qualitative methods, as illustrated in the following table.[1]

Strengths of Q	Weaknesses of Q
Ideal for phenomena that naturally occur in real life (i.e., in natural settings).	Not focused on establishing cause-and-effect statements.
Objective and dependent on subjects' operations, reducing the influence of the researcher on the outcomes (the researcher is not the "instrument" and data interpretations are limited by subjects' responses).	Historically, not well understood by either quantitative researchers or qualitative researchers since it does not fully fit either set of expectations.
Useful for a basic description of new (previously unstudied) phenomena in terms of the "factors" (shared points of view) present among persons of interest.	The relative prevalence of "factors" cannot normally be generalized to larger populations, except by pairing with a quantitative study.
Useful whenever human points of view must be understood.	
Useful for program and policy evaluations.	
Excels in complex analysis, resisting the "temptation" to simplify what is observed.	
Relatively quick to complete; often only requiring days or weeks to finish.	

---

1. See the tables in chapter 23 entitled, "Qualitative and Quantitative Research."

A Q study begins with a question about shared perceptions within a group (or groups). It is an ideal tool for investigating questions such as the following.[2]

Do a certain denomination's set of churches planted in Southeast Asia by US missionaries experience the same denominational (and/or spiritual or theological) identity as US pastors and missionaries?

What are the perceptions about the most important concerns in church planting among candidate Ugandan church planters before and after a seminar on church planting?

STEP-BY-STEP THROUGH A Q STUDY

A typical Q study consists of the following five steps:

1. **Identify the concourse.** Resolving a research question using Q starts by identifying a "concourse," defined as a diverse conversation or flow of meanings about a topic. A concourse can be gathered through interviews, library research, personal conversations, internet searches, and so on. For instance, in a study on perceptions of church planting among pastors in Uganda, the concourse was compiled partly from interviews with leaders before training on the topic and partly from the training curriculum itself (Shipley 2010).

2. **Sample the concourse.** In Q methodology it is important to adequately sample the whole concourse in a manageable number of statements. Usually a *structured* sample (Brown 1980) of forty to fifty statements is used to ensure that statements are available to reflect (model) whatever point of view the participants may have. This sample, labeled the "Q-set" is prepared for administration as a Q-sort by constructing a target grid in the shape of a flattened normal curve.

   The researcher then prepares one or more conditions of instruction for sorting the Q-set onto that grid. For example, statements can be sorted into seven columns from "Most unlike me" or "Most unimportant" on the far left to "Most like me" or "Most important" on the far right, with the middle column reserved for neutral statements.

---

2. Q methodology seems to be enjoying a much-deserved resurgence as mixed-method studies are becoming more common. Q's solid methodological approach to questions of human subjectivity make it well suited for many applications in missiological research.

-3 Least Important	-2	-1	0 Neutral	1	2	3 Most Important

Figure 1: Q "target grid" for 29 statements (Donner 2001, 28).[3]

3. **Collect Q-sort data.** The persons, labeled the "P-set," who do the sorting are selected logically because of their connection to the research question (not randomly sampled from a population). The P-set need not be large—usually the Q-set is larger than the P-set. Though online administration is possible, the researcher typically presents and explains the sorting task in person to each participant, then records the completed Q-sort. Ideally, the researcher does some follow-up interviewing to validate the Q-set and to better understand what participants were thinking during the sort. For example, the researcher might ask, "What is it about this statement that made you put it in the 'Most like me' column?" By completing the Q-sort, each participant produces a "snapshot" of his or her unique view of the concourse at one point in time. The Q-sort can then be directly and statistically compared with the Q-sorts of other participants.

4. **Statistical analysis.** Participants Q-sorts are entered into a statistical program such as the special-purpose PQMethod.[4] The software is designed to:

   • compares every sort with every other sort and identifies sorting patterns called "factors";

---

3. The figure's caption states, "Once you have completed the Q sort, please double-check that there is one number in each cell and no duplicates."

4. PQMethod software is free and available for download from http://www .lrz-muenchen.de/~schmolck/qmethod.

- calculates a kind of "averaged" sort for each factor that idealizes what the pattern-defining sorts had in common;
- and indicates what statements were most influential for each factor, including which statements were treated in significantly different ways by different factors.

As with most computerized statistical tools, it is possible for a beginner to simply put data from sorts in and get results out. Additional options are available for experienced Q researchers. Extra care in the statistical-analysis step is rewarded by ease of interpretation in the final step.[5]

5. **Factor interpretation.** The final step in a Q study is to interpret the factors that emerged from the statistical analysis. Each factor represents a point of view shared by two or (usually) more sorts. The researcher interprets these points of view contextually, emphasizing the most important statements in defining the factor. Factor interpretation also takes into account what was learned during the post-sort interviews. Usually, factor interpretation directly answers one or more of the original research questions. It is also possible for the researcher to find something totally unexpected, which is part of the power of Q.

CONCLUSION

Q methodology allows *participants* to make their subjective judgments observable through the Q-sort. Q then allows *researchers* to comprehend the patterns among sorts using statistical tools, providing a structured, relatively objective path to deeper understanding of the views of a selected group's perspective.

REFERENCES AND RESOURCES FOR ADDITIONAL READING

Brown, Steven R. 1980. *Political Subjectivity: Applications of Q Methodology in Political Science.* New Haven, CT: Yale University Press.[6]

---

5. The last step in phase 3. See chapter 4 entitled, "The Four-Phase Model of Missiological Research."

6. The most comprehensive, authoritative reference on Q. This is a hard to find in hard copy but available online: http://qmethod.org/papers /Brown-1980-PoliticalSubjectivity.pdf.

Donner, Jonathan C. 2001. "Using Q-sorts in Participatory Processes: An Introduction to the Methodology." In *Social Analysis: Selected Tools and Techniques*. Social Development Papers, 36, 24–59. Washington, DC: The World Bank, Social Development Department.[7]

McKeown, Bruce, and Dan Thomas. 1988. *Q Methodology*. Thousand Oaks, CA: Sage Publications.

Shipley, Robert. 2010. "Rabbit Churches: An Enquiry into the Enabling Assumptions of the Uganda Assemblies of God Church Planting Movement." PhD diss., Pan-Africa Theological Seminary.

WEBSITES OF INTEREST

Q Methodology: A Method for Modern Research (Official website of Q's professional organization, links to Q papers, resources, and tutorials)
http://qmethod.org/about

Q-method@listserv.kent.edu. (Offers friendly and knowledgeable answers to Q-related questions from Brown, McKeown, Schmolck, Braswell, and others)
http://www.lsoft.com/scripts/wl.exe?sl1=q-method&h=listserv.kent.edu

Schmolck, P., PQManual
http://www.lrz.de/~schmolck/qmethod/pqmanual.htm

Schmolck, P., QMethod page (Provides links to free PQMethod software, as well as bibliography of Q studies)
http://www.lrz-muenchen.de/~schmolck/qmethod/

---

7. Available at: http://siteresources.worldbank.org/INTCDD/Resources/SAtools.pdf.

JOURNAL ARTICLE WITH ABSTRACT

Kiser, Laurel J., Deborah Medoff, Maureen M. Black, Winona Nurse, Barbara H. Fiese. 2010. "Family Mealtime Q-sort: A Measure of Mealtime Practices." *Journal of Family Psychology* 24, no. 1: 92–96. doi: 10.1037/a0017946

Studies outlining the protective functions of shared family meals suggest that helping families experience successful meals is an important goal. Measuring the effectiveness of family mealtime interventions necessitates the ability to quantify both the frequency and context of shared mealtimes. This article introduces a new instrument, the Family Mealtime Q-Sort, describes its development, and presents preliminary data about its psychometric properties. Data from initial evaluation of the Family Mealtime Q-Sort using family mealtime videos (N = 51) demonstrate acceptable interrater reliability, promising validity, and the ability to compare family mealtimes to an independently derived, culturally appropriate standard. The results suggest that the Q-sort adequately measures important dimensions of a successful mealtime including a positive atmosphere. . . . Further research on the tool is warranted.

47
PILE SORT METHODOLOGY
Beth Grant, PhD

Using the qualitative methodology of pile sorting, a researcher will ask participants (informants) to organize a set of items (typically terms or phrases printed on cards) into piles based on their similarity or proximity. This methodology facilitates investigation of the semantic categories of the informants and the relationship between key terms. The items normally emerge from previous interviews, surveys, and the literature review.

Pile sorting is both empirically effective and non-threatening, especially in cultures that do not value transparency and directness. It may also be the method of choice when the topic under investigation may be culturally sensitive.

PRELIMINARY INVESTIGATION TO IDENTIFY THE ITEMS

Pile Sort research often utilizes "freelists," which De Munck (2009) labeled the "single most powerful and informative systematic date-collection technique available" (47). By asking simple but carefully crafted freelist questions, researchers can glean an emic "snapshot" of the items belonging together in a category, as perceived by informants in a specific culture, group, or institution. This can be accomplished with relatively few informants. A missiological researcher could, for example, ask Indian church leaders or laypersons a simple question: "What are the qualities of a good leader in the church in India?" Those qualities would then become the items used in a later pile sort.

THE PILE SORTING PROCESS

Pile sorting requires at least a half-hour per informant: the informant must sort the cards, then the researcher must record the sorting ranking, and then ask the informant to explain his or her decisions. This third task is an important part of the research methodology.

Six steps are required to complete a single sort:

1. The items (terms, names, etc.) chosen during the preliminary investigation are printed on index cards (or equivalent paper) and numbered on the back. The numbers are assigned arbitrarily but cannot be changed once the pile sort starts.

2. The researcher shuffles the cards into random order before presenting the card to each informant.

3. The researcher explains that the terms on the cards were chosen during an earlier part of the study and are, therefore, not random.

4. The researcher gives the informant simple card-sorting instructions: "What goes with what?" or "Which items belong together?" It is vital that the same instructions are presented to each informant.

5. The researcher should hold any question about the informant's thinking while sorting until the sort is complete. Interruptions or distractions can influence the sort.

6. After completing the first sort into two piles, the informant reads the numbers on the back of the cards in each pile, and attempts to label each pile. If an informant is unable to label the category/pile, he or she can identify the most typical term in each pile.[1]

This six-step process of recording and requesting labels or explanation is repeated with each informant.[2]

The resultant data from all informants' pile sorts are then compiled and analyzed. Statistical software packages can facilitate the analysis: two examples are ANTHROPAC and AGPROX, an aggregate proximity matrix. Alternatively, the data can be analyzed manually, focusing on the basic ranking.

PILE SORTING VARIATIONS

Researchers have created interesting variations on the basic process described above:

---

1. Alternatively, the informant can explain why he or she placed a group of cards in that particular pile.

2. A volunteer may be recruited to help with the exercise.

Successive constrained pile sorts. The researcher determines the number of sub-piles, beyond the basic two described above, into which the cards must be sorted.[3] The informant continues to divide each pile into two additional sub-piles until only two cards are left per pile. This procedure can take up to ninety minutes and requires considerable patience.

Single free pile sorts.[4] In this variation, the informant sorts the cards into as many piles as he or she desires. This variation pile sorting is frequently used by researchers.

Small-group sorts. While pile sorting is generally conducted with individuals, it is possible to conduct with small groups. In a study conducted in Bangladesh to investigate household food insecurity, researchers administered pile sorts to several small groups of respondents; the results between groups appeared to be consistent (Frongillo et al. 2003). In a highly collectivistic culture, this small-group alternative may encourage dialogue and active participation in the research.

Simple rankings. An informant is given the cards and asked to rank items or objects in order of importance. The researcher then records the ordered stack, with the most important item given the highest number of points (e.g., 15 in a 15-card sort; down to 1 for least important).

Strengths of Pile Sorting	Weaknesses of Pile Sorting
One of most popular sorting-task research methodologies because of its flexibility.	Can be time-intensive compared to other research methodologies.
Allows comparison of more terms than other methodologies	It requires patience, organizational skills, and constantly double-checking one's progress as a researcher or volunteer.
Effective method for finding themes in previously gathered data.	The variable meanings of terms make it essential that informants understand the terms used as the researcher intends.*
Facilitates research into the social structure of organizations and institutions.	The "lumper/splitter" problem can occur: some informants tend to put many items in a pile or want to put many items in single piles since they view each item as unique in some way.
Allows researchers to map cognitively defined social dynamics of groups and communities.†	The method often requires at least one volunteer. Some payment or reward is recommended for the time and patience required.

---

3. This is generally two piles, as described in the preceding section.
4. This method is also called an unconstrained pile sort.

Strengths of Pile Sorting	Weaknesses of Pile Sorting
A useful tool for generating taxonomic trees.[‡]	A pilot test is highly recommended to estimate the time per informant and confirm accuracy of word meaning between initial free lists and pile sorting.
Can include a large number of items in the study (20–100).	Without prior familiarity with the cultural context, data and research problem, inaccurate interpretation of findings is likely.
Provides great flexibility of design and implementation; it can even use physical objects in place of written words and phrases.	Manual analysis of the data can be time-consuming and tedious; computer program analysis can be difficult without a background in statistical analysis.
Facilitates the emergence of cognitive categories not easily articulated, including culturally sensitive topics.	

[*] This concern is most likely addressed if terms are carried into the pile sort from an earlier methodology in the study and if the researcher has an emic perspective.

[†] That is, who goes with whom, how people view the grouping of people within a social organization.

[‡] See examples in Bernard (2011, 399) and De Munck (2009, 73).

REFERENCES AND RESOURCES FOR ADDITIONAL READING

Alasuutari, Pertti, Leonard Bickman, and Julia Brannen, eds. 2009. *The Sage Handbook of Applied Social Research Methods.* Thousand Oaks, CA: Sage Publications.

Bernard, H. Russell. 2011. *Research Methods in Anthropology: Qualitative and Quantitative Approaches.* 5th ed. Lanham, MD: AltaMira Press.

De Munck, Victor. 2009. *Research Design and Methods for Studying Cultures.* Lanham, MD: AltaMira Press.

Frongillo, Edward A., Nusrat Chowdhury, Eva-Charlotte Ekström, and Ruchira T. Naved. 2003. "Understanding the Experience of Household Food Insecurity in Rural Bangladesh Leads to a Measure Different Fromm that Used in Other Countries." *Journal of Nutrition* 133: 4158–4162.

Guest, Greg, and Kathleen M. MacQueen, eds. 2008. *Handbook for Team-Based Qualitative Research.* Lanham, MD: AltaMira Press.

Ross, James L., Sandra L. Laston, Pertti J. Pelto, and Lazeena Muna. 2002. "Exploring Explanatory Models of Women's Reproductive

Health in Rural Bangladesh." *Culture, Health and Sexuality* 4: 173–90. doi: 10.1080/13691050110096189.

WEBSITE OF INTEREST

Three Pile Sorting Instructions
http://www.cawst.org/assets/File/Three%20Pile%20Sorting%20Instructions.pdf

JOURNAL ARTICLE WITH ABSTRACT

Quintiliani, Lisa M., Marci K. Campbell, Pamela S. Haines, and Kelly H. Webber. 2008. "The Use of the Pile Sortmethod in Identifying Groups of Healthful Lifestyle Behaviors Among Female Community College Students." *Journal of the American Dietetic Association* 108: 1503–1507. doi:10.1016/j.jada.2008.06.428

When encountering new or understudied populations, it is useful to build an understanding of the needs and perceptions of the target audience. This study investigated the application of the qualitative pile sort method for gaining information about nutrition and physical activity behaviors. In a pile sort, individuals make a list of topics relevant to a particular subject, and then they group these topics into related piles. This study investigated whether there was consistency in the ways in which participants grouped behaviors related to having a healthful lifestyle. Pile sorts were conducted during six focus groups among 28 female community college students (46% white; 39% had a 2-year degree or higher). A total of 74 piles of grouped behaviors were coded from the transcripts. Analyses revealed good consistency (identified nine to 12 times) for four groupings: exercise, lifestyle, how you eat, and positive foods. The pile sort method represents an activity that can be incorporated into formative research for interventions focused on complex behaviors with multiple components; in addition, this method may provide structure to counseling sessions and facilitate a better understanding of the perceptions of healthful eating and physical activity from patients' perspectives.

UNIT 5

Theological and Empirical Integration

48
INTEGRATING DISCIPLINES
Exploration of a Methodology

Anita L. Koeshall, PhD

THE UNIQUE NATURE OF MISSIOLOGY

Missiology is a cross-cultural discipline that investigates the theories and methods employed by churches as they seek to fulfill their mandate to participate in the mission of God. Such investigations incorporate multiple disciplines, such as anthropology, education, historiography, linguistics, philosophy and epistemology, psychology, and sociology. Each of these disciplines is marked by its own theories, body of knowledge, and best-practice methods for research. Interdisciplinarity is a hallmark of the field of missiology.

Missiology is by nature a cross-cultural discipline. Two or more academic disciplines are incorporated in every missiological research endeavor in order to explicate the complexities of church and missionary structures, methods, communication, patterns of cooperation, and leadership. More recently developed fields of inquiry such as communication, management, and technology may also be included in a given missiological study.

In addition to the secular disciplines listed above, a missiological study must engage the biblical text by investigating arenas such as theology, church tradition, world religions, and church-growth theories. Together, these disciplines create the lens by which cross-cultural workers examine key topics, such as ecclesiology, Christology, pneumatology, and salvation as experienced in local communities.

Missiology engages the task of understanding cultures, as do secular anthropologists. It also investigates the effect of culture on theologizing, communication, leadership, organizational structures, relationships, contextualization, and a wide range of practices that characterize the tasks of church and mission. Thus, missiology is the only field of inquiry that combines the three domains of social science, intercultural studies, and theology in every research project.

Eric L. Johnson (2011) argues that modernity teaches the segregation of knowledge into disciplines and sub-disciplines. Particularly relevant to missiology, modernity insists on the separation of the natural or scientific discoveries from biblical or theological truth. To the researcher raised in modernity, compartmentalization seems almost instinctive; causing the researcher to struggle with integration, finding it to be problematic and abstruse. As a result, each field of study fosters reductionistic tendencies, restricting analysis and solutions to its own sphere of reference. In addition, social scientists typically allow no space for biblical reflection, faith, or supernatural intervention. Similarly, theologians tend to value and pursue culture-free, knowable truth. Accordingly, "missiology must find a way to integrate spirituality, psychology, anthropology and sociology in a holistic understanding that more closely approximates reality" (Van Engen 1996, 256). The purpose of this chapter is to reflect on possible methodologies for integration.

HEURISTICS: THE RESEARCHER AS A MASTER ARCHITECT

Paul G. Hiebert employs the heuristic of architectural blueprints to describe the integration of theology and anthropology (2008, 75). Every building, when being constructed, has a unique set of plans for each of its systems; all those systems must be integrated into the whole finished edifice. Heating, electrical, plumbing, and the physical structure must be coordinated. Looking at any one set of blueprints does not explain the complex whole. Similarly, one discipline is not capable of producing a "thick" description of the social, historical, ecclesial, and missional context being explored. Therefore, a missiological researcher must become a "master architect," capable of examining a relevant researchable problem by "layering" disparate perspectives or "blueprints" together in order to understand the complex and often perplexing reality.

This layering process requires the researcher, as master architect, to invest the time and develop the skills needed to do in-depth research. This implies the need for literature searches in multiple libraries, the use of several research methodologies, and, most importantly, the personal development as an expert in more than one field of study. Only a multidiscipline researcher can attempt an adequate and valid integration without compromising the truth or overlooking insights from any of the fields of knowledge.

Little has been written about specific methodologies of integration in missiology. However, practical theologians researching within a single culture face a similar challenge of interdisciplinarity; they have proposed useful methods for meaningful integration. For example, Stephen Pattison (2000) encourages a mutual critical conversation between three "dialogue partners": the researcher's "own ideas, beliefs, feelings, perceptions, and assumptions, the beliefs, assumptions and perceptions provided by the Christian tradition (including the Bible), and the contemporary situation which is being examined" (139). According to Pattison, each of these dialogue partners must ask questions of the other two. Through this process of mutual exchange, the problem will be resolved.

John Swinton and Harriet Mowat (2006) explored Pattison's mutual critical conversation method as a research strategy, viewing it as a hermeneutical cycle. First, the situation is researched by a qualitative or quantitative social science method to "uncover hidden meanings" and understand the resulting practices. These results then are brought into "constructive dialogue with Scripture and tradition with a view to developing revised forms of practice that will impact upon and transform the original situation" (2006, 81–82).

Challenging Pattison's idea of "mutual" conversation, Swinton and Mowat press for an interdisciplinary method that elevates the contribution of theology. They respect the clarification and complexity that qualitative research reveals about a given situation, while maintaining theology's significance as "logically prior to and independent of qualitative research data" (2006, 87).

Swinton and Mowat (2006) also argue that theologians must have the humility to employ a "hermeneutic of suspicion as to whether or not . . . [their] interpretation of revelation is pure, faithful or otherwise" (89). A theological perspective can be clarified and enriched by a social scientist who approaches the text from outside the constraints of theological methodology. Such a researcher can make explicit the blinders that prevent the theologian from seeing his or her own biases.

Practical theologians may need to consider only the social science and theological blueprints; however, a missiologist must add the cross-cultural component to this methodological dialogue. Although cross-cultural inquiry is a social science, this blueprint plays a crucial role in all missiological studies, since missiology by definition seeks to facilitate Christian witness across cultures. The missiologist must cultivate expertise in cross-cultural interaction in order to (1) minimize the influence of his or her own cultural lenses, and (2) expose those influences that hinder both a mono-cultural theologian *and* a single-discipline, mono-cultural social scientist.

Therefore, a missiologist researches a problem using at least three sets of blueprints:

1. The social science blueprint—best chosen to explicate the situation.
2. The cultural blueprint—used to examine the cultural context in which the problem is embedded, as well as to explore the role that culture plays in the exacerbation, alleviation, or explanation of the problem.
3. The biblical blueprint—details the theological basis on which the problem is centered.

From a missiological perspective, most research problems lie within social constructs that spring from a culturally legitimized biblical understanding of church or mission. A missiological researcher must thoroughly examine the problem using all three blueprints, applying best-practice methodology for each discipline.

INTEGRATION: LAYERING THE BLUEPRINTS

The task of missiological inquiry is not finished with the application of these individual disciplines. Throughout the process, the missiologist, as the master architect, must remain conscious of the dynamic influence that the layers of blueprints have on each other. That dynamic influence is most evident in the study's findings, which proceed from the interdisciplinary interaction (see following figure). During that interaction, findings from one discipline critique findings from other disciplines. Specific multi-directional critiques are demonstrated in the following principles, with examples given for each parenthetically:

1. Social sciences can aid in understanding the Truth in Scriptures because that Truth is embedded in the social context of the biblical narrative. (For example, the anthropological theories of honor and shame, or collectivism and individualism, illuminate Scriptures such as 1 Cor 11:1–16, or Eph 5:21–6:9).
2. Cross-cultural theories can explicate a theologian's conclusions, revealing possible cultural biases in his or her

interpretations. (For example, theologians may attempt to describe Trinitarian relationships as either hierarchical or egalitarian through a process of anthropomorphism, thus legitimizing their own preferred church structures.)

3. Biblical Truth, in turn, can evaluate or judge the rightness or validity of theories used by social scientists. (For example, Hofstede defines "high power distance" in terms of power striving; when evaluated against John 13:1–5, for example, such striving cannot be justified in church leadership.)

Finally the blueprints of biblical Truth, social science theory, and cross-cultural understanding must be layered to reveal the complexity of the central research problem, and to resolve it. Through that layering process, the researcher crafts the integrated findings needed to reveal a way forward for biblically faithful, empirically valid mission theory and praxis.

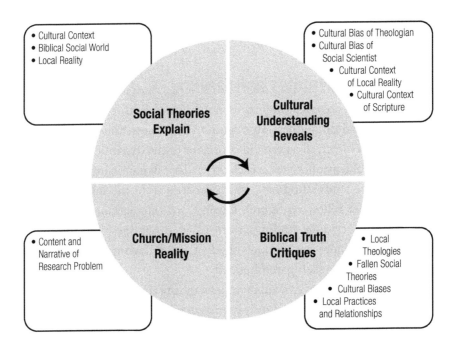

Figure 2: Integrating Biblical Truth, Social Science Theory, and Cross-Cultural Understanding to Create a Master Blueprint by Which to Investigate a Research Problem

Therefore, several of the following tasks are pertinent to any missiological study:

1. Identify the theological idea, assumption, goal, or framework that is central to this research project or dissertation.
2. Describe how biblical Truth will be applied to critique a sociological or anthropological theory that the researcher intends to use as an instrument to understand a church or missional reality.
3. Indicate how a social science theory will make explicit the biases that are implicit in a locally legitimized biblical understanding, ecclesiological practice, missional paradigm, or theology.
4. Explore the role cultural differences play in the local setting.
5. Create, evaluate, or apply theory.
6. Develop practical and concrete application steps in order to point the way towards more faithful embodiment of God's Truth in Church and mission organizations.

REFERENCES AND RESOURCES FOR ADDITIONAL READING

Geertz, Clifford. 1977. *The Interpretation of Cultures*. New York, NY: Basic Books.

Hiebert, Paul G. 2008. *Transforming Worldviews: An Anthropological Understanding of How People Change*. Grand Rapids, MI: Baker.

Hofstede, Geert. 2001. *Culture's Consequences: Comparing Values, Behaviors, Institutions, and Organizations Across Nations*. 2nd ed. Thousand Oaks, CA: Sage Publications.

Johnson, Eric L. 2011. "The Three Faces of Integration." *Journal of Psychology & Christianity* 30: 339–55.

Pattison, Stephen. 2000. "Some Straw for the Bricks: A Basic Introduction to Theological Reflection." In *The Blackwell Reader in Pastoral and Practical Theology*, edited by James Woodward and Stephen Pattison, 135–48. Malden, MA: Blackwell Publishing.

Swinton, John, and Harriet Mowat. 2006. *Practical Theology and Qualitative Research*. London: SCM Press.

Van Engen, Charles. 1996. *Mission on the Way: Issues in Mission Theology*. Grand Rapids, MI: Baker.

Verkuyl, Johannes. 1998. *Contemporary Missiology: An Introduction*. Grand Rapids, MI: Eerdmans.

49
INTEGRATION IN WRITING UP MISSIOLOGICAL RESEARCH

Alan R. Johnson, PhD

In this chapter, I want to bring some personal reflections on the *process* of integrative writing to this subject.

TWO CENTRAL BELIEFS

My own journey in research has benefitted from two central beliefs that continually inform how I approach the research process and how I write. The first belief is that all research is embedded in a theoretical framework. One of my research supervisors compared the primary function of theory to a sieve, each theory forms a unique sieve that "catches" a specific type of data in the life-stream being investigated. After I pose a research problem, reflecting on this first belief or assumption helps me to consider the various "sieves" available to me as a theory-informed researcher. I can then begin to envision what each sieve would catch if it was utilized in my research. Perhaps I wish to understand how Africans in tribe X in country Y influence each other to get things done (often called "leading" in our contexts). I can envision how this question would be addressed by an economist, a political scientist, an anthropologist, a psychologist, or a cultural materialist who focuses on counting calories and measuring energy intake. I can even envision how a liberation theologian or other theologian might seek to resolve this research question. Each theory-informed perspective, as a unique sieve, "catches" a unique chunk of the "reality" occurring in that particular African tribal social setting.

My second major belief is that creating an empirical "account" is essential to problem resolution. Every epistemological and ontological framework can account for what, how, and why something happens as it does in tribe X of country Y. Accounts grow through research, accumulating evidence, and rationales for the claims they are making. This process is often expressed in terms of some kind of mid-level theoretical construct that makes sense of what is happening in a particular slice of social life. As suggested above, I can envision what might be contained in a shamanistic account, a cultural account, a psychological account, or a genealogical account. Each is supported by the worldview in which such an account makes sense and provides meaningful explanation.

As such, missiological research is inherently interdisciplinary. As a result, a missiological researcher approaches his or her findings with multiple perspectives to help elucidate the subject matter. DeLonn Rance[1] refers to this iterative process of drawing upon all of these perspectives as "looping." As the researcher develops a construct or interacts with a finding from, for instance, the social science arena, the researcher can loop back and connect that finding with biblical/theological understandings and cross-cultural understanding. The goal is to strengthen the interdisciplinary account, demonstrating in the process why that account explains more of a given social reality than other potential accounts.

THREE KEY HABITS OR PERSONAL DISCIPLINES

Given the above perspective, it is easy to understand why missiological writing is inevitably more demanding than other forms of dissertation writing. Rather than writing from within one research paradigm or framework, a missiological researcher must write from multiple perspectives: scriptural, empirical, and cultural.

This kind of integrative work constitutes a major challenge, especially when completing a large research and writing like a dissertation. In order to succeed in such efforts, development of certain habits and personal disciplines can facilitate the process; three are discussed here.

Memoing

The first involves continually memoing key insights gained from the various perspectives as they emerge. That memoing process represents the researcher's initial search for connection points with insights in other perspectives. This must happen long before the "write-up" begins as it provides the grist for such work.

---

1. See chapter 15 entitled, "Doing Theology Missiologically."

Visual Mapping

The second habit or personal discipline necessitates finding some way to display what the frameworks and research disciplines have "caught" in their sieves. This visual mapping is critically important, for visually experimenting with interrelationships greatly facilitates integrative writing. Using large sheets of paper in order to draw things out and begin connecting or organizing them in meaningful ways, the researcher begins to see connections previously not seen. Placing major findings from the biblical, social, and cultural inquiry strategically, enables the researcher to "think" about their relationships visually.

Incremental Writing

Finally, writing itself is a form of learning; certain insights are possible only while actually engaged in the physical act of writing. Therefore, those who do best at dissertation writing do a little bit of writing every day, as a habit or personal discipline, rather than trying to write it all in one brief period of time. One is able to "see" things previously not seen when writing. This third habit suggests the wisdom of capturing thoughts, even in rough form, so that those thoughts can be reshaped through self-editing. This is why writing more frequently in smaller chunks is so valuable; this strategy allows a writer to increase the time available to make connections and engage in that process of looping back to examine existing findings or seek new data across the different domains of missiological research.

In the long run, these three daily disciplines facilitate the integrative thinking necessary for missiological research, as well as creating the writing habits necessary for a successful dissertation write up.

While missiological writing is demanding, there is a special joy in the task as well. We as researchers focusing on God's mission in the world get the privilege of participating in what God is doing, and can draw upon the rigors of research work to help as part of the process of Spirit discernment in our ministry context.

50

MY JOURNEY IN INTEGRATION
The Spirit of God in Integration
DeLonn L. Rance, PhD

When I was in sixth grade, my teacher attempted to explain Newton's first law of motion: that an object in motion will not change its velocity unless an external force acts upon it. She illustrated for us farm boys by stating that if we were riding in the back of a pickup truck, the speed of our bodies and the speed of the pickup would be constant; so if we jumped up at a ninety degree angle, we would land exactly in the same spot from which we jumped. This scientific affirmation did not match my sixth-grade experience; Newton's theory did not resonate with my reality. Despite my introverted personality, I doggedly argued that any time I stood riding on the tailgate of my uncle's pickup and jumped straight up in the air, I always landed with significant discomfort in the dirt and dust behind the pickup.

After several hours of trying to get through to me, my teacher finally gave up and called in reinforcements. The high school physics teacher arrived to put me in my place, yet he found himself in the awkward position of having to say that both my teacher and I were correct. She was correct if the illustration of Newton's law occurred in a vacuum (e.g., space). I was correct, however, on planet earth where wind resistance exists. Thus began my journey in integration that now focuses on missiological theory. That theory must be congruent with praxis, or the missionary may be painfully "left in the dirt."

Anita Koeshall[1] and Alan Johnson[2] provide key insights on (1) the integration of the various disciplines that facilitate missiological research, and (2) on the relationship between

---

1. See chapter 48 entitled, "Integrating Disciplines: Exploration of a Methodology."
2. See chapters 2 and 49 entitled, "Epistemological Frameworks in Qualitative Research," and "Integration in Writing Up Missiological Research," respectively.

- theory and praxis
- theological inquiry and social science research
- biblical Truth and empirical truth
- the natural and supernatural
- the Word, the Church, and the world.

Koeshall's "layering" and "multi-directional" task both articulate and illustrate an integrative approach to the missiological research process; I describe this process as "looping." The social sciences provide tools that allow the missiologist, with the Spirit's guidance, to discern the Truth revealed in both a specific cultural context and in the biblical text, while also critiquing the missiologist's own cultural interpretive biases. The Truth revealed in Scripture calls the missiologist-as-researcher to acknowledge that humans can only "know" in part, not in full. Ultimately, encountering Truth requires total surrender to the Spirit of God.

The Truth of Scripture confronts the researcher, the research participants, and the theories that attempt to explain a given reality. Missiological theories must be sourced in biblical Truth and Spirit dependence. Even if research findings meet the academic standards of validity and reliability, it does not mean that those findings are truth. Rather, for the missiological researcher, empirical findings are perceived to be true and must then be critiqued by the Truth revealed in Scripture.

As Koeshall and Johnson both affirm, the explanation (theory) and recommendations that emerge from missiological research must accomplish three essential tasks. They must[3]

- "reveal a way forward for faithful mission theory and praxis,"
- "assess how biblical truth is known and relevant to a particular context,"
- "point the way towards more faithful embodiment of God's Truth in Church and mission organizations" (i.e., reveal the will of God in the specific missionary enterprise).

Dissertations and projects written by missiologists, especially in their findings, recommendations, and outcomes, must provide an explanation (theory) and application (action steps/praxis) sourced in the will of God

---

3. All three quotations are from Koeshall, Chapter 48, "Integrating Disciplines: Exploration of a Methodology Integrating Disciplines: Exploration of a Methodology."

that can be embraced and obeyed by the missionary/apostolic people of God. Koeshall's comparison of a missiologist's research task to that of a "master architect" illumines the interrelationship and integration of the various disciplines ("blueprints") and competencies necessary to do missions. In this research enterprise to build effectively, however, missiological researchers must never forget that "unless the Lord builds the house, the builders labor in vain" (Ps 127:1).

I find a simile (one that reflects my rural roots) in the work and skills of a farmer. Like a farmer, a missiological researcher is a generalist whose work is not limited to a single task or discipline. A farmer must be a meteorologist, agronomist, mechanic, commodities broker, and chemist, among other professions. Similarly, a missiologist as a scholar-practitioner utilizes the tools of the academy (e.g., social sciences, history, natural sciences, theology) to prepare the soil, remove the rocks, plant the seed, and bring in the harvest (i.e., make disciples by communicating the gospel in word and deed, plant, nurture and develop the church, its leadership, and eventually its own mission). Unlike the architect who can build from the blueprint through human effort, neither the farmer nor the missiological researcher can:

- create the seed (the unchanging revealed truth of the Gospel, the grand narrative of the reconciliation of the universe in Christ: see Eph 1)
- cause the plant to grow, the sun to shine, nor the rain to fall (the continuing activity of the Holy Spirit in the world)
- produce a harvest (the Community of the redeemed, the Body of Christ) for only God gives the increase: see 1 Cor 3:6–7)

Missiological research needs to "preach," providing Spirit–inspired answers to real-life missional challenges, "so that some might be saved" (1 Cor 9:22) and bring glory to God, the ultimate purpose of missiological research. Simultaneously, missionary practice must be critiqued by missiology. This happens as the missiological researcher asks, "What is the source of power for this action? Who gets the glory?" and similar questions. This constant questioning helps to ensure that all missionary endeavors are directed and empowered by the Spirit.

Missiological research swings between the unseen and the seen; it is fundamentally a process of prayer and spiritual discernment that "loops" between the natural and the supernatural. It requires hard work, dedication, consecration, and surrender (the natural), but only bears fruit as the impossible is made possible by the work of the Spirit (the supernatural). The Word affirms that it is "not by might nor by power, but by my Spirit" (Zech 4:6): the Spirit of Jesus who is the same yesterday, today, and forever (Heb 13:8). For missiological research to bear fruit, it must be integrated and empowered by the Spirit.

51
INTEGRATION AND THE MISSIONARY LIFE[1]

Mark A. Hausfeld

The importance of integration in the missionary life cannot be overstated, and missiology and its study cannot be separated from the foundations of being a missionary. Further, without the integration of life with research, there cannot be an integrated missionary research and missiology. The missionary not only speaks from a context of knowing the biblical and theological foundations of the Christian faith, but also models that faith in a holistic fashion. Family life, personal care, the spiritual walk, and day-to-day experiences are part and parcel of life for any minister with the designated elements of preaching, teaching, and various other traditionally identifiable missionary activities. The missionary must demonstrate an integrated life-style from the Sunday morning throughout the rest of the week, and from the home culture to the new one. He or she must not embrace a fragmented existence; a genuine, Spirit-led missionary of integrity must pursue the goal, a fully integrated life.

Integration into the missionary's (and missiologist's) context is not merely a cognitive process. Though it may be understood as a given, it is important to place the Person and work of the Holy Spirit intentionally at the beginning of this complex, whole-person process. Therefore, this interdisciplinary process must include the missional and spiritual formation. The call of God to a person begins in the spirit as the Spirit of God communicates information and brings inspiration. This process of information to inspiration resulting in a call is, above all, a spiritual dynamic. Here is the genesis of integration, as theological reflection,

---

1. For this essay, while the focus is on integration within the missionary life, it is understood that the missiologist and missological researcher are founded on their missionary life and experience.

cultural analysis and historic and historical perspectives develop into strategic formation for contextualized mission. Koeshall's essay (chapter 48) explicates this process of integration through her adopted nomenclature and process, as in the following figure reproduced from her chapter:

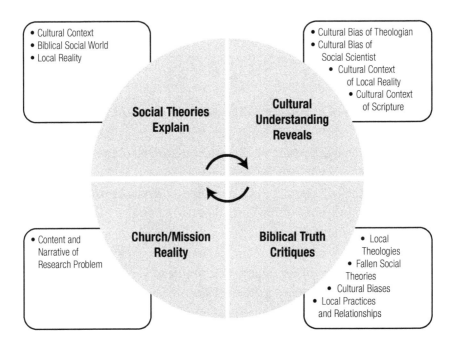

Figure 3: Integrating Biblical Truth, Social Science Theory, and Cross-Cultural Understanding to Create a Master Blueprint by Which to Investigate a Research Problem

What I perceive needs to be further emphasized is the Person and work of the Holy Spirit in this process of integration. The revolving arrows caught my attention; it provides a natural/supernatural link in the integration movement. This dynamic of the Holy Spirit with the missionary in the integration effort is the continued praxis of reflection/action and action/reflection that began with the missionary's call. I am particularly struck by what Koeshall writes before presenting the above figure:

> The task of missiological inquiry is not finished with the application of these individual disciplines. Throughout the process, the missiologist, as the master architect, must remain conscious of the dynamic influence that the layers of blueprints have on each other. That dynamic influence

is most evident in the study's findings, which proceed from the interdisciplinary interaction.

Credible integration demands the intentional guidance and counsel of the Holy Spirit. Thus, the revolving arrows could be understood not only as a symbol of the integration process but also the dynamic of the Person and work of the Holy Spirit in the integration of theological, sociological and missiological effort.

This intentionally pneumatological perspective will fulfill the challenge posed by Charles Van Engen, quoted by Koeshall: "Missiology must find a way to integrate spirituality, psychology, anthropology and sociology in a holistic understanding that more closely approximates reality" (1996, 256). By maintaining an emphasis on the activity of the Holy Spirit throughout the integration process, the spirituality element in Van Engen's quote keeps the spiritual formation practice a vibrant constant in the missiologist's integration.

The accomplishment of missions certainly spirals through cultural, ecclesiastical, biblical-theological, and social components. Ultimately, it is the work of the Spirit that guides the integration process and brings meaning and understanding to both the missionary and to the recipients of the missionary message. The missionary enterprise cannot ever accomplish the task nor facilitate the mission of God without the integrating presence of the Spirit of God. Ultimately, the mission is His mission!

REFERENCE CITED

Van Engen, Charles. 1996. *Mission on the Way: Issues in Mission Theology.* Grand Rapids, MI: Baker.

52
VALUING THE INTEGRATION OF THE SOCIAL SCIENCES IN MISSION PRACTICE

John L. Easter, PhD

On any given day on the campus of the *Assemblies of God School of Theology* in Lilongwe, Malawi, you will find students gathered together under a mango tree discussing theological matters, and how it applies to their life and ministry in the world in which they live. As a missionary educator, I soon discovered the significance of the mango tree in Malawian life. The mango tree serves as a focal point for the community, a place of decision-making by village elders, in addition to the relief from the heat and rain it provides. Beneath its shade, relationships are reinforced, dialogue transpires, and networks are built: the place where nourishment—both physical and social—is found, and where history transmitted and remembered becomes part of oral tradition.

Under that mango tree, I once had a conversation with a close friend, culturally and religiously shaped by his upbringing among his Muslim tribe, the Yao. Sharing his heart about how missionaries had failed to understand his tribal culture, he expressed concern that mission workers from outside had not taken the task of learning his people seriously:

> If missionar[ies] could be free to associate with my people at any time without boundaries or limitations, they would be most effective. The missionaries should be free to move around and go to any family and learn from them. If food is offered, [they] should accept the food. Missionar[ies] associating with the people in such a way would be very welcome in our society. Also, [they] must come and stay for a few years with the people, associating with them, trying to understand them and what they are doing, visit[ing] all the homes in the villages. . . . Most people

see missionaries as being distant from us. (Machemba, personal communication)

The integrative nature of missiology, drawing from both theology and the social sciences, can help us construct bridges to close the distance between the mission worker and the host culture.

THE VALUE OF INTERDISCIPLINARY INTEGRATION

Koeshall's "layering blueprint" analogy and Johnson's "multi-directional" task describes key elements that constitute the missiological research process. That process can aid cross-cultural workers to understand and relate to a culture-sharing people more meaningfully. When these elements interface, an integrated framework emerges that expands their understanding of embedded or hidden values, beliefs, and perceptions. Understanding these cultural factors can give enlightenment regarding observable social behaviors and attitudes, which in turn enhance social interaction with individuals in a ministry context.

Missiology is inherently a dynamic interdisciplinary field. The secular presuppositions that influence the social sciences must be governed by a sound biblical hermeneutic in order to help prioritize these disciplines, and clarify how they relate to God's mission. Indeed, a cross-cultural researcher must prayerfully cultivate sensitivity to the leading and guidance of the Holy Spirit as they seek to draw from the well of the social sciences and their cognate disciplines. Yet, our mission theology needs the added value of cultural insights that enhance ministry practice.

The contribution of the behavioral sciences can positively inform our contextualized efforts to share the gospel, plant the church, and make disciples. Though we look through a *glass darkly* when it comes to working in different cultural settings, the social disciplines can shed some light on the forces that shape the lives of the people we seek to reach. The interface between theological foundations, missiological principles, and the social science findings converge to provide different lenses to inform our strategy of ministry under the Spirit's direction. Two areas in particular can benefit from the use of the social sciences and, thus, positively inform our missiological practice: the understanding of (1) oneself and the mission team, and (2) one's ministry context (Whiteman 1997, 137).

UNDERSTANDING OF SELF AND THE MISSION TEAM

One of the most important contributions we gain from the social sciences is a better understanding of ourselves. The social sciences make us aware of the degree to which our own social, cultural, and economic backgrounds shape our own worldview and behavior, and that of our mission team. Specifically, anthropology, linguistics, and sociology, can help us see the blind spots in our cultural lenses. Our cultural framework has tremendous influence on how we function in the body of Christ, relate to our mission team and national believers, and interface with non-Christian people. Our cultural framework also strongly impacts our theological framework. Our gospel witness can be negatively impacted because we fail to recognize attitudes of ethnocentrism and cultural bias. Not understanding our own cultural disposition can lead us to confuse our cultural values with biblical values (Whiteman 1997, 137).

Clearly, we should take into account the regenerative and sanctifying work of the Spirit in our lives. The effectual work of the Spirit illuminates our values, affections, attitudes, and behaviors in light of God's Word. Yet, this does not preclude us from utilizing the social disciplines to discover the complicating "layers" of our cultural selves.

UNDERSTANDING OUR MINISTRY CONTEXT

Culture powerfully influences how social groups understand the gospel. It can also positively inform how the gospel should be delivered to a culture-sharing group. Research by Geert Hofstede, Gert Jan Hofstede and Michael Minkov underscores the degree to which people's cultural environs determine how they interpret their world (2010). By utilizing the tools of anthropology and linguistics, we learn how to better relate to a culture-sharing community and respond to behaviors that emerge from its embedded values, beliefs, and perceptions.

These cultural realities are expressed in a variety of ways. For example, many African tribal communities reflect a high-grid social context, in which issues of authority, collectivism, gender roles, and avoidance reflect their frame of reference. Signs and symbols within the context of community life also play an important role, and affect cultural and spiritual attitudes by community members. Rituals centered on birth rites, marriage, funerals, rainfall, and dance all form the basis for tribal perceptions concerning the people's relationship with one another and the spirit world. Those rituals assign highly symbolic meaning to the most basic of physical contexts. A mountain becomes more than an elevated land mass; an accident becomes much more than a fateful event. Meaning is never divorced from context.

The social sciences can aid our understanding of the ministry context to which we are called; it can do this by enabling us to:

- recognize that expressions of a culture-sharing group influence how they perceive the gospel message being communicated.
- study and analyze phenomenological features. It is not enough to study biblical texts; careful evaluation of emic perceptions and predispositions will help us discover culturally unique layers of hidden values and attitudes that influence people's understanding of Scripture and the Holy Spirit's work in their lives.
- endure cultural ambiguity in communication. How the missionary acts when experiencing cultural uncertainty may hinder how the community, the Yao tribe for example, understands and receives the gospel message (Elmer 2006, 53–55).
- trust the Holy Spirit to operate within the communication and hermeneutical processes to illuminate the understanding of individuals in the culture-sharing group concerning their relationship with Christ (Shaw and Van Engen 2003, 35).

FINAL THOUGHTS

Communication requires interaction, and interaction always takes place within a socio-cultural context. The goal is to integrate the "Truth" of Scripture with the "truth" of social science so that ministry strategies are both biblically sound and culturally relevant. Effective use of Scripture and the social sciences can positively inform our strategy to better facilitate cross-cultural relationships; this will enable us to plant and nurture viable communities of faith for Christ's glory.

Cross-cultural missionaries who strategically engage their ministry context will draw on the disciplines of missiology. It is critically important for our strategy to be governed by a Christ-centered hermeneutic and a Spirit-empowered ecclesiology. Nonetheless, the social disciplines can positively aid us in the practical arenas of linguistics, ethnographic inquiry, and cultural exegesis. As a result, we are empowered to construct contextually appropriate strategies for reaching the culture-sharing groups we are called to serve.

REFERENCES CITED

Elmer, Duane. 2006. *Cross-Cultural Servanthood: Serving the World in Christlike Humility*. Downers Grove, IL: InterVarsity Press.

Hofstede, Geert, Gert Jan Hofstede, and Michael Minkov. 2010. *Cultures and Organizations, Software of the Mind: Intercultural Cooperation and Its Importance for Survival*. 3rd ed. New York: McGraw-Hill.

Shaw, R. Daniel, and Charles E. Van Engen. 2003. *Communicating God's Word in a Complex World: God's Truth or Hocus Pocus?* New York: Rowman & Littlefield Publishers.

Van Rheenen, Gailyn. 1991. *Communicating Christ in Animistic Contexts*. Pasadena, CA: William Carey Library.

Whiteman, Darrell. 1997. "The Role of the Behavioral Sciences in Missiological Education." In *Missiological Education for the Twenty-First Century: The Book, the Circle, and the Sandals*, edited by J. Dudley Woodberry, Charles Van Engen, and Edgar J. Elliston. Eugene, OR: Wipf and Stock Publishers.

53

MISSIOLOGICAL RESEARCH AS WORSHIP

A Pneumatological Journey of Discovery

DeLonn L. Rance, PhD

> But when he, the Spirit of truth, comes, he will guide you into all the truth. He will not speak on his own; he will speak only what he hears, and he will tell you what is yet to come. He will glorify me because it is from me that he will receive what he will make known to you. (John 16:13–14)[1]

The text above clearly expresses truth that Jesus declared and recorded in John; it constitutes the thesis of this chapter: the researcher yielded to the Spirit encounters truth and eschatological hope that glorifies Christ. As a missiologist engaged in research and writing, I am consistently overwhelmed by the magnitude of the task. While research and writing are not in my natural "gift mix," yet I sense the Spirit's empowering presence as I write, believing that this comes as a divine directive. I choose to surrender to that directive, stepping out by faith (with my fingers on keyboard) to communicate thoughts about the nature and process of research. In so doing, the God I serve empowers me to do what I cannot do.

This process of Spirit-directed and Spirit-empowered obedience is spiritual worship, an expression of a living sacrifice (Rom 12:1). It is much like the Philippians' gift to Paul, which became "a fragrant offering, an acceptable sacrifice, pleasing to God" and for his glory (Phil 4:18, 20). This chapter addresses the missiologist's approach to research as worship. It does so with reverence, humility, submission, passion, and expectancy. Those foundational thoughts are followed by practical recommendations from personal experience.

---

1. All Scripture references are from the New International Version.

RESEARCH AS WORSHIP

"God is spirit, and his worshipers must worship in the Spirit and in truth" (John 4:24). Missiological research is founded on the theological truth that the God of the Bible speaks and acts, both in history and in the present, bringing order out of chaos (Gen 1). For his own glory, God reveals himself. He does so in order to provide reconciliation between himself and humankind. His reconciliation extends to humankind and all of creation. Through the obedience of the Son, expressed consistently in his life, death and resurrection, God will restore all things under his Headship, his rule (Eph 1:10).

Research is a special act of worship because it seeks to discover truth in both general and special revelation, and in direct communication from the Spirit. Research thus becomes a process of divine discernment of how the Church, individually and corporately, serves and worships God, builds itself up in the faith, and communicates the gospel to the world. Researchers are "transformed by the renewal" of their minds as they respond to Paul's exhortation to present their bodies "as a living sacrifice, holy and acceptable to God, which is . . . spiritual worship" (Rom 12:1b, 2b). Thus, the Spirit empowers authentic worship. Every act of obedience, including research, is worship, for it reveals the God who calls researchers to "declare the praises of him who called you out of darkness into his wonderful light" (1 Pet 2:9b).

> Each of you should use whatever gift you have received
> to serve others, as faithful stewards of God's grace in
> its various forms. . . . so that in all things God may be
> praised through Jesus Christ. To him be the glory and the
> power for ever and ever. Amen. (1 Pet 4:10–11)

In essence, worship is an activity of the Spirit in the followers of Jesus that brings glory to God. Spirit-motivated worship acknowledges the true relationship between humans and the Trinity. God is worthy of complete devotion and total surrender, for only he is worthy of all glory, honor, praise. Worship only occurs by the activity of the Spirit within believers; it requires attitudes (mind, will) and actions (body, words) that bow before Jesus in complete surrender and dependence.

RESEARCH WITH REVERENCE, HUMILITY, AND SURRENDER

> The fear of the Lord is the beginning of wisdom;
> all who follow his precepts have good understanding.
> To him belongs eternal praise. (Ps 111:10)

The fear of the Lord is the beginning of wisdom; further, the Spirit leads to the discovery of Truth. These foundational truths lead the missiologist to approach research with reverence (God is worthy of worship), humility (the missiologist is incapable of knowing God without the activity of the Spirit in Christ), and surrender (the appropriate response to the God who is the source of all truth). All missiological research should, therefore, be centered in Christ and dependent on the activity of the Spirit. "Unless the Lord builds the house, the builders labor in vain. Unless the Lord watches over the city, the guards stand watch in vain" (Ps 127:1). Unless the Spirit guides and empowers the research, the missiologist labors in vain.

Truth is revealed and disseminated to others as the missiologist yields to the Spirit's direction and empowerment in the process of research, the reporting of findings and the formulation of recommendations. Research is a sacred trust, a divinely inspired vocation, focused on making Christ known through the agency of the Church. Truth discovered in the examination of general revelation through the disciplines of secular research are valid for the missiologist only when submitted to, and integrated with, special revelation through robust biblical and theological research.

RESEARCH WITH PASSION

> When Jesus landed and saw a large crowd, he had compassion
> on them, because they were like sheep without a shepherd.
> So he began teaching them many things. (Mark 6:34)

The Bible describes God in emotional terms: for example, Jesus expressed emotions, and the Spirit touches the emotions of the Christ follower. God created humans with emotions; worship is both an emotional and an intellectual process. Therefore, missiological research should not be sterile, but full of passion: passion for God, for fellow believers, for the lost, and for the research task to which the researcher has been called.

To disavow emotions in the research process is to reject a God-given gift to encourage, motivate, and move to change and action. To deny emotion in research is to limit a tool in the hands of the Spirit, particularly in research related to (emotional) human subjects. However, human emotion and human reason are only trustworthy when subject to the Spirit.

The missiologist approaches research with passion because research as worship is a divine invitation to partner with God in the fulfillment of his mission. In the creation story, God creates the universe *ex nihilo*, but also commissions humankind to participate in his work in the Dominion Mandate (Gen 1:23). God continues to bring order out of chaos by the power of the Spirit. Developing new theory based on research findings or executing a kingdom-relevant research project should be a Spirit-empowered act of bringing order out of missional chaos.

RESEARCH WITH EXPECTANCY

> My message and my preaching were not with wise and persuasive words, but with a demonstration of the Spirit's power, so that your faith might not rest on human wisdom, but on God's power (1 Cor 2:4-5).

> And this gospel of the kingdom will be preached in the whole world as a testimony to all nations, and then the end will come (Matt 24:14).

The missiologist approaches research with expectancy for when God's truth is communicated, he reveals himself with "a demonstration of the Spirit's power." The anticipation of this manifestation of power, where God breaks into history bringing order to chaos, and life to death, fills the researcher with expectancy and empowers the declaration of gospel truth. The fruitfulness of the missiologist's research does not rest on human wisdom, but God's power.

Missiological research should therefore be prophetic, an anticipation of the future, communicating God's will in specific contexts to individuals, to local and national churches, and to the world. Spirit-driven research empowers the missionary people of God to communicate in word and deed the good news to lost peoples and persons. The missiologist works with the end in view, Christ's return and coming of the fullness of the kingdom of God, at the preaching of the gospel "as a testimony to all nations." (Matt 24:14)

PRACTICAL RECOMMENDATIONS FROM PERSONAL EXPERIENCE

Missiological research creates space to perceive God's reality, not the researcher's notions or best guesses about reality. As a practitioner, the missiologist deals with real-world issues. Therefore, the missiological researcher needs the clearest picture of that reality, because truth sets people free. Dallas Willard, speaking to the advantage of believing in the reality of the Trinity, states:

> Remember, to believe something is to act as if it is so. To believe that two plus two equals four is to behave accordingly when trying to find out how many dollars or apples are in the house. The advantage of believing it is not that we can pass the tests in arithmetic; it is that we can deal much more successfully with reality. Just try dealing with it as if two plus two equals six. (1997, 317–18)

The advantage of research as worship for the missiologist is not to get a grade as a missiologist, a researcher, or an academic; the true advantage is that research enables a missiologist to deal "more successfully with reality" in missions.

Missiological research is a process of prayer that prepares the way, creates space for the Spirit to work in revealing truth, and empowers a response to that truth. There is no prescribed way of bathing the research process in prayer because each researcher and research context is unique. However, creating space to be sensitive to the Spirit must be intentional and accompanies the entire research journey.[2]

In times of confusion, frustration, or when simply overwhelmed by research's challenges, a missiologist should pause, ask the Spirit for guidance, and listen for his response. When confronted by evil in the world, by the brokenness and lostness of the human condition, by sin even in the community of faith, a missiologist must weep before the Lord and intercede for those in need. When sensing the Spirit's direction,

---

2. Specific prayers could include: (1) the choice of research topic, (2) the articulation of purpose and problem statements, (3) the formulation of research questions, (4) the choice of methodology and sampling group, (5) the execution of the research, (6) the coding of the data, (7) the interpretation and reporting of the findings, and (8) the proclamation of the prophetic word—the "so what" of God for the researcher, the church, and the world.

experimenting with an insight, or sensing awe at what God is doing in and through the research, the wise missiological researcher will stop and give thanks, allowing praise to rise before God's throne. Research as worship must be intentional and all consuming.

A PERSONAL ILLUSTRATION

When I began my own research journey, I perceived it as a giant puzzle to which I could apply my problem-solving skills to in order to facilitate the work that I felt called to do. Yes, I had prayed about whether to pursue a PhD degree, where I should study, and what topic I should focus on. Once I was into the research, it initially seemed like just another task to complete. However, two main issues prompted me to be more intentional in worship as I researched. The first issue concerned my struggle to be bring focus to the research, complicated by the overwhelming scope of the data I generated. I distinctly remember a moment as I was developing my research proposal, pounding my fist on the table and audibly crying out to God, "I can't do this! I can't wrap my head around this, God. Where are you? If you want me to do this, you have to show up!" . . . and he did.

Second, as I read the literature and analyzed the data, truth and the significance of my findings would occasionally overwhelm me. Seemingly out of nowhere, an insight would "bubble up" out of the findings—an insight I knew came from the Spirit. In my research "cave," I would begin to weep and simply have to lift my hands and my voice in adoration of the living God. Particularly moving were the stories and testimonies that emerged out of my interviews with Salvadoran Assemblies of God missionaries: stories of healing, provision, direction, exorcism, even the raising of the dead. Most importantly, though, were the stories of women and men who heard the gospel and were transformed by their encounter with the Savior, Jesus Christ.

CONCLUSION

The missiologist approaches research as worship with reverence, humility, submission, and passion. Research as worship generates keen expectancy, as the missiologist pursues a pneumatologically guided and motivated journey of discovery that brings meaning and significance to service. I resonate with Rueben Job:

As I write, I hope that my ordinary life and ordinary capacity will be energized, directed, and used by the One who gives me life and has called me to this ministry. If I allow myself to think that this ministry and this project are all up to me, I risk feelings from despair to arrogance. However, if I remember that I am not alone, but think, work, and live in the presence of the living Christ, I remain hopeful that even the most simple and ordinary task carried out in that presence and with the assistance of Jesus Christ is sacred, meaningful, and useful. (2003, 171)

Many missiological researchers often divide the secular and sacred in their professional lives (i.e., ministry is done through human efforts with no sense of the immediacy and empowerment of the Spirit). The antidote to missiological drift in the missionary enterprise and the temptation to separate what we do from what the Spirit does, is to be totally dependent on the Spirit and passionately in love with the One who guides us into all truth. Missiological research as worship seeks to integrate human and divine action in the power of the Spirit. Worship in response to God brings glory to his name and reveals God to us—and through us to the nations of the earth, that they might also worship him.

> Great and marvelous are your deeds,
> Lord God Almighty.
> Just and true are your ways,
> King of the nations.
> Who will not fear you, Lord,
> and bring glory to your name?
> For you alone are holy.
> All nations will come
> and worship before you,
> for your righteous acts have been revealed.
> (Rev 15:3–4)

REFERENCES CITED

Job, Rueben P. 2003. "Readings for Reflection." In *A Guide to Prayer for All Who Seek God*, edited by Norman Shawchuck and Rueben P. Job. 171. Nashville: Upper Room Books.

Willard, Dallas. 1997. *The Divine Conspiracy: Rediscovering Our Hidden Life in God*. New York: Harper Collins.

APPENDICES

APPENDIX 1
Four-Phase Model of Missiological Research

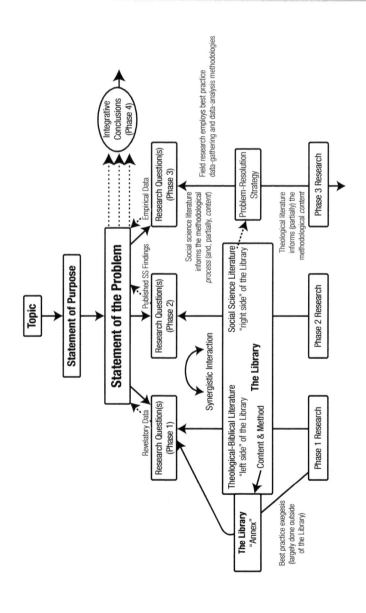

APPENDIX 2

Four-Phase Model in Academic Context

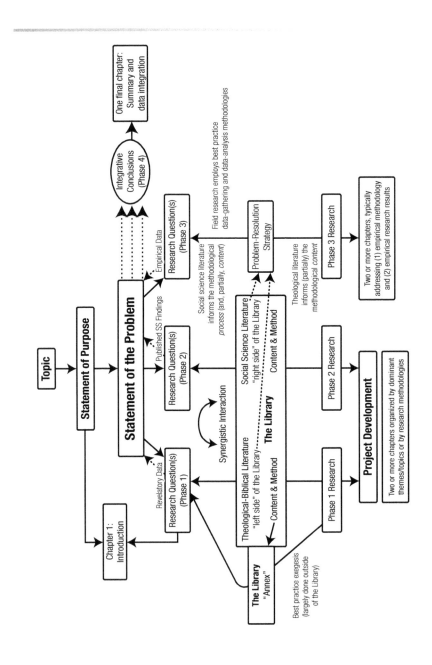

APPENDIX 3
Interdisciplinary Researchers' Needs and Behaviors[1]

Information-seeking Needs	Information-seeking Behaviors
To become familiar with cultural assumptions, language and organization of several disciplines rather than one.	**Orientation:** Beginning with the most familiar of academic discipline, become familiar with the less familiar by comparing key concepts, vocabulary, research methodologies, theories and epistemology.
To become aware of key terminology that may have different meanings in different disciplines.	**Chaining/citation linking:** While cited reference searches are standard practice in academic research, this skill is even more essential for cross-disciplinary research. It facilitates identifying newer relevant resources across disciplines (i.e., EbscoHost-related sources in search results)
To gather more information sources when researched interdisciplinary area is "high scatter."*	**Browsing/probing:** Exploring a semi-defined area of interest and determining research networks and linkages (multidisciplinary databases, i.e. WorldCat). Leads to new research areas, even change in direction.
To identify key researchers of topic, disciplines and associated research areas.	**Monitoring:** After becoming oriented to new disciplines, email alerts to strategic journal updates and updates from professional society websites can help monitor new developments in relevant studies.
To learn how to articulate information needs and where to find them.	**Differentiating:** Making judgments about the status, orientation or quality of sources
To locate other researchers with similar interests	**Extracting:** Pulling out specific information of interest
To develop methods for staying current with new research in several disciplines rather than one.	**Consolidation and integration:** Refining research focus, integrating insights gained and determining when enough information has been gathered.

* The term "scatter" refers to the number and structure of resources in an academic discipline (see O'Connor & Newby, 2011: 225). For traditional academic disciplines, information resource scatter is low and readily identified in library research. In contrast, topics researched by interdisciplinarians tend to have highly disbursed information resources (high scatter) require more contacts, more research time across disciplines, and a higher learning curve.

1. Adapted from O'Connor and Newby: pages 225–28. See O'Connor, Lisa, and Jill Newby. 2011. Entering unfamiliar territory: Building an information literacy course for graduate students in interdisciplinary Areas. *Reference & User Services Quarterly* 50 (3): 224–29. http://blog.rusq.org/wp-content/uploads/2011/04 /Information-Lit.pdf (accessed September 24, 2011).

APPENDIX 4
Pentecostal Research Resources
Martin Mittelstadt, PhD[1]

Assemblies of God (USA): Flower Pentecostal Heritage Center
http://www.agheritage.org/
Hollenweger Center for the Interdisciplinary Study of Pentecostal and
Charismatic Movements
http://hollenwegercenter.net/
International Pentecostal Holiness Church:
Archives and Research Center
http://www.iphc.org/archives/inventory
Lee University: Dixon Pentecostal Research Center
(Pentecostal Church of God)
http://cogheritage.org/site/resources/
Oral Roberts University: Holy Spirit Research Center
http://www.oru.edu/library/special_collections/holy_spirit
_research_center/index.php
Pentecostal and Charismatic Churches in the UK:
Center for Pentecostal and Charismatic Studies
http://www.bangor.ac.uk/trs/centres/pcs/publications.php
Pentecostal Assemblies of Canada: Academic and Archive Resources
http://www.paoc.org/about/archives/academic-archival-resources
Pentecostal World Fellowship: World Directory of Pentecostal Journals
http://www.pentecostalworldfellowship.org/pub/pub.htm
Pentecostal/Charismatic Churches of North America: Online Resources
http://www.pccna.org/resources.htm

---

1. Martin Mittelstadt is Professor of New Testament at Evangel University, Springfield, Missouri.

Pentecostal-Charismatic Theological Inquiry International
>http://www.pctii.org/
>[User-friendly links to other sites and resources: e-journal, online publications, etc.]

Pew Forum: http://pewforum.org/
>See also: "Spirit and Power: A 10-Nation Survey of Pentecostals"

Pneuma Foundation: Resources of Spirit-empowered Ministry
>http://www.pneumafoundation.com/links_articles.jsp;jsessionid =C01D1187FC84FD429352C5DEE0FFFB9C
>http://www.pneumafoundation.com/links_study.jsp

Regent University: Pentecostal Research Center
>http://www.regent.edu/lib/special-collections/pentecostal -research.cfm

Society for Pentecostal Studies: Resource Sites
>http://www.sps-usa.org/resources/sites.html

University of Birmingham:
>Research Unit for Pentecostal and Charismatic Studies
>http://artsweb.bham.ac.uk/aanderson/Main/research_unit _for_pentecostal.htm

APPENDIX 5
Dictionaries of Interest to Missiologists

MISSIOLOGICAL DICTIONARIES

Title	Author / Editor	Publisher	Year	Pages
Biographical Dictionary of Christian Missions	Gerald H. Anderson	Eerdmans	1999	845
Dictionary of Mission Theology: Evangelical Foundations	John Corrie, et al (eds.)	IVP Academic	2007	461
Dictionary of Mission: Theology, History, Perspectives	Karl Muller, et al (eds.)	Wipf & Stock	2006	518
Evangelical Dictionary of World Missions	A. Scott Moreau (ed.)	Baker Academic	2000	1,072

BIBLICAL/THEOLOGICAL DICTIONARIES AND LEXICONS

Title	Author / Editor	Publisher	Year	Pages
A dictionary of the Holy Bible, for general use in the study of the Scriptures: with engravings, maps, and tables	American Tract Society	American Tract Society	2007	362
Evangelical Dictionary of Biblical Theology	Walter A. Elwell (ed.)	Baker Publishing Group	1996	933
Biographical Dictionary of Christian Theologians	Patrick Carey and Joseph Lienhard	Greenwood	2000	608
Concise Dictionary of Christian Theology (Rev., updated ed.)	Millard J. Erickson	Crossway Books	2001	224
Dictionary of Early Christian Biography	Henry Wace and William C. Piercy (eds.)	Hendrickson	1999	1,040
Dictionary of the Bible	John L. McKenzie	Touchstone	1995	975
New Dictionary of Theology	David F. Wright, Sinclair B. Ferguson, J. I. Packer (eds.)	IVP Academic	1986	757
Hitchcock's Bible Names Dictionary	Roswell D Hitchcock	Benediction Classics	2010	138

Title	Author / Editor	Publisher	Year	Pages
Holman Illustrated Bible Dictionary (Rev. ed.)	Charles W. Draper, Chad Brand, Archie England (eds.)	Holman Reference	2003	1704
Greek-English Lexicon of the New Testament and Other Early Christian Literature (3rd ed.)	Frederick William Danker (ed.)	University Of Chicago Press; 3rd edition	2001	1,188
New Westminster Dictionary of Christian Spirituality	Philip Sheldrake (ed.)	Westminster John Knox Press	2005	704
Brown-Driver-Briggs Hebrew and English Lexicon	Francis Brown, S. R. Driver, and Charles A. Briggs	Hendrickson	1996	1,216
Vine's Complete Expository Dictionary of Old and New Testament Words: With Topical Index	W. E. Vine, Merrill F. Unger, and William White, Jr.	Thomas Nelson	1996	848
Westminster Theological Wordbook of the Bible	Donald E. Gowan (ed.)	Westminster John Knox Press	2003	551

SELECTED DICTIONARIES FROM RELATED DISCIPLINES

Title	Author / Editor	Publisher	Year	Pages
Biographical Dictionary of Social and Cultural Anthropology	Vered Amit (ed.)	Routledge	2004	640
Dictionary of Anthropology (11th ed.)	Thomas Barfield	Wiley-Blackwell	1998	640
Dictionary of Concepts in Cultural Anthropology	Robert H. Winthrop	Greenwood Press	1991	360
Dictionary of Race, Ethnicity, and Culture	Guido Bolaffi et al. (eds.)	Sage Publications	2002	356
Evangelical Dictionary of Christian Education	Michael J. Anthony (ed.)	Baker Academic	2001	752
Greenwood Dictionary of Education	Nancy O'Brien and John Collins	Greenwood Press	2008	448
International Dictionary of Adult and Continuing Education (2nd ed.)	Peter Jarvis	Routledge	2002	208

APPENDIX 6
Encyclopedias of Interest to Missiologists

MISSIOLOGICAL ENCYCLOPEDIAS

Title	Author / Editor	Publisher	Year	Pages
Outreach Ministry in the 21st Century: The Encyclopedia of Practical Ideas	Group Publishing	Group Publishing	2007	224
Philosophy, Science, and Theology of Mission in the 19th and 20th Centuries: A Missiological Encyclopedia	Jan A. B. Jongeneel	Peter Lang Publishing	1996	428
Religions of the World: A Comprehensive Encyclopedia of Beliefs and Practices (2nd ed.)	J. Gordon Melton	Abc-Clio	2010	2,740
Routledge Encyclopedia of Missions and Missionaries	Jonathan Bonk (ed.)	Routledge	2007	494
Encyclopedia of Missions: Descriptive, Historical, Biographical, Statistical	Edwin M Bliss et al. (eds.)	Nabu Press	2010	872
World Christian Encyclopedia: A Comparative Survey of Churches and Religions in the Modern World (2nd ed.) (2nd vol.)	David B. Barrett et al. (eds.)	Oxford University Press	2001	1,730
Encyclopedia of Christianity	John Stephen Bowden	Oxford University Press	2005	1,364
Encyclopedia Mythica (internet encyclopedia)	http://www .pantheon.org/	(internet)	—	—

BIBLICAL AND THEOLOGICAL ENCYCLOPEDIAS (A SAMPLE)

Title	Author / Editor	Publisher	Year	Pages
Blackwell Encyclopedia of Modern Christian Thought	Alister E. McGrath	Blackwell Publishers	1993	720
Catholic Encyclopedia (multi-volume set)	Charles George Herbermann et al. (eds.)	The Encyclopedia Press	1918	—
Encyclopedia of Evangelicalism	Randall Herbert Balmer	Westminster John Knox	2002	654

APPENDIX 7

Electronic Theses and Dissertations (ETD)
Major Collections[1]

Marvin Gilbert, EdD

Major Portals—Multiple Universities	Description of the Collection*
ABES	Collection of **French** dissertations from multiple universities
Cyberthesis	**French**-language dissertations from University of Lyon
DART-Europe	Collection of 685,723,550 ETDs from 593 European universities
EthOS	British ETDs: e.g., "Africa" (3,806), "African theology" (44), "Asia" (1727), and "Asian theology" (14).
Networked Digital Library of Theses and Dissertations	◀Primary source Use "Basic Search": type in a topic/key word Multi-lingual ETD collection provided by a large consortium of universities. (some African universities included). "leadership emergence" (57)
Theses Canada	Consortium of almost seventy Canadian universities Some in **French**
Theological Research Exchange Network	◀Primary source (especially for Herm/Bib Theo searches)
Trove: National Library of Australia	Consortium of Australian universities and seminaries: 560,000 ETDs
WorldCat	◀Primary source (Meta-search engine) Not all are open-source (free) NOTE: Limit "Content" to "Thesis/dissertations"
[PhD Data]	Dissertations in progress: various disciplines and nations
[Social Science Research Network]	[No ETD's: Academic papers, conference proceedings, etc.]

* The numbers in parentheses following the sample keywords (e.g., "Africa") are the number of "hits" (dissertations) available in that university's ETD collection.

---

1. Updated June 23, 2016.

ELECTRONIC THESIS AND DISSERTATION COLLECTIONS:[2]
EXAMPLES OF SELECTED SOUTH AFRICAN UNIVERSITIES[3]

Name of University or Portal	Using the Collection[4]
Free State (University of the) http://etd.uovs.ac.za/cgi-bin/ETD-search/search	Search by Keyword at lower left (scroll down a bit). "theology" (9), "leadership" (3)
Johannesburg (University of)	Search within this community and its collections: Enter one or more key words. "theology" (90), "transformational leadership" (52)
North-West University http://dspace.nwu.ac.za/handle/10394/2	In:(choose) Electronic Theses and Dissertations Search for: Enter one or more key words "theological education" (5), "servant leadership" (10), "missionaries" (102)
Pretoria (University of) http://upetd.up.ac.za/ETD-db/ETD-search/search	Search by Keyword at lower left (scroll down a bit). "theological education" (2 in English), "theological" (17"), "missions" (4)
Rhodes University http://eprints.ru.ac.za/view/subjects/	Keyword at upper right: enter one or more key words "theological education" (31),
Stellenbosch University https://scholar.sun.ac.za/search	Full Text SearchEnter one or more key word. "servant leadership" (30), "theological education" (34), "missionaries" (237)
UNISA http://uir.unisa.ac.za/handle/10500/507	Search within this collection at upper left. "leadership" (836), "theology" (430)
Western Cape (University of the) http://etd.uwc.ac.za/	Keyword at left on side bar. "theology" (25), "leadership" (26)

2. For greatly increased search power, use the "National ETD Portal" (http://www.netd.ac.za/). This web site searches the ETD collections of sixteen South African universities (or individual departments within a university).

3. Some ETDs will be in Afrikaans. In some search engines, put the phrase (e.g., theological education) in quotation marks ("theological education") when searching for phrases. This chart is listed as an example from South Africa, but each region/country will have their own relevant resources like this.

4. The numbers in parentheses following the sample keywords are the number of "hits" (dissertations) available in that university's ETD collection.

APPENDIX 8
Sources of Quotable-Citable Information
Marvin Gilbert, EdD

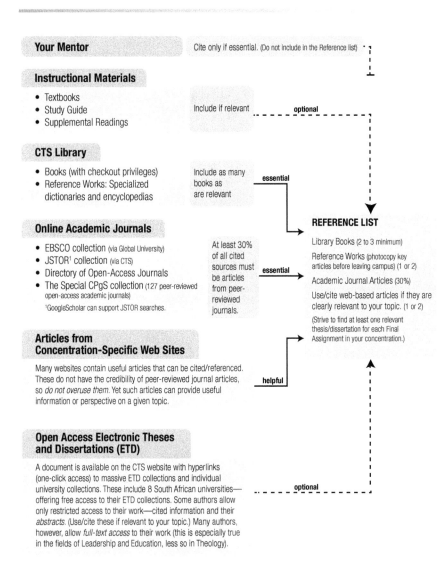

Your Mentor

Cite only if essential. (Do not include in the Reference list)

Instructional Materials

- Textbooks
- Study Guide
- Supplemental Readings

Include if relevant — optional

CTS Library

- Books (with checkout privileges)
- Reference Works: Specialized dictionaries and encyclopedias

Include as many books as are relevant — essential

REFERENCE LIST

Library Books (2 to 3 minimum)

Reference Works (photocopy key articles before leaving campus) (1 or 2)

Academic Journal Articles (30%)

Use/cite web-based articles if they are clearly relevant to your topic. (1 or 2)

(Strive to find at least one relevant thesis/dissertation for each Final Assignment in your concentration.)

Online Academic Journals

- EBSCO collection (via Global University)
- JSTOR[1] collection (via CTS)
- Directory of Open-Access Journals
- The Special CPgS collection (127 peer-reviewed open-access academic journals)

  [1]GoogleScholar can support JSTOR searches.

At least 30% of all cited sources must be articles from peer-reviewed journals. — essential

Articles from Concentration-Specific Web Sites

Many websites contain useful articles that can be cited/referenced. These do not have the credibility of peer-reviewed journal articles, so *do not overuse them.* Yet such articles can provide useful information or perspective on a given topic. — helpful

Open Access Electronic Theses and Dissertations (ETD)

A document is available on the CTS website with hyperlinks (one-click access) to massive ETD collections and individual university collections. These include 8 South African universities—offering free access to their ETD collections. Some authors allow only restricted access to their work—cited information and their *abstracts.* (Use/cite these if relevant to your topic.) Many authors, however, allow *full-text access* to their work (this is especially true in the fields of Leadership and Education, less so in Theology). — optional

APPENDIX 9
Open-Access Journals in Five Disciplines[1]
Marvin Gilbert, EdD

BIBLICAL STUDIES, RELIGION, AND THEOLOGY[2]

Acta Theological.
> http://www.scielo.org.za/scielo.php?script=sci_serial&pid=1015
> -8758&lng=en&nrm=iso
> **ISSN:** 10158758
> **Year Started:** 2009 University of the Free State (South Africa)

American Theological Inquiry.
> http://www.atijournal.org/
> **ISSN:** 19422709
> **Year Started:** 2008

Approaching Religion.
> http://ojs.abo.fi/index.php/ar/index
> **ISSN:** 17993121
> **Year Started:** 2011

---

1. Journals listed here appear in the Directory of Open-Access Journals (DOAJ) or are known by the editors. All listed in this document are published only in English, or English is the first of only two languages (e.g., English and French). All links (121 total) were tested on October 24, 2011. In some cases, the url addresses in the DOAJ are outdated and were updated in this document at that time.

2. Journals listed in this document have not been screened for content or theological position (with some exceptions). Inclusion in this document does not equate to our endorsement as editors of all content. The reader should use sound judgment when reviewing any article.

Asian Journal of Pentecostal Studies.
> http://www.apts.edu/index.cfm?menuid=94&parentid=54 Asia
> **ISSN:** 01188534
> **Year Started:** 1998
> Pacific Theological Seminary (Philippines)[3]

Australian e-Journal of Theology.
> http://aejt.com.au/
> **ISSN:** 14486326
> **Year Started:** 2003 Australian Catholic University

Common Ground Journal.
> http://www.commongroundjournal.org/
> **ISSN:** 15479129 Year started 2003

Cyberjournal for Pentecostal-Charismatic Research.
> http://www.pctii.org/cyberj/.
> **ISSN:** 15231216
> **Year Started:** 1997

Denver Journal: An Online Review of Current Biblical and Theological Studies.
> **ISSN:** d0000900
> http://www.denverseminary.edu/dj/index.php
> **Year Started:** 1998 Denver Seminary

Evangelical Quarterly, The.
> http://www.biblicalstudies.org.uk/articles_evangelical
> _quarterly-08.php

Harvard Divinity Bulletin.
> http://www.hds.harvard.edu/news/bulletin
> _mag/
> **ISSN:** 00178047
> **Year Started:** 2001 Harvard Divinity School

Homiletic: A Review of Publications in Religious Communication.
> http://www.homiletic.net/
> **ISSN:** 07380534
> **Year Started:** 2008

---

3. The nation in which the university publishing the journal is located will be cited parenthetically is outside the USA and if not obvious in the journal's title.

Hope's Reason: A Journal of Apologetics.
> http://apologeticsjournal.com/Home.html
> **ISSN:** 19238185
> **Year Started:** 2010

HTS Teologiese Studies/Theological Studies.
> http://www.hts.org.za/index.php/HTS
> **ISSN:** 02599422
> **Year Started:** 2002

Journal for Christian Theological Research.
> http://www2.luthersem.edu/ctrf/JCTR/default.htm
> **ISSN:** 10871624
> **Year Started:** 1996

Journal of Hebrew Scriptures.
> http://www.arts.ualberta.ca/JHS/
> **ISSN:** 12031542
> **Year Started:** 1996 University of Alberta

Journal of Latin American Hermeneutics.
> http://www.isedet.edu.ar/jolah/journal.htm
> **ISSN:** 16682610
> **Year Started:** 2004 Instituto Universitario (Buenos Aires, Argentina)

Journal of Southern Religion.
> http://jsr.fsu.edu/
> **ISSN:** 10945253
> **Year Started:** 1998 West Virginia University

Practical Matters.
> http://www.practicalmattersjournal.org/about
> **ISSN:** 21552355
> **Year Started:** 2009

Religions.
> http://www.mdpi.com/journal/religions/
> **ISSN:** 20771444
> **Year Started:** 2010

Review of Biblical Literature.
> http://bookreviews.org/default.asp
> **ISSN:** 10990046
> **Year Started:** 1970 (Not a journal: RBL provides extensive book reviews of Bible-related texts)

Rutgers Journal of Law and Religion.
> http://org.law.rutgers.edu/publications/law-religion/Home.shtml
> **ISSN:** d0000989
> **Year Started:** 1999 Rutgers University

Studies in Christian-Jewish Relations.
> http://ejournals.bc.edu/ojs/index.php/scjr/
> **ISSN:** 19303777
> **Year Started:** 2005 Boston College Libraries and Center for Christian-Jewish Learning

TC: A Journal of Biblical Textual Criticism.
> http://purl.org/ TC
> **ISSN:** 10897747
> **Year Started:** 1996

Theological Librarianship. https://journal.atla.com/ojs/index.php/theolib
> **ISSN:** 19378904
> **Year Started:** 2008

EDUCATION

Adult Education and Development.
> http://www.eaea.org/news.php?aid=3191&k=-3&%20d=2004-04
> **ISSN:** 03427633
> **Year Started:** 2000

African Symposium, The.
> http://www.ncsu.edu/aern/symposium_main.htm
> **ISSN:** TX6342323
> **Year Started:** 2001

Australasian Journal of Educational Technology.
> http://www.ascilite.org.au/ajet/ajet.html
> **ISSN:** 13240781
> **Year Started:** 1985

Australian Journal of Educational & Developmental Psychology.
> http://www.newcastle.edu.au/group/ajedp/
> **ISSN:** 14465442
> **Year Started:** 2001 School of Education—University of Newcastle (Australia)

Canadian Journal of Higher Education.
> http://ojs.library.ubc.ca/index.php/cjhe/index
> **ISSN:** 03161218
> **Year Started:** 2007

Canadian Journal of Learning and Technology.
> http://www.cjlt.ca/index.php/cjlt
> **ISSN:** 14996677
> **Year Started:** 2002

Canadian Journal of University Continuing Education.
> http://ejournals.library.ualberta.ca/index.php/cjuce-rcepu/index
> **ISSN:** 03189090
> **Year Started:** 2009

Christian Perspectives in Education.
> http://digitalcommons.liberty.edu/cpe/
> **ISSN:** 2159807X
> **Year Started:** 2007 Liberty University

College Quarterly, The.
> http://www.collegequarterly.ca/
> **ISSN:** 11954353
> **Year Started:** 1993 Seneca College (Canada)

Current Issues in Comparative Education.
> http://www.tc.columbia.edu/cice/index.html
> **ISSN:** 15231615
> **Year Started:** 1998 Teachers College—Columbia University

Education Review.
> http://edrev.asu.edu/index.html
> **ISSN:** 10945296
> **Year Started:** 2002 College of Education—Arizona State University (Book review and essay articles only)

Educause Quarterly.
> http://www.educause.edu/eq
> **ISSN:** 15285324
> **Year Started:** 2000

European Journal for Research on the Education and Learning of Adults.
> http://www.rela.ep.liu.se/
> **ISSN:** 20007426
> **Year Started:** 2010 Linköping University (Sweden)

Higher Education Perspectives.
> http://hep.oise.utoronto.ca/index.php/hep
> **ISSN:** 17101530
> **Year Started:** 2004 University of Toronto (Canada)

InterActions: UCLA Journal of Education and Information Studies.
> http://repositories.cdlib.org/gseis/interactions/
> **ISSN:** 15483320
> **Year Started:** 2004 Graduate School of Education &
> Information Studies

International Education Journal.
> http://www.iejcomparative.org/
> **ISSN:** 14431475
> **Year Started:** 1999

International Journal for Educational Integrity.
> http://www.ojs.unisa.edu.au/index.php/IJEI
> **ISSN:** 18332595
> **Year Started:** 2005

International Journal of Multicultural Education.
> http://ijme-journal.org/index.php/ijme
> **ISSN:** 19345267
> **Year Started:** 2007 Eastern University

Journal of Academic and Business Ethics.
> http://www.aabri.com/jabe.html.
> **ISSN:** 1941336X
> **Year Started:** 2009.

Journal of Distance Education.
> http://www.jofde.ca/index.php/jde
> **ISSN:** 08300445
> **Year Started:** 1986

Journal of Education for International Development.
   http://www.equip123.net/JEID/default.htm
   ISSN: 15542262
   Year Started: 2005
Journal of Educational Enquiry.
   http://www.ojs.unisa.edu.au/index.php/EDEQ
   ISSN: 14445530
   Year Started: 2000 Centre for Research in Education—
   University of South Africa (UNISA)
Journal of Extension.
   http://www.joe.org/
   ISSN: 00220140
   Year Started: 1978
Journal of Learning Design.
   http://www.jld.qut.edu.au/
   ISSN: 18328342
   Year Started: 2005
   Queensland University of Technology (Australia)
Journal of University Teaching and Learning Practice.
   http://jutlp.uow.edu.au/
   ISSN: 14499789
   Year Started: 2004 University of Wollongong (Australia)
New Horizons in Adult Education and Human Resource Development.
   http://education.fiu.edu/newhorizons/
   ISSN: 19394225
   Year Started: 1987 Florida International University
Radical Pedagogy.
   http://radicalpedagogy.icaap.org
   ISSN: 15275558
   Year Started: 1999
Reflecting Education.
   http://www.reflectingeducation.net/index.php/reflecting
   ISSN: 17469082
   Year Started: 2005 Institute of Education—University of
   London (UK)

South African Journal of Education.
>   http://www.scielo.org.za/revistas/saje/iaboutj.htm
>   **ISSN:** 02560100
>   **Year Started:** 1981 North-West University (South Africa)

Studies in Learning, Evaluation, Innovation and Development.
>   http://www.sleid.cqu.edu.au/index.php
>   **ISSN:** 18322050
>   **Year Started:** 2004 Central Queensland University (Australia)

LEADERSHIP

Academic Leadership.
>   http://www.academicleadership.org
>   **ISSN:** 15337812
>   **Year Started:** 2000

Advancing Women in Leadership.
>   http://advancingwomen.com/awl/awl_wordpress/
>   **ISSN:** 10937099
>   **Year Started:** 1997

Canadian Journal of Educational Administration and Policy.
>   http://www.umanitoba.ca/publications/cjeap/
>   **ISSN:** 12077798
>   **Year Started:** 1995 Faculty of Education—University of
>   Manitoba (Canada)

E-Journal of Organizational Learning and Leadership.
>   http://www.leadingtoday.org/weleadinlearning/
>   **ISSN:** d0000925
>   **Year Started:** 2002

Electronic Journal of Business Ethics and Organization Studies.
>   http://ejbo.jyu.fi/
>   **ISSN:** 12392685
>   **Year Started:** 1996

Emerging Leadership Journeys.
>   http://www.regent.edu/acad/global/publications/elj/
>   **ISSN:** 19414684
>   **Year Started:** 2008 Regent University School of Global
>   Leadership and Entrepreneurship

Inner Resources for Leaders.

> http://www.regent.edu/acad/global/publications/innerresources/
> **ISSN:** 19422989
> **Year Started:** 2009 Regent University School of Global Leadership and Entrepreneurship

International Electronic Journal for Leadership in Learning.

> http://www.ucalgary.ca/~iejll/
> **ISSN:** 12069620
> **Year Started:** 1997 (inactive) University of Calgary Press (Canada)

International Journal of Education Policy and Leadership.

> http://journals.sfu.ca/ijepl/index.php/ijepl
> **ISSN:** 15555062
> **Year Started:** 2006 Simon Fraser University and George Mason University

International Journal of Leadership Studies.

> http://www.regent.edu/acad/global/publications/ijls/new/home.htm
> **ISSN:** 15543145
> **Year Started:** 2005 Regent University School of Global Leadership and Entrepreneurship

International Journal of Teacher Leadership.

> http://www.csupomona.edu/~ijtl/
> **ISSN:** 19349726
> **Year Started:** 2008 (temporarily inactive) California State Polytechnic University, Pomona

Journal of Behavioral and Applied Management.

> http://www.ibam.com/pubs/jbam/default.asp
> **ISSN:** 19300158
> **Year Started:** 1999

Journal of Biblical Perspectives in Leadership.

> http://www.regent.edu/acad/global/publications/jbpl/
> **ISSN:** 19414692
> **Year Started:** 2008 Regent University School of Global Leadership and Entrepreneurship

Journal of Leadership Education.
> http://www.fhsu.edu/jole/index.html
> **ISSN:** 15529045
> **Year Started:** 2002

Journal of Management and Strategy.
> http://www.sciedu.ca/journal/index.php/jms
> **ISSN:** 19233965
> **Year Started:** 2010

Management.
> http://management-aims.com/
> **ISSN:** 12864892
> **Year Started:** 1998

Online Journal of Distance Learning Administration.
> http://www.westga.edu/%7Edistance/jmain11.html
> **ISSN:** 15563847
> **Year Started:** 1998 State University of West Georgia

Research and Practice in Human Resource Management.
> http://rphrm.curtin.edu.au/
> **ISSN:** 02185180
> **Year Started:** 1993 Curtin Business School—Curtin University
> and the Singapore Human Resources Institute

MISSIONS, ANTHROPOLOGY, AND CROSS-CULTURAL STUDIES

African Sociological Review.
> http://ajol.info/index.php/asr
> **ISSN:** 10274332
> **Year Started:** 2006

African Studies Quarterly: The Online Journal for African Studies.
> http://www.africa.ufl.edu/asq/
> **ISSN:** 10932658
> **Year Started:** 1999 University of Florida

Akademika.
> http://www.ukm.my/penerbit/jademik.html
> **ISSN:** 01265008
> **Year Started:** 2006
> Universiti Kebangsaan (Malaysia)

Anthropological Notebooks.
> http://www.drustvo-antropologov.si/anthropological_
> notebooks_eng.html
> **ISSN:** 1408032X
> **Year Started:** 2006

Anthropological Review.
> http://versita.metapress.com/content/120923/
> **ISSN:** 18986773
> **Year Started:** 2007 Versita Open University (Poland)

Anthropology Matters Journal.
> http://www.anthropologymatters.com/index.html
> **ISSN:** 17586453
> **Year Started:** 1999

Antrocom: Online Journal of Anthropology.
> http://www.antrocom.net/
> **ISSN:** 19732880
> **Year Started:** 2005

Asian Social Science.
> http://ccsenet.org/journal/index.php/ass/
> **ISSN:** 19112017
> **Year Started:** 2008

Canadian Journal of African Studies.
> http://ejournals.library.ualberta.ca/index.php/cjas-rcea
> **ISSN:** 19233051
> **Year Started:** 1967

Childhood in Africa: An Interdisciplinary Journal.
> http://www.afrchild.ohio.edu/CAJ/index.html
> **ISSN:** 19486502
> **Year Started:** 2009 Ohio University

Cross–Cultural Communication.
> http://www.cscanada.net/index.php/ccc
> **ISSN:** 17128358
> **Year Started:** 2005 Canadian Academy of Oriental and
> Occidental Culture

Culture and Society: Journal of Social Research.
>   http://culturesociety.vdu.lt/
>   **ISSN:** 20294573
>   **Year Started:** 2010 Vytautas Magnus University (Lithuania)

Diversities.
>   http://www.unesco.org/new/en/social-and-human-sciences
>   /resources/periodicals/diversities/
>   **ISSN:** 20796595
>   **Year Started:** 2010 (formerly *International Journal on
>   Multicultural Societies*)

Durham Anthropological Journal.
>   http://www.dur.ac.uk/anthropology.journal/
>   **ISSN:** 17422930
>   **Year Started:** 2004 Department of Anthropology–University of
>   Durham (UK)

Ethne: Online Journal for Pentecostal and Missional Leadership.
>   **ISSN:** 2071940X
>   **Year Started:** not stated
>   http://www.antsonline.org/aboutus.htmlAll Nations Theological
>   Seminary (Malawi)

Journal for Cultural and Religious Theory.
>   http://www.jcrt.org/
>   **ISSN:** 15305228
>   **Year Started:** 1999

Journal of Asia Pacific Studies.
>   http://www.japss.org/Journal-Asia-Pacific-Studies.html
>   **ISSN:** 19480091
>   **Year Started:** 2009

Journal of Asian Missions.
>   http://www.apts.edu/index.cfm?menuid=94&parentid=54
>   **ISSN:** 01193228
>   **Year Started:** 1999 Asia Pacific Theological Seminary
>   (Philippines)

Journal of Ethnology and Folkloristics.
>   http://www.jef.ee/index.php/journal
>   **ISSN:** 17366518
>   **Year Started:** 2007 University of Tartu (Estonia)

Journal of Intercultural Communication.
>   http://www.immi.se/jicc/index.php/jicc/
>   **ISSN:** 14041634
>   **Year Started:** 1999

Journal of International Women's Studies.
>   http://www.bridgew.edu/SoAS/jiws/
>   **ISSN:** 15398706
>   **Year Started:** 2000 Bridgewater State University
>   (Massachusetts)

Journal of Pan African Studies.
>   http://www.jpanafrican.com/
>   **ISSN:** 08886601
>   **Year Started:** 1987

Journal of Religion and Popular. Culture
>   http://www.usask.ca/relst/jrpc/
>   **ISSN:** d0000983
>   **Year Started:** 2002 Religious Studies Faculty—University of
>   Saskatchewan (Canada)

Journal of Religion and Society.
>   http://moses.creighton.edu/JRS/
>   **ISSN:** 15225658
>   **Year Started:** 1999 Creighton University

Journal of World Christianity.
>   http://www.journalofworldchristianity.org/index.php/jowc
>   **ISSN:** 19431538
>   **Year Started:** 2008 New York Theological Seminary

Michigan Discussions in Anthropology.
>   http://quod.lib.umich.edu/m/mdiag/
>   **ISSN:** 01937804
>   **Year Started:** 1971 University of Michigan

Middle East Studies.
>   http://www.middle-east-studies.net/
>   **ISSN:** 21099618
>   **Year Started:** 2009

Oral Tradition.
>   http://journal.oraltradition.org/
>   **ISSN:** 08835365
>   **Year Started:** 1986

Quotidian: Dutch Journal for the Study of Everyday Life.
>   http://www.quotidian.nl/
>   **ISSN:** 1879534X
>   **Year Started:** 2009 Amsterdam University (Netherlands)

Studies in Gender and Development in Africa.
>   http://ajol.info/index.php/sigada/index
>   **ISSN:** 08559449
>   **Year Started:** 2007

Studies in Social Justice.
>   http://ojs.uwindsor.ca/ojs/leddy/index.php/ssj
>   **ISSN:** 19114788
>   **Year Started:** 2007 University of Windsor (Canada)

Studies of Tribes and Tribals.
>   http://www.krepublishers.com/02-Journals/T%20&%20T/T
>   %20&%20T-00-0-000-000-2003-Web/T%20&%20T-00-0
>   -000-000-2003-1-Cover.htm
>   **ISSN:** 0972639X
>   **Year Started:** 2003

Transcience: A Journal of Global Studies.
>   http://www.transcience-journal.org/
>   **ISSN:** 21911150
>   **Year Started:** 2010

Transit.
>   http://german.berkeley.edu/transit/
>   **ISSN:** 15519627
>   **Year Started:** 2005 Department of German—University of
>   California at Berkeley

Ufahamu: A Journal of African Studies.
>   http://escholarship.org/uc/international_asc_ufahamu
>   **ISSN:** 21505802
>   **Year Started:** 2009 University of California at Los Angeles

RESEARCH JOURNALS

AIDS Research and Treatment.
>http://www.hindawi.com/journals/art/
>**ISSN:** 20901240
>**Year Started:** 2010

Australian Educational Researcher.
>http://www.aare.edu.au/aer/aer.htm
>**ISSN:** 03116999
>**Year Started:** 2003

Electronic Journal of Research in Educational Psychology.
>**ISSN:** 16962095
>**Year Started:** 2003
>http://www.investigacion-psicopedagogica.org/revista/new/
>english/index.php University of Almeria (Spain)

Forum: Qualitative Social Research.
>http://qualitative-research.net/fqs/fqs-eng.htm
>**ISSN:** 14385627
>**Year Started:** 2000

International Journal of Qualitative Methods.
>http://ejournals.library.ualberta.ca/index.php/IJQM/index
>**ISSN:** 16094069
>**Year Started:** 2002 University of Alberta

Journal of Educational and Social Research.
>http://www.mcser.org/index.php?option=com_
>content&view=category&layout=blog&id=34&Itemid=70
>**ISSN:** 22400524
>**Year Started:** 2011

Journal of Research Practice.
>http://jrp.icaap.org/
>**ISSN:** 1712851X
>**Year Started:** 2005 Athabasca University (Canada)

Qualitative Report, The.
>http://www.nova.edu/ssss/QR/index.html
>**ISSN:** 10520147
>**Year Started:** 1990 School of Social and Systemic Studies—
>Nova Southeastern University

Qualitative Studies.
>   http://ojs.statsbiblioteket.dk/index.php/qual/index
>   **ISSN:** 19037031
>   **Year Started:** 2010 Aalborg University (Denmark)

Reconceptualizing Educational Research Methodology.
>   http://www.rerm.hio.no/index.php/rerm.
>   **ISSN:** 1892042X
>   **Year Started:** 2010

Survey Research Methods.
>   http://w4.ub.uni-konstanz.de/srm/.
>   **ISSN:** 18643361
>   **Year Started:** 2007

Turkish Online Journal of Qualitative Inquiry.
>   http://www.tojqi.net/
>   **ISSN:** 13096591
>   **Year Started:** 2010

APPENDIX 10
Informed Consent Essential Content
Johan Mostert, DPhil

The content of the informed consent document should contain, as a minimum:

1. The purpose of the research
2. The participant's right to withdraw from participation, at any time during the research, without any penalty or loss
3. The estimated time that would be involved in the research
4. Any potential risk or adverse effect that could result through participation
5. A guarantee of anonymity and confidentiality, including how the records will be kept confidential and/or disposed of and if there are any limits of confidentiality
6. The prospective research benefits
7. That any questions about the research the participant may have will be answered at the conclusion of the process
8. Whom to contact if the participant has questions about the research or participant's rights
9. An offer to provide a summary of the findings

APPENDIX 11
Techniques in Interviewing
John L. Easter, PhD and Alan R. Johnson, PhD

As an expansion of chapter 29, Foundations of Interviewing, and chapter 30, Strategies of Effective Interviewing, this appendix offers some specific techniques and rules of thumb to keep in mind in the interview process.[1]

1. Respondents interpret and reply to questions based on their own experience, present concerns, and interests. A common problem is to formulate questions and assume the interviewer frame is the same as respondents. Whenever the reply to a major question has not made clear the frame of reference, try to ascertain the respondent's frame of reference by additional questioning such as "Why is that?" "What did you have in mind?" (Kahn and Cannell 1969, 156)

2. An alternative is to stipulate the frame of reference as part of the question. Instead of "How are things?" ask "How are things–financially I mean?" (Kahn and Cannell 1969, 155–56)

3. Avoid taking the actor's point of view as an explanation. "Naïve interviewers believe that the supposed limits of quantitative research are overcome by an open-ended interview schedule and a desire to catch 'authentic' experience" (Silverman 2006, 381). Interview data is never simply raw but are both situated and textual.

4. Study the interrelationships between elements. Multi-element explanations are better than single ones. (Silverman 2006, 386)

---

1. The primary source material is from Agar 1996, 141-49; Kahn and Cannell 1969; Knight, 2002, 139; and Silverman, 2006.

5. Make sure that you understand the response. If you do not then do non-directive probing, asking them to tell you more about that. Repeat the question if needed (Knight 2002, 139).

6. When people answer inadequately or answer a different question from what you asked, thank the respondent for the answer and then repeat the original question. Sometimes the very fact that people will not answer a particular question is revealing in and of itself, when they continue to evade and answer (Knight 2002, 139).

7. Do not answer questions for the respondent.

8. Use rephrasing an answer and ask the respondent if you are understanding them correctly. If you have not grasped something, follow that point up with the respondent until you are clear.

9. Use natural settings and situations for talking and asking questions. People are often intimidated if you want to "interview" them, and will say they have no time, and so on. If you change the frame and spend time in natural settings you can often ask your questions and people are very happy to talk. Using wisdom in framing what you are doing will help you to gain access and avoid being marginalized.

10. In interviews, people often answer with espoused logic rather than logic-in-use. One way to get at logic-in-use is to try and explore an action as soon as possible after they have done it when their memory is most vivid (Knight 2002, 68–69).

11. In many settings the outside participant observer is given "correct" answers or "public" answers to questions, particularly if they deal with cultural issues and values. Often the only way to learn about private scripts and actual thoughts is through unobtrusive means, observation, or picking up on comments rather than "answers" to interview questions.

REFERENCES

Agar, Michael. 1996. *The Professional Stranger: An Informal Introduction to Ethnography*. San Diego, CA: Academic Press.

Kahn, David, and Charles F. Cannell. 1968. "Interview." In *International Encyclopedia of the Social Sciences*, ed. David L. Sills, 8: 149–161. New York: MacMillan Co. and Free Press.

Knight, Peter T. 2002. *Small-Scale Research: Pragmatic Inquiry in Social Science and the Caring Professions*. London: Sage Publications.

Silverman, David. 2006. *Interpreting Qualitative Data: Methods for Analysing Talk, Text and Interaction*. 3rd ed. London: Sage Publications.

APPENDIX 12
Sampling Error:
The 1936 US Presidential Prediction Poll

Selecting a sample from a larger group is always a bit risky! Sampling error can distort the findings, leading to conclusions that are wrong— embarrassingly wrong sometimes. A classic case in point was the valiant attempt to predict the outcome of the US Presidential election in 1936. A popular magazine of that era, *Literary Digest,* selected a huge sample of people from telephone directories and automobile registration lists. Those in the sample, 10 million strong, were asked which presidential candidate they would choose. An overwhelming majority stated they were going to vote for the Republican candidate Alfred Landon, not his Democratic opponent Franklin Roosevelt. So the editors of the magazine concluded that Landon would win a landslide victory. As it turned out, Landon was overwhelmingly defeated.

Meanwhile, a young man named George Gallup correctly predicted the election's outcome. He was able to do this even though his team had chosen a much smaller sample (300,000 people). As it turned out, Gallup's sample, based on the developing science of demographics, was far more representative of *all* the voters.

Gallup's success in 1936 launched a career of sampling, with increasing accuracy, from very large populations. Those who carefully follow polit-ical trends today through the polling efforts by news networks and other pollsters have built on the science of large-scale sampling pioneered by Gallup and others.

Literary Digest's incorrect prediction was due to the selection of a sample that did not represent the entire voter population. The sample included only middle-and upper-class people, those who could afford telephones and automobiles during those Depression years. Not surpris-ingly (in retrospect), such people were largely Republicans who voted for Republican candidates. The more economically disadvantaged voting population, who later voted for the winning Democratic candidate, were in effect excluded from the *Literary Digest* sample.

Those working for *Literary Digest* apparently assumed that since they had contacted a huge number of people, they could accurately predict the election from their sample. They did not realize, as Gallop did, that it is not the *size* but the *representativeness* of the sample that ensures prediction accuracy. A sample as large as 10 million can produce misleading findings if it is not representative of the population. In contrast, a sample as small (comparatively) as Gallup's 300,000 can be accurate if it represents adequately the entire population. A representative sample, then, is essential when generalizing to the larger population as a whole.

APPENDIX 13
Sample Size Required for a Known Population

RECOMMENDED SAMPLE SIZES FOR 5 PERCENT
SAMPLING ERROR OF PRECISION[1]

Population size	Sample size	Population size	Sample size
10	10	275	163
15	14	300	172
20	19	325	180
25	24	350	187
30	28	375	194
35	32	400	201
40	36	425	207
45	40	450	212
50	44	475	218
55	48	500	222
60	52	1000	286
65	56	2000	333
70	59	3000	353
75	63	4000	364
80	66	5000	370
85	70	6000	375
90	73	7000	378
95	76	8000	381
100	81	9000	383
125	96	10000	385

1. Source: Isaac, William B., and Stephen Michael. 1971. *Handbook in Research and Evaluation*. 2nd ed. San Diego, CA: R. R. Knapp.

Population size	Sample size	Population size	Sample size
150	110	15000	390
175	122	20000	392
200	134	25000	394
225	144	50000	397
250	154	100000	398

USEFUL WEBSITES

http://www.google.co.za/search?q=Minimum+Sample
+Size+table&ie=utf-8&oe=utf-8&aq=t&rls=org
.mozilla:en-US:official&client=firefox-a
http://edis.ifas.ufl.edu/pd006

APPENDIX 14
Steps in Qualitative Data Analysis
John L. Easter, PhD and Alan R. Johnson, PhD

The chapter on qualitative data analysis emphasized that researchers must go beyond description to explanation. No set formula exists for making sense of qualitative data. Listed below, however, are some key steps that will help researchers move from data, through sensemaking, to theory development.

The steps described are broadly taken from Bernard (2011), and supplemented by ideas, tips, and rules of thumb from Knight (2002, 182–90), who drew upon Miles and Huberman (1994). Where applicable, chapters in this volume are also referenced.

Steps two through four must be worked through recursively and often, as researchers go back to collect more data for further clarification and expansion of previous rounds of analysis.

1. Prepare and organize transcribed texts, all interview and observational data, and documents involved with the research site or research questions.

   Since qualitative research generates such large amounts of material, it is critical to organize data from the very beginning and to keep refining the system for easy retrieval. See chapter 33 entitled, "Field Work and Field Notes: Building an Ethnographic Database" for a discussion of working with field notes.

2. Identify analytical categories (themes) and concepts that emerge from the texts.

   Steps two through four in this model are all involve the work of coding and memoing which are discussed in separate chapters in this volume (chapters 34 and 35, respectively).

   Here are some rules of thumb to keep in mind during this initial work. Since the analytic process starts from the beginning of data-collection activities, querying the data will provide new lines of inquiry to get more material.

- *Stand back and seek new perspectives.* Sometimes one must step back and widen the angle of view on the data to try and pick up previously unseen connections. In Alan's research in a single slum community, it was not till near the end after working through the data for a long time that he saw how geography in the community played a part in what was happening.
- *Work with contradictions.* When an apparent contradiction is found, seek for conditions, perspectives that could reconcile it, or evidence to support it. In Alan's work, he discovered that the same slum leader who was seen as the most trustworthy person in the community was also viewed as having acted out of self-interest while serving as committee president. Trying to make sense of this contradiction led to some very fruitful and significant interpretation.
- *Explore new relationships.* Discerning the relationships between categories represents a fundamental step for gaining deeper understanding of complex information. In his research, John discovered key relationships; similar patterns of invocation exist in both African Traditional Religion and Pentecostalism towards satisfying certain felt needs and spiritual expectations of the participant, which helps to explain the attractive nature of Pentecostalism within the African context. By discovering these relationships, John gained insight into implications at work in light of these relational dynamics.
- *Turn the problem around.* Once problematics are discovered it helps to look at a problem through fresh angles by asking more specific questions and by making useful applications. For instance, if you are working in a society where the conventional wisdom is that all relationships work on a patron-client basis and you discover evidence that there are kinds of relationships that operate differently. You began your research trying to understand how people lead in the context of these patron-client relationships. To "turn the problem around" in this instance would mean to ask new questions about how people lead others outside of patron-client relations. This would mean asking new questions and

checking your findings by applying them in new situations to see if they "work" the same or not.

- *Try to understand basic motivations and apply them to new data.* Take findings and apply it to other situations in the data, or new material to see if it makes sense and clarifies that material. If not, revise the findings.

- *See behind rationalizations.* One of the mentors in Alan's program had a saying that a good research question was not to answer "what is going on" but rather to try to answer "what is going on when what is going on is going on." Informants have interests, there are the "right" things to say and things that foreigners should be told, versus what people actually think or do. The researcher must constantly interrogate sources to see what else is happening.

- *Try to ask and answer the question "what is the meaning of this?"* In Alan's work he heard the word "trustworthy" used in reference to why people would cast a vote for a person, and realized that while knowing the dictionary definition, he did not know what that term meant, how it was built, maintained and so on.

3. Compare the data from each of the categories identified.

In initial runs through the material the search is for categories and themes, but then there is a move towards connecting, comparing, and contrasting these things. This is the beginning stage of seeking interrelationships and configurations.

- Look for patterns and themes
- Try imagining clusters of themes, concepts, cases
- Explore metaphors for drawing data together
- Count to see if it really as rare or common as it seems
- Compare and contrast to see whether categories are distinctive
- Try unclustering things that initial analysis linked together
- Check the suitability of categories-revise definitions if needed, look for examples and counter-examples.
- Explore relationships between variables by trying to identify stories that might link them all.
- Look for mediators/moderators in the chain of cause X causes Y causes Z-may have Y1, Y2, Y3.

4. Examine how the categories are connected to each other.

Here is where the researcher attempts to identify central categories (and the subcomponent categories that compose them) and relationships between them. In the beginning, there will be a lot of discrete categories, but further analysis and data collection will help show how things are related, which things are similar and dissimilar, and where there are polarities and positions on a continuum.

- See if they cover everything that matters, if not revise (Knight 2002, 189).
- Look for opportunities to reduce the number of categories to a manageable number-recommend seven plus or minus two.
- Begin defining of categories so that they are clear enough that another researcher could to use it to code the same material (Knight 2002, 189).

5. Build a theoretical model in light of relational dynamics between the major themes

Once major themes emerge, it is better to reduce the findings to five or six central categories—attempting to harness every finding becomes too broad and cumbersome in the reporting phase of the study. Knight advises that at this point to check if the emerging account is plausible and explore whether it can be extended to other people's insights (2002, 188). See chapter 10 entitled, "Theory Development" for more details on this process.

REFERENCES

Bernard, H. Russell. 2011. *Research Methods in Anthropology: Qualitative and Quantitative Approaches*. 5th ed. Lanham, MD: AltaMira Press.

Knight, Peter T. 2002. *Small-Scale Research: Pragmatic Inquiry in Social Science and the Caring Professions*. London: Sage Publications.

Miles, Matthew, and A. Michael Huberman. 1994. *Qualitative Data Analysis*. 2nd ed. Thousand Oaks, CA: Sage Publications.

APPENDIX 15

Guidelines for Biblical and Theological Research[1]

Douglas A. Oss, PhD[2]

GENERAL GUIDELINES

1. Determine the topic or text that will be the focus of your research.
2. Keep in mind the acceptable format for footnotes/endnotes, bibliography, spacing, title page, grammar, style, etc.
3. When writing an exegetical theological paper:
    - Include an explanation of any interpretive difficulties.
    - Assess the impact the passage had within its immediate literary and redemptive-historical contexts.
    - Explore the canonical redemptive-historical connections and determine the christocentric bearing of the passage.
4. When writing a dogmatic[3] theological paper:
    - Determine why a correct understanding of this issue is important; don't waste the church's time on foolish and unedifying controversies (1 Tim 1:4; 6:4; Tit 3:9).
    - Explore the canonical material that can properly be brought to bear on this issue.

---

1. I am indebted to Prof. Vern Poythress (Westminster Theological Seminary, Philadelphia, PA) for portions of this guideline. For further help read John Frame, *The Doctrine of the Knowledge of God* (Phillipsburg, NJ: Presbyterian and Reformed, 1987), "Evaluating Theological Writings" (369–70); "How to Write a Theological Paper" (371–79); and "Maxims for Theologians and Apologists" (375–79).

2. Douglas A. Oss is the director of the Cordas C. Burnett Center for Biblical Preaching, and professor of Biblical Theology and New Testament Interpretation at the Assemblies of God Theological Seminary, Springfield, Missouri. This document was provided by the author with permission to use.

3. The term *dogmatic* here means that which based on the foundational dogmas or beliefs of the church.

- Include an explanation of any interpretative difficulties that affect our ability to formulate doctrine on this topic.
- Include any helpful discussion from the history of the church's approach to this issue.

THE HOLY SPIRIT'S ILLUMINATION

The "doctrine of illumination" refers to the teaching function of the Spirit. Every effort of the Christian scholar must arise from, be sustained by, and bear fruit through the Holy Spirit's illumination. The starting point for all scholarly research must therefore be prayer. Let prayerful submission to the Lord and His Word characterize your whole theological enterprise ask God to give you sound biblical-theological insight at each step of your research and writing. The disciplines of both scholar and saint are yours by calling; they must be joined together your lives since you are charged to feed the flock. Your labor in your studies is not merely academic and temporary, but spiritual and lifelong. Acknowledge God's grace throughout this process: ask Him for help, and thank Him when He gives it—He will you know.

ESSENTIAL ACTIONS

1. Be organized, cogent, and persuasive. For exegetical theological papers, you may find it useful to develop a separate section for motific analysis. This is where biblical theology functions as a method. It may be fruitful to pursue a given motif at some length.

2. For dogmatic theological papers, you may find it useful to organize your material in ways specifically tailored to the demands of your topic.
   - If the issue has been the subject of historical controversial, set out a history of the debate, analyze and critique the various viewpoints, and conclude with your own understanding of the Bible's teaching on this matter.
   - If the issue has several key facets, determine what they are and treat them methodically one after another in separate sections.
   - If the issue is a matter of current debate, outline the main rival positions, assess their respective strengths and/or

weakness, and offer your assessment of the Bible's teaching on this matter.

3. Provide proper and thorough documentation of materials used in research.
   - Two commonly used style-guides are *MLA Handbook* (8th ed., 2016), and *Publication Manual of the American Psychology Association* (6tht ed., 2009) (APA) in related areas.
   - However, Kate L. Turabian, et al., *A Manual for Writers of Research Papers, Theses, and Dissertations* (8th ed., 2013) is the standard for biblical studies and will be your most helpful resource for questions about documentation and formatting; this work is consistent in style and gives many examples for both footnote and bibliographical format (see below).
   - A more detailed manual that Turabian is related to is *The Chicago Manual of Style* (16tht ed., 2010).
   - In the area specifically tied to biblical studies, *The SBL Manual of Style* (2nd ed., 2014) has become the manual of choice in some venues. Note that it contains an extensive collection of abbreviations for books, documents, manuscripts, journals, etc. related to biblical studies.

4. Exercise care in handling your passage in an exegetical theological paper.
   - Give due consideration to each verse of the passage.
   - Pay attention to how the passage as a whole fits together.
   - Focus on the influence the immediate context in the book, both literary and historical.
   - View the passage in the light of major concerns, emphases, themes, and other illumination provided by the book as a whole (crucial).
   - Reflect on any allusions by the human writer to other Scripture passages (essential for a canonical understanding).
   - See the *whole* of Scripture from the point of view of this verse, but in a way that acknowledges the remoteness of what is only remotely connected.
   - Distinguish what the original human author and audience could have understood from additional connections that we now see in the light of the completed canon.

5. Exercise care in covering the biblical teaching in a dogmatic theological paper.

- Deal with all the key texts that bear on your doctrinal position.
- Assess each passage's meaning in its own context to determine its applicability to your topic.
- Spell out any complexities that render a sure decision difficult.
- Respect the theological contribution of those who have gone before you in the church.
  - Do not lightly dismiss or ignore the consensus of the Church throughout its history.
  - Do not misrepresent even those with whom you differ.
  - Do not argue against implications that you attach to someone's view without determining that they are in fact necessary implications of that viewpoint.[4]
  - Do not set up a straw man and knock that down rather than wrestling with your opponent's theological strengths.
- Be bold where Scripture is clear and cautious where Scripture is vague.

INCONSEQUENTIAL ACTIONS

1. A discussion at any length harmonizing problems and objections of liberals.
2. Grammatical minutiae (except as these may bear on a major interpretive question).
3. Making preaching-type applicants in the body of the paper.
4. Providing an extended introduction and discussion of the setting (except as these may bear on a major interpretive question).

ACTIONS AND CONTENT THAT HURT AN ARGUMENT

1. Majoring on minors.
2. Neglecting to comment at all about an important verse.
3. Approaching a passage from the framework of systematic theology in a way that overwhelms the fine nuances of the passage itself (e.g.,

---

4. See D. A. Carson, *Exegetical Fallacies* (Grand Rapids: Baker, 1984), "Logical Fallacies," 91–126.

reading in systematic theological meaning with no redemptive-historical appreciation).
4. Failing to interpret a passage with proper canonical awareness:
   • Keeping your eyes too exclusively fixed on one text.
   • Missing a key OT background, or background from the book in question, for a given verse or topic.
   • Missing a key NT fulfillment.
   • Focusing too extensively on the whole of Scripture (being too broad).
   • Failing to distinguish between the emphasis of an individual text on the one hand and the whole counsel of God on the other hand.
   • Failing to show an organic connection between the emphasis of an individual text on the one hand and the whole counsel of God in on the other hand. Examples include:
     - giving priority in interpretation to a reconstructed historical situation about which you hypothetically suppose the passage to be speaking, rather than to the passage itself as it comes from author to reader.
     - etymologizing, or otherwise using a word study as though it were a method of doing biblical theology.
     - emphasizing verbal parallels more than conceptual (real) parallels when doing motific analysis.
     - making a passage speak more definitely and/or precisely than what it will bear.
     - allegorizing.

STEPS IN INTERPRETATION: EXEGETICAL THEOLOGICAL DEVELOPMENT

1. Preliminary acquaintance with the text:
   • Memorize the passage (and some context).
   • Define the limits of the passage (the NIV paragraphs are generally reliable).
   • Pray for the Holy Spirit's illumination: for insight, courage, and humility to understand and present the passage faithfully.

- Read and re-read the passage in the larger literary context of the book. View the whole of Scripture from the standpoint of this passage and this passage from the standpoint of the whole of Scripture. Strive for a maximum number of different perspectives.

2. Exegesis in the original setting (observant and interpretation in uniqueness):
   - Learn as much as you can about the speaker, the audience, and the circumstances of the utterance (historical background).
   - Check out difficulties with reference tools: commentaries, Bible encyclopedias, atlases, lexicons, grammars, etc.
   - Analyze the passage syntactically.
   - Outline the passage using whatever forms of outlining are most promising.
   - Determine how the passage relates conceptually to its immediate literary context.
   - Identify the genre of the text and of larger sections in which it is imbedded.

3. Exegesis in the canonical setting (interpretation in relationship to the entire canon and to the unfolding of God's plan and purpose in redemptive history).
   - Locate the passage in its epoch in the history of redemption, and determine its contribution to revelation at that point.
   - Do motific analysis of your passage in:
     - antecedent Scripture.
     - subsequent Scripture.
   - Do a diachronic analysis of the earlier canonical sources and later use of this passage in Scripture, and its application to various audiences.
     - Does your passage quote or allude to a text from an earlier portion of the canon?
     - Does a later portion of the canon quote or allude to your passage?
   - Pick key words and trace their usage through OT and NT. Be alert:
     - for parallel motifs where these words are used.

- to the fact that every instance of a word will not indicate a parallel motif or concept.
- Use cross-references and other resources to locate passages most similar or most contrasting to the given passage.
- Identify theological issues raised or solved.
- Compare the passage with other passages dealing with similar issues.
- Reevaluate exegesis in the light of the canon already available to the original hearers of the given passage.
- How does the passage preach Christ?
- Assess how differences in redemptive-historical epoch and/or cultural situation will affect current application.
- Summarize the message of the passage in a single declarative sentence. Try to make the summary precise enough that a person familiar with the Bible might guess the passage just from the summary.
- Check your work against *exegetical* commentaries.

4. When preparing for preaching (application):
   - Formulate three or four applications to our time, and to yourself.
   - Make the applications concrete by forming them in one sentence summaries.
   - Adapt the application to your audience. What should they *do* differently because of this passage?
   - Choose a principal application, then work backward from the application to the sermon outline, with the audience constantly in view. Decide whether following the text consecutively or motifically would be more effective. Organize the outline so that each major section answers a question the audience might well ask about the principle motif.
   - Fill in the outline in detail: illustrate, do more application, etc.

STEPS IN INTERPRETATION: DOGMATIC THEOLOGICAL DEVELOPMENT

1. Define the scope of the issue: Do not pick too large nor too small a topic for the goal at hand.

2. Collect the relevant biblical data that will help you develop a full grasp of the matter.
   - Use a concordance, cross-references, and your memory of the Bible to assemble the initial scriptural data.
   - Check your findings against other's work to discover any oversight that might hinder you from dealing comprehensively with the issue.
   - Follow the steps for exegetical theological development listed above.
     - For key passage: follow these steps as closely as time constraints will allow.
     - For subsidiary passages:
       - follow these steps loosely when you are clear about the meaning of the passage.
       - follow these steps closely when you realize an exegetical problem must be settled before you can be sure of how to apply it to your own topic.
3. Check off your work against the work of others who have gone before you.
   - Determine what the Church Fathers, Reformers, and contemporary evangelical theologians have said about the issue.
   - Recheck your exegetical work when your results are at odds with established evangelical positions.
   - Where your difference remains in spite of careful reconsideration, assess and critique the views that differ from yours.
     - Attempt to demonstrate where they go wrong, anticipating objections as if the one whom you are critiquing would be responding to your critique.
     - Show what the church gains in doctrinal clarity and/or fidelity by following the path you prescribe over the one you critique.

APPENDIX 16
Using Indices and Abstracts for Biblical and Theological Research[1]
James Hernando, PhD[2]

PRELIMINARY STEPS

Take your topic and make a list of topical subjects that are intrinsic to your study. For example, your doctoral project might involve developing a discipleship curriculum for the elderly in an elderly community center in your city. Some related topics might include:

1. Discipleship
2. Christian discipleship
3. Christian education
4. Adult education for the elderly
5. Christian life
6. Spiritual formation

You can always identify additional topics. Start with *broader*[3] topics and categories, ones that are inclusive of your topic and work toward a *narrower*[4] focus (e.g., "care for the elderly" may lead you toward "learning for the aged"). Thus, you must "mine" the bibliographies of wisely chosen, narrowly focused articles.

---

1. Biblical theology spans the teaching of Scripture on your topic and how that works through Scripture with *progressive revelation*. See for example *New Dictionary of Biblical Theology* regarding "eras": patriarchal, non-writing prophets, monarchy-both N&S and prophetic literature, Exilic prophets, post-exilic prophets, Gospels, Acts, Epistles, Revelation.

2. James D. Hernando is professor of New Testament at the Assemblies of God Theological Seminary, Springfield, Missouri. This document was provided by the author with permission to use.

3. Broad: encyclopedias. Get a jump off point from encyclopedia bibliographies, see those listed in Appendix 18, "Selected Bibliography for Biblical and Theological Research."

4. *New International Dictionary of New Testament Theology* (4 vols), see in Appendix 18, "Selected Bibliography for Biblical and Theological Research."

The indices below often contain book reviews. A well-selected mono-graph on your topic or a related topic will include a large numbers of relevant bibliographic entries.

REFERENCE INDICES FOR LOCATING BOOKS AND JOURNAL ARTICLES

1. *Humanities Index.*[5] Works indexed in this resource focus on the humanities and social science, but are useful for theological research. Check, for example, the following biblical-theological topics: Church, Christian/Church, Christianity, and Christians, then look at the sub-categories: for example, Christian ethics, Christian life, Christian missions, Missions.

   Some indexed categories present a list of sources which can be related to the "biblical teaching" on a particular topic. For example, the topic "Christianity" contains a host of sub-categories in the Humanities Index, including Christianity and _____:

2. Culture

3. Economics

4. Education (cf. Discipleship)

5. Literature

6. Science

7. Other religions: Paganism, Buddhism, Hinduism, Islam, Judaism

8. Politics: race relations, slavery, social problems, the world, war, and so forth.

9. *Social Science Index*. This resource uses many of the same headings as those used in the *Humanities Index*, but you will find more social science journals.

10. *Religion Index.*[6] This resource has the broadest scope of topics. Abbreviations for all periodicals are given in the list of periodicals; make a copy for future reference and footnotes. Note that the 8th edition of Turabian's *A Manual for Writers of Research Papers, Theses, and Dissertations* allows for abbreviations of journals and periodicals.

---

5. These are indexed by year.
6. This is by topic *and* author.

For Bible-theology research, focus on headings like *Bible* or *Christian*[7] with sub-categories:

11. Bible—authority, canon, commentaries,[8] criticism etc.
12. Bible—social teachings
    - Bible-study
    - Bible-psychology
    - Bible-theology
13. Christian—education, discipleship, epistemology, counseling, psychology, etc.

NOTE: A biblical theology considers the entire scope and progress of divine revelation across the biblical canon.[9] Thus, a credible biblical theology:

> seeks both a *diachronic* (through time) description of what biblical authors were saying in texts set in a specific historical-cultural setting. It looks to see the development of a topic as biblical history unfolds.

> seeks a holistic or *synchronic* (in time) description of what the Bible (or some portion of it) teaches on a given subject. This is essentially a prescriptive task of describing what this teaching means for contemporary faith and praxis.

Assumed in these two approaches is both the authority of Scripture and its relevance, that Scripture has something to say to our time and situation, and that we *should* seek to respond to it.

14. *Guide to Social Science and Religion in Periodical Literature.* This index attempts to integrate social science and humanities, and includes some periodicals that are omitted in the Religion Index.
15. *Christian Periodical Index.* This resource includes more popular Christian periodicals (e.g. *Christian Science Monitor, Christianity Today,* and published church journals); it also includes a limited number of

---

7. Focus on the most helpful, most exhaustive of categories.

8. For best commentaries only for particularly troubling or obscure passages see Appendix 20.

9. A helpful article that defines and describes the work of "Biblical Theology" is found in Richard H. Soulen and R. Kendall Soulen, *Handbook of Biblical Criticism,* 3rd ed. (Louisville, KY: Westminster John Knox, 2011), 26–27.

scholarly journals. Topics identified in this index it will also appear in the Religion Index.

16. *Old Testament Abstracts* **and** *New Testament Abstracts.* These two abstracts will help you *before* you go into the library holdings, or get on line at *EBSCO Host* to access online resource. They will prevent random copying of any and every article that looks relevant. These two abstracts accomplishing this by providing a brief abstract or descriptive summary of what is in a book or journal article.

17. *Old Testament Abstracts:*[10] See contents page for the following categories: Pentateuch, Historical Books, The Writings, Major Prophets, Minor Prophets, Biblical Theology, Intertestamental, Apocrypha, NT Use, and Qumran. Note especially the book notices under Biblical Theology.[11] Make a copy of the abbreviation of periodicals abstracted and the authors so you do not have to write each one out each time.

18. *New Testament Abstracts:*

    Note organization: NT General, Gospel-Acts, Epistles-Revelation, NT World

    See especially Biblical Theology

    Note Scripture Text Index or key passages and text related to your study.

---

10. Old Testament Abstracts/New Testament Abstracts are published quarterly, then bound. Good starting places for searches in these two abstracts include 10, 15, 20 years ago, depending on how narrow your topic is. In contrast to EBSCO Host, these resources will give you an *abstract* of the article (saving you the time needed to read through the article).

11. See for example, Elmer Martens' *Old Testament Theology* and the contents in the abstract – vol. 21, page 165.

APPENDIX 17
Bibles and Bible Versions
Bible Versions—English (with abbreviations)

Benny C. Aker, PhD, and Douglas A. Oss, PhD[1]

NIV: New International Version (readable, but made many translation decisions)

TNIV: Today's New International Version (known for simple syntax and readability)

NASB: New American Standard Bible ("translationese" instead of real English)

CEV: Contemporary English Version (the best translation for unchurched and new converts; 3rd grade level English)

ESV: English Standard Version (excellent, conservative, more literal version)

NLT: New Living Translation (very good, recent, simpler, version)

NKJV: New King James Version (good but still has some of the weaknesses of the KJV text and tradition)

NET: New English Translation (excellent modern conservative translation)

---

1. Benny C. Aker is professor emeritus of New Testament Exegesis, and Douglas A. Oss is the Director of the Cordas C. Burnett Center for Biblical Preaching, and Professor of Biblical Theology and New Testament Interpretation, both at the Assemblies of God Theological Seminary, Springfield, Missouri. This document was provided by the authors with permission to use.

UNDERSTANDING BIBLE TRANSLATIONS

Paraphrases	Translations	
Not translations	Functional	Formal
No regard for grammar, syntax or vocabulary	Phrase/idiom-based	Grammar/syntax-based
Theological commentary	Grammar and syntax considered	No vocabulary or syntax restrictions
disguised as a Bible	Restricted vocabulary	ESV
The Message	Restricted syntax	NASB
The Living Bible	NLT	KJV
The Amplified Bible	NIV	NKJV
	TNIV	

BIBLE DICTIONARIES AND ENCYCLOPEDIAS

One Volume Dictionaries
Eerdmans Dictionary of the Bible
Harper's Bible Dictionary
New Bible Dictionary[2]
New International Dictionary of the Bible, Pictorial Edition

Multi-volume Dictionaries and Encyclopedias
Douglas, J. D., ed. 1980. *Illustrated Bible Dictionary.* 3 vols. Wheaton, IL: Tyndale House.[3]
Freedman, David Noel, Editor-in-chief. 1992. *The Anchor Bible Dictionary.*[4] 6 vols. New York: Doubleday.
International Standard Bible Encyclopedia. 4 vols. 1995. Grand Rapids, MI: Eerdmans.[5]
Sakenfeld, Katharine Doob, ed. 2009. *The New Interpreter's Dictionary of the Bible.* 5 vols. Nashville, TN: Abingdon Press.[6]

---

1. This bibliography—originally prepared by Lois E. Olena, DMin and modified by Paul W. Lewis, PhD—is a compilation of various bibliographies used by members of the Assemblies of God Theological Seminary's Bible-Theology Department: Benny C. Aker, PhD; Roger D. Cotton, ThD; James D. Hernando, PhD; Paul W. Lewis, PhD; Douglas A. Oss, PhD; James H. Railley, DTh; and Charles E. Self, PhD.
2. Many of the best British and US conservative scholars.
3. This is a conservative work.
4. The quality of the scholarship is mixed. This work is being revised.
5. The 1939 version is available at http://www.internationalstandardbible.com/. The quality of scholarship is mixed.
6. The NIDB is generally well to the left (i.e., liberal) of Evangelical positions.

InterVarsity Series: Downers Grove, IL: InterVarsity.
- Alexander, Bill T., and H. G. M. Williamson, eds. *Dictionary of the Old Testament: Historical Books*, 2005.
- Alexander, T. Desmond, and David Baker, eds. *Dictionary of the Old Testament: Pentateuch*, 2002.
- Boda, Mark J., and J. Gordon McConville, eds. *Dictionary of the Old Testament: Prophets*, 2012.
- Evans, Craig A., and Stanley E. Porter, eds. *Dictionary of New Testament Backgrounds*, 2000.
- Green, Joel B., Scot McKnight, and I. Howard Marshall, eds. *Dictionary of Jesus and the Gospels*, 1992.
- Hawthorne, Gerald F., Ralph P. Martin, and Daniel G. Reid, eds. *Dictionary of Paul and His Letters*, 1993.
- Longman III, Tremper, and Peter Enns, eds. *Dictionary of Old Testament: Wisdom, Poetry and Writings*, 2008.
- Martin, Ralph P., and Peter H. Davids, eds. *Dictionary of the Later New Testament & Its Developments*, 1997.
- Rosner, Brian S., T. Desmond Alexander, Graeme Goldsworthy, and D. A. Carson, eds. *New Dictionary of Biblical Theology*, 2000.
- Ryken, Leland, James C. Wilhoit, and Tremper Longman III, eds. *Dictionary of Biblical Imagery*, 1998.

Bible Works 10 and Logos[7]

Biblical Language Concordances

Hatch, Edwin, and Henry Redpath. 1998. *Concordance to the Septuagint and the other Greek Versions of the Old Testament*. 2nd ed. Grand Rapids, MI: Baker.

Kohlenberger III, John R., and James A. Swanson. 1998. *The Hebrew-English Concordance to the Old Testament: With the New International Version*. Grand Rapids, MI: Zondervan.

Wigram, George. 1972. *The New Englishman's Greek Concordance*. South Pasadena, CA: William Carey Library.

---

7. These works include the Older Version of *ISBE*. The newer one is available in hardcopy. Logos also has a good dictionary in its Scholar's Library. Take care with public domain sources within: some are dated or not relevant.

————. 1984. *The New Englishman's Hebrew Concordance*. Peabody, MA: Hendrickson.

Exegetical Methodology

Chisholm, Robert B., Jr. 1998. *From Exegesis to Exposition: A Practical Guide to Using Biblical Hebrew*. Grand Rapids, MI: Baker.[8]

Duvall, J. Scott, and J. Daniel Hays. 2001. *Grasping God's Word: A Hands-On Approach to Reading, Interpreting, and Applying the Bible*. Grand Rapids, MI: Zondervan.

Fee, Gordon. 2002. *New Testament Exegesis: A Handbook for Students and Pastors*. 3rd ed. Philadelphia, PA: Westminster.

Hernando, James D. 2005. *Dictionary of Hermeneutics: A Concise Guide to Terms, Names, Methods, and Expressions*. Springfield, MO: Gospel Publishing House.

Kaiser, Walter C. Jr. 1981. *Toward An Exegetical Theology*. Grand Rapids, MI: Baker.[9]

Klein, William W., Craig L. Blomberg, and Robert L. Hubbard, Jr. 1993. *Introduction to Biblical Interpretation*. Dallas, TX: Word.[10]

Osborne, Grant R. 1991. *The Hermeneutical Spiral: A Comprehensive Introduction to Biblical Interpretation to Biblical Interpretation*. Downers Grove, IL: InterVarsity Press.

Stuart, Douglas. 2001. *Old Testament Exegesis: A Primer for Students and Pastors*. 3rd ed. Philadelphia: Westminster.

Vyhmeister, Nancy Jean. 2008. *Quality Research Papers: For Students of Theology and Religion*, 2nd ed. Grand Rapids, MI: Zondervan.

---

8. This is an excellent tool for how to use Hebrew in interpreting Scripture.

9. This is an excellent resource for understanding principalizing, and diagramming.

10. This work and the *The Hermeneutical Spiral* are the best; they should be read by every graduate Bible student.

WORD BOOKS/THEOLOGICAL DICTIONARIES[11]

Old Testament

Botterweck, G. Johannes, and Helmer Ringgren, eds. 1974. *Theological Dictionary of the Old Testament*. (TDOT) 10 Vols. Grand Rapids, MI: Eerdmans.[12]

Harris, R. Laird, Gleason L. Archer, Jr., and Bruce K. Waltke, eds. 2003. *Theological Wordbook of the Old Testament*. (TWOT) 2 Vols. Chicago: Moody.[13]

Jenni, Ernst, and Claus Westermann. 1997. *Theological Lexicon of the Old Testament*. 3 Vols. Translated by Mark E. Biddle. Peabody, MA: Hendrickson.[14]

Van Gemeren, Willem A., ed. 1997. *New International Dictionary of Old Testament Theology and Exegesis*. (NIDOTTE) 5 vols. Grand Rapids, MI: Zondervan.[15]

New Testament

Balz, Horst, and Gerhard Schneider, eds. 1990–1993. *Exegetical Dictionary of the New Testament*. Vols. 3. Trans. publisher. Grand Rapids, MI: Eerdmans.

Brown, Colin, Gen. ed. 1986. *The New International Dictionary of New Testament Theology*. (NIDNT) 4 vols. Grand Rapids, MI: Zondervan.[16]

---

11. Take care regarding word study fallacies of older tools (e.g., TDNT and to lesser degree TDOT). Note that these tools are useful for technical terms, but often misleading otherwise. We recommend stronger tools, including TWOT, NIDOTTE, and NIDNT.

12. Has several translators.

13. This work is not as thorough as NIDOTTE; it is brief: more like a lexicon.

14. This work is not really a "lexicon;" it is, rather, a theological dictionary of the OT.

15. This work is required for any OT word studies. The OT was done by some of the best of U.S. scholars and is much better than the NT one. It provides longer exegetical comments on words in the Old Testament. Its indexes include correlations of Strong's numbers with Goodrick/ Kohlenberger numbers.

16. Gives the Greek translation of terms and discusses the etymology, use in classical literature, Old Testament literature, and New Testament literature. It has good indexes to words and phrases. (See abridged version)

Kittel, Gerhard, and Gerhard Friedrich, eds. 1976. *Theological Dictionary of the New Testament.* (TDNT) Trans. Geoffrey W. Bromiley. 10 Vols. Grand Rapids, MI: Eerdmans.

Kittel, Gerhard, and Gerhard Friedrich, eds. 1985. *Theological Dictionary of the New Testament.* Trans. Geoffrey W. Bromiley. Abridged ed. Grand Rapids, MI: Eerdmans.[17]

Spicq, Ceslas. 1994. *Theological Lexicon of the New Testament.* 3 vols. Trans. James D. Ernest. Peabody, MA: Hendrickson.[18]

Verbrugge, Verlyn, ed. 2000. *The NIV Theological Dictionary of New Testament Words: An Abridgment of the New International Dictionary of New Testament Theology.* Grand Rapids, MI: Zondervan.[19]

Lexicons[20]

Brown, Francis, S. R. Driver, and Charles A. Briggs, eds. 1907. (BDB) *A Hebrew and English Lexicon of the Old Testament.* Oxford: At the Clarendon Press.[21]

Arndt, William, Frederick W. Danker, and Walter Bauer. 2000. *A Greek-English Lexicon of the New Testament and Other Early Christian Literature.* (BDAG) 3rd ed. Ed. Frederick W. Danker. Chicago: University of Chicago Press.[22]

Holladay, William L. 1971. *A Concise Hebrew and Aramaic Lexicon of the Old Testament.* Grand Rapids, MI: Eerdmans.[23]

Koehler, Ludwig, and Walter Baumgartner. 1994-2000. *The Hebrew and Aramaic Lexicon of the Old Testament.*(HALOT) 5 vols. Revised

---

17. This is an abridged version of Kittel's 10-vol. set.

18. This is not really a lexicon; it is, rather, a theological dictionary of NT Greek.

19. This is now called *The New International Dictionary of New Testament Theology* (2004).

20. Warnings: (1) weak resources, such as Vines, Wuest, Spiros Zohdiates, etc.; (2) misusing classical Greek dictionaries, such as Liddell-Scott. Recommend standards: HALOT and BDB for OT; and BDAG for NT.

21. The classic scholarly lexicon but not user friendly or up to date. Still useful as a "concordance" of potential usage.

22. The standard scholarly lexicon for the Greek NT.

23. The best affordable lexicon.

by Walter Baumgartner and Johann Jakob Stamm. Trans. and ed.
M. E.J. Richardson. New York: Brill.[24]

Lampe, G. W. H. 1984. *A Patristic Greek Lexicon.* Oxford: Clarendon Press.

Liddell, Henry George, Robert Scott, Henry Stuart Jones, and Roderick
McKenzie. 1996. *A Greek-English Lexicon.* 9th ed. New York:
Oxford University Press.[25]

Louw, Johannes P., and Eugene A. Nida, eds. 1988-89. *Greek-English
Lexicon of the New Testament Based on Semantic Domains.* 2nd ed.
New York: United Bible Societies.[26]

Lust, Johan, Erik Eynikel, and Karin Hauspie, eds. 2003. *A Greek-English
Lexicon of the Septuagint.* Stuttgart: Deutsche Bibelgesellschaft.

Bible Works 10 and Logos (Scholar's Library) both have some of these—
some are on both CDs. You may have to order them separately. For
a concordance, Bible Works 10 cannot be beat. Bible Works 10 and
Logos (Scholar's Library) also have several good Hebrew lexicons
and Liddell & Scot's Greek lexicon. This lexicon will have words
that other lexicons do not have. It covers classical Greek onwards.

BIBLICAL THEOLOGIES

General

Alexander, T. Desmond, and Brian S. Rosner, eds. 2000. *New Dictionary
of Biblical Theology: Exploring the Unity & Diversity of Scripture.*
Downers Grove, IL: InterVarsity Press.

Barr, James. 1976. "Biblical Theology." In *Interpreter's Dictionary of the
Bible, Supplement*, ed. Keith Crim, 104–11. Nashville, TN:
Abingdon.[27]

———. 1999. *The Concept of Biblical Theology: An Old Testament Perspective.*
Minneapolis, MN: Fortress.[28]

---

24. The best lexicon.

25. Not a lexicon of NT Greek, but still useful as a supplement on classical
Greek background of terms. (However: be careful about misreading classical Greek
definitions into NT exegesis.)

26. Uses a semantical field approach.

27. Reviews the biblical theology movement and key themes associated with it.

28. Helpful but also more liberal.

Charlesworth, James H. 1993. "What Has the Old Testament to Do with the New?" In *The Old and New Testaments: Their Relationship and the "Intertestamental" Literature*, ed. James H. Charlesworth and W. P. Weaver, 39–87. Valley Forge, PA: Trinity.[29]

Childs, Brevard S. 1992. *Biblical Theology of the Old and New Testaments*. Minneapolis, MN: Fortress.

Hafemann, Scott J., ed. 2002. *Biblical Theology: Retrospect and Prospect*. Downers Grove, IL: InterVarsity.

Hafemann, Scott J., and Paul R. House, eds. 2007. *Central Themes in Biblical Theology: Mapping Unity in Diversity*. Grand Rapids, MI: Baker.[30]

Horton, Stanley. 1977. *What the Bible Says About the Holy Spirit*. Springfield, MO: Gospel Publishing House.

Leon-Dufour, Xavier, ed. 1973. *Dictionary of Biblical Theology*. 2nd ed. New York: Seabury.[31]

Webb, Barry G. 1998. "Biblical Theology and Biblical Interpretation." In *Interpreting God's Plan: Biblical Theology and the Pastor*, edited by J. R. Gibson, 47–74. Adelaide, Aus.: Open Book.

Westermann, Claus. 1982. *Elements of Old Testament Theology*. (Originally published as *Theologie des Alten Testaments in Grundzügen*. Göttingen: Vandenhoeck & Ruprecht, 1978). Trans. Douglas W. Stott. Atlanta: John Knox.

Old Testament Theology

*Bibliography: Martens, Elmer A. 1997. *Old Testament Theology*. IBR Bibliographies 13. Grand Rapids, MI: Baker.[32]

Alexander, T. Desmond, and David W. Baker, eds. 2003. *Dictionary of the Old Testament: Pentateuch*. Downers Grove, IL: InterVarsity.

---

29. Surveys Eichrodt ('covenant'), von Rad (typology), Childs (canon), Sanders (Torah as canon), and Terrien (presence). Argues for the promise-fulfillment, or promise-expectation approach with typology serving to connect much of this.

30. 1. Scott J. Hafemann, "Covenant Relationship," 2. Thomas R. Schreiner, "Commands of God," 3. Frank S. Thielman, "Atonement," 4.Stephen G. Dempster, "Servant of the Lord," 5. Paul R. House, "Day of the Lord," 6. Elmer Martens, "People of God," 7. Roy E. Ciampa, "History of Redemption."

31. A translation of a 1968 French Roman Catholic work. Contains signed articles by seventy scholars on the major theological themes in the Bible.

32. Best OT Theology bibliography available.

Beckwith, Roger T., and Martin J. Selman, eds. 1995. *Sacrifice in the Bible.* Grand Rapids, MI: Baker.

Beale, Greg K. 2004. *The Temple and the Church's Mission: A Biblical Theology of the Dwelling Place of God.* Downers Grove, IL: Apollos/ InterVarsity.

———. 2011. *A New Testament Biblical Theology: The Unfolding of the Old Testament in the New.* Grand Rapids, MI: Baker Academic.

Brueggemann, Walter. 1977. *The Prophetic Imagination.* Philadelphia, PA: Fortress.

———. 1992. "Old Testament Theology." In *Old Testament Theology: Essays on Structure, Theme, and Text.* In OT Theology: Essays, ed. Patrick D. Miller. Minneapolis, MN: Fortress.[33]

———. 1997. *Theology of the Old Testament: Testimony, Dispute, Advocacy.* Minneapolis, MN: Fortress.[34]

Childs, Brevard S. 1979. *Introduction to the Old Testament as Scripture.* Philadelphia: Fortress.

———. 1986. *Old Testament Theology in a Canonical Context.* Philadelphia: Fortress.

Clowney, E. P. 1977. *Preaching and Biblical Theology.* Nutley, NJ: Presbyterian and Reformed.

Dumbrell, William J. 1984. *Covenant and Creation: A Theology of the Old Testament Covenants.* Carlisle, UK: Paternoster.

Dyrness, William A. 1979. *Themes: Old Testament Theology.* Downers Grove, IL: InterVarsity.[35]

Eichrodt, Walther. 1961. *Theology of the Old Testament.* 2 vols. (Originally published as *Theologie des Alten Testaments* 3 vols. Göttingen : Vandenhoeck und Ruprecht, 1961). Translated by J. A. Baker. Old Testament Library. Philadelphia: Westminster.[36]

---

33. Fifteen theological contributions by Brueggemann: Two essays deal with structure and organization of biblical theology, seven deal with various themes, and six present theological development of specific texts. He asserts the absurdity of the notion of a theology of either the Old or the New Testament in isolation from the other. Focus on literary and rhetorical studies.

34. Provoking, if over-inclined to dialectical thought.

35. Good for missions and culture.

36. Finds its organizing center to be "covenant."

Ellis, E. Earle. 1992. *The Old Testament in Early Christianity: Canon and Interpretation*. Grand Rapids, MI: Baker.

Goldingay, John. 2003. *Israel's Gospel*. Vol. 1 of *Old Testament Theology*. Downers Grove, IL: InterVarsity.

———. 2006. *Israel's Faith*. Vol. 2 of Old Testament Theology. Downers Grove, IL: InterVarsity.

———. 2009. *Israel's Life*. Vol. 3 of Old Testament Theology. Downers Grove, IL: InterVarsity.

Greidanus, Sidney. 1999. *Preaching Christ from the Old Testament: A Contemporary Hermeneutical Method*. Grand Rapids, MI: Eerdmans.

Hafemann, Scott J., ed. 2002. *Biblical Theology: Retrospect and Prospect*. Downers Grove, IL: InterVarsity.

Hasel, Gerhard D. 1991. *Old Testament Theology: Basic Issues in the Current Debate*. 4th ed. Grand Rapids, MI: Eerdmans.

Hildebrandt, Wilf. 1995. *An Old Testament Theology of the Spirit of God*. Peabody, MA: Hendrickson.

House, Paul R. 1998. *Old Testament Theology*. Downers Grove, IL: InterVarsity.

Hubbard, Robert L., Jr., Robert K. Johnston, and Robert P. Meye, eds. 1992. *Studies in Old Testament Theology: Historical and Contemporary Images of God and His People*. Dallas: Word.

Kaiser, Walter C., Jr. 1973. *The Old Testament in Contemporary Preaching*. Grand Rapids, MI: Baker.

———. 1978. *Toward an Old Testament Theology*. Grand Rapids, MI: Zondervan.

———. 1983. *Toward Old Testament Ethics*. Grand Rapids, MI: Zondervan.

———. 1985. *The Uses of the Old Testament in the New*. Chicago: Moody.

———. 1987. *Toward Rediscovering the Old Testament*. Grand Rapids, MI: Zondervan.

———.1995. *The Messiah in the Old Testament*. Grand Rapids, MI: Zondervan.

———. 1998. *The Christian and the "Old" Testament*. Pasadena, CA: William Carey Library.

———. 2003. *Preaching and Teaching from the Old Testament: A Guide for the Church*. Grand Rapids, MI: Baker.

———. 2008. *The Promise-Plan of God: A Biblical Theology of the Old and New Testaments*. Grand Rapids, MI: Baker.

Martens, Elmer A. 1994. *God's Design*. 2nd ed. Grand Rapids, MI: Baker.

Niehaus, Jeffrey J. 1995. *God at Sinai: Covenant and Theophany in the Bible and Ancient Near East*. Studies in Old Testament Biblical Theology. Carlisle, UK: Paternoster Press.

Payne, J. Barton. 1962. *The Theology of the Older Testament*. Grand Rapids, MI: Zondervan.

Von Rad, Gerhard. 1963. *Old Testament Theology*. 2 vols. Philadelphia: The Westminster.

Ryken, Leland, James C. Wilhoit, and Tremper Longmen III, eds. 1998. *Dictionary of Biblical Imagery*. Downers Grove, IL: InterVarsity.

Smith, Ralph L. 1993. *Old Testament Theology: Its History, Method, and Message*. Nashville, TN: Broadman and Holman.

Waltke, Bruce K., with Charles Yu. 2006. *An Old Testament Theology: An Exegetical, Canonical, and Thematic Approach*. Grand Rapids, MI: Zondervan.

Watts, James Washington. 1967. *Old Testament Teaching*. Nashville. TN: Broadman.

Webb, William J. 2001. *Slaves, Women, & Homosexuals: Exploring the Hermeneutics of Cultural Analysis*. Downers Grove, IL: InterVarsity.

Wright, Christopher J. H. 1992. *Knowing Jesus through the Old Testament*. Downers Grove, IL: InterVarsity.

———. 1995. *Walking in the Ways of the Lord: The Ethical Authority of the Old Testament*. Downers Grove, IL: InterVarsity.[37]

———. 2004. *Old Testament Ethics for the People of God*. Downers Grove, IL: InterVarsity.

———. 2006. *Knowing the Holy Spirit through the Old Testament*. Downers Grove, IL: InterVarsity.

———. 2007. *Knowing God the Father through the Old Testament*. Downers Grove, IL: InterVarsity.

Wright, N. T. 1993. *Climax of the Covenant: Christ and the Law in Pauline Theology*. Minneapolis, MN: Fortress.

Zuck, Roy B., ed. 1991. *A Biblical Theology of the Old Testament*. Chicago: Moody.

---

37. See http://www.langhampartnership.org/chris-wright/bibliography/ for full Christopher Wright bibliography.

New Testament Theology

Achtemeier, Paul J., Joel B. Green, and Marianne M. Thompson. 2001. *Introducing the New Testament: Its Literature and Theology*. Grand Rapids, MI: Eerdmans.

Beale, G. K. 2011. *New Testament Biblical Theology: Unfolding the Old Testament in the New*. Grand Rapids, MI: Zondervan.

———, ed. 1994. *The Right Doctrine from the Wrong Text: Essays on the Use of the Old Testament in the New*. Grand Rapids, MI: Baker.

Beale, G. K., and D. A. Carson, eds. 2007. *Commentary on the New Testament Use of the Old Testament*. Grand Rapids, MI: Baker Academic.

Beasley-Murray, G. R. 1991. *Gospel of Life: Theology in the Fourth Gospel*. Peabody, MA: Hendrickson.

Burge, Gary M. 2010. *Jesus and the Land: The New Testament Challenge to "Holy Land" Theology*. Grand Rapids, MI: Baker Academic.

Caird, G. B. 1994. *New Testament Theology*. Completed and edited by L.D. Hurst. New York: Oxford University Press.

Conzelmann, Hans. 1969. *An Outline of the Theology of the New Testament*. New York: Harper & Row.

Cullmann, Oscar. 1950. *Baptism in the New Testament*. Trans. J.K.S. Reid Studies in Biblical Theology, no. 1. London: SCM.

Dumbrell, William J. 1985. *The End of the Beginning: Rev. 21–22 and the Old Testament*. Sydney, Aus.: Lancer.[38]

Dunn, James D. G. 1970. *Baptism in the Holy Spirit: A Re-Examination of the New Testament Teaching on the Gift of the Spirit in Relation to Pentecostalism Today*. Studies in Biblical Theology, 15, 2nd Series. London: SCM Press.

———. 1987. *New Testament Theology in Dialogue*. Biblical Foundations in Theology. London: SPCK.

———. 1998. *The Theology of Paul the Apostle*. Grand Rapids, MI: Eerdmans.[39]

———. 2009. *New Testament Theology: An Introduction*. Library of Biblical Theology. Nashville, TN: Abingdon.

---

38. Superb motific analysis of New Jerusalem, new temple, new covenant, new Israel, and new creation.

39. Great for conceptualizing ministry.

————, and James P. Mackey. 1987. *New Testament Theology in Dialogue: Christology and Ministry.* Philadelphia: Westminster.

Ellis, E. Earle.1978. *Prophecy and Hermeneutic in Early Christianity.* Grand Rapids, MI: Eerdmans.

Esler, Philip F. 2005. *New Testament Theology: Communion and Community.* Minneapolis, MN: Fortress.

Fee, Gordon. 1987. *The First Epistle to the Corinthians.* New International Commentary on the New Testament. Grand Rapids, MI: Eerdmans.

————. 1994. *God's Empowering Presence: The Holy Spirit in the Letters of Paul.* Peabody, MA: Hendrickson.[40]

————. 1996. *Paul, the Spirit, and the People of God.* Peabody, MA: Hendrickson.[41]

France, R. T. 1971. *Jesus and the Old Testament: His Application of Old Testament Passages to Himself and His Mission.* Downers Grove, IL: InterVarsity.[42]

Goppelt, Leonard. 1964. *Jesus, Paul, and Judaism: An Introduction to New Testament Theology.* London: Thomas Nelson.

————. 1981, 1982. *Theology of the New Testament.* 2 vols. Grand Rapids, MI: Eerdmans.

Guelich, Robert A., ed. 1978. *Unity and Diversity in New Testament Theology: Essays in Honor of George E. Ladd.* Grand Rapids, MI: Eerdmans.

Guthrie, Donald. 1981. *New Testament Theology.* Downers Grove, IL: InterVarsity.[43]

Hunter, Archibald Macbride. 1966. *Introducing New Testament Theology.* London: SCM Press.

Jeremias, Joachim. 1971. *New Testament Theology.* New York: Scribner.

Keener, Craig S. 1997. *The Spirit in the Gospels.* Grand Rapids, MI: Baker.

Kümmel, Werner Georg. 1996. *The Theology of the New Testament: According to Its Major Witnesses, Jesus - Paul - John.* Trans. John E. Steely. London: Xpress Reprints.

---

40. See especially 146-261 on the Gifted Minister.

41. Excellent condensation of some of Fee's most significant conclusions.

42. Distinguishes between allegory and typology, arguing that typology is the theological interpretation of the Old Testament. Denies that typology was predictive; rather, it displays consistency in the principles of God's working in the world.

43. See especially 21–74.

Ladd, George Eldon. 1993. *A Theology of the New Testament*. Ed. Donald A. Hagner. Grand Rapids, MI: Eerdmans.

Lindars, Barnabas. 1991. *The Theology of the Letter to the Hebrews*. New Testament Theology. New York: Cambridge University Press.

Lincoln, Andrew T., and A. J. M. Wedderburn. 1993. *The Theology of the Later Pauline Letters*. New Testament Theology. Cambridge, UK: Cambridge University Press.

Marshall, I. Howard. 1990. *Jesus the Saviour: Studies in New Testament Theology*. Downers Grove, IL: InterVarsity.

———. 1990. *The Origins of New Testament Christology*. Issues in Contemporary Theology. Leicester, UK: Apollos.

———. 2004. *New Testament Theology: Many Witnesses, One Gospel*. Downers Grove, IL: InterVarsity.

———. 2008. *A Concise New Testament Theology*. Downers Grove, IL: InterVarsity.

———, and David Peterson. 1998. *Witness to the Gospel: The Theology of Acts*. Grand Rapids, MI: Eerdmans Publishing Co.

Matera, Frank J. 1999. *New Testament Christology*. Louisville, KY: Westminster/John Knox.

———. 2007. *New Testament Theology: Exploring Diversity and Unity*. Louisville, KY: Westminster/John Knox.

Morris, Leon. 1986. *New Testament Theology*. Grand Rapids, MI: Zondervan.

O'Toole, R. F. 1984. *The Unity of Luke's Theology*. Wilmington, DE: Michael Glazier.

Richardson, Alan. 1974. *An Introduction to the Theology of the New Testament*. London: SCM Press.[44]

Ridderbos, Herman N. 1975. *Paul an Outline of His Theology*. Grand Rapids, MI: Eerdmans.

Schreiner, Thomas R. 1990. *Interpreting the Pauline Epistles*. Guides to New Testament Exegesis. Grand Rapids, MI: Baker.

———. 1993. *The Law and Its Fulfillment: A Pauline Theology of Law*. Grand Rapids, MI: Baker.

———. 2001. *Paul, Apostle of God's Glory in Christ: A Pauline Theology*. Downers Grove, IL: InterVarsity.

---

44. Thematic Approach.

———. 2008. *New Testament Theology: Magnifying God in Christ*. Grand Rapids, MI: Baker Academic.

Stauffer, Ethelbert. 1963. *New Testament Theology*. Trans. John Marsh. London: SCM Press.

Stronstad, Roger. 1995. *Spirit, Scripture, and Theology: A Pentecostal Perspective*. Baguio City, Philippines: Asia Pacific Theological Seminary Press.[45]

Thielman, Frank. 2005. *Theology of the New Testament: A Canonical and SyntheticApproach*. Grand Rapids, MI: Zondervan.

Zuck, Roy B., and Darrell L. Bock, eds. 1994. *A Biblical Theology of the New Testament*. Chicago: Moody.

Historical Theology

Allison, Gregg. 2011. *Historical Theology: An Introduction to Christian Doctrine*. Grand Rapids MI: Zondervan.

Alston, Wallace M. Jr., and Welker, Michael. 2007. *Reformed Theology: Identity and Ecumenicity II: Biblical Interpretation in the Reformed Tradition*. Grand Rapids, MI: Eerdmans.

Arand, Charles P., Robert Kolb, and James A. Nestingen. 2012. *The Lutheran Confessions*. Philadelphia, PA: Fortress Press.

Berkhof, Louis. 1969. *The History of Christian Doctrine*. (Originally published in 1937 as *Reformed Dogmatics*) Carlisle, PA: Banner of Truth

Burgess, Stanley M., ed. 2011. *Christian Peoples of the Spirit: A Documentary History of Pentecostal Spirituality from the Early Church to the Present*. New York: NYU Press.

Curran, Charles E. 2013. *The Development of Moral Theology*. Washington DC: Georgetown University Press.

Gonzalez, Justo. 2009–2010. *A History of Christian Thought*. Rev. ed. 3 Vols. Nashville, TN: Abingdon Press.

Hägglund, Bengt. 2007. *History of Theology*. Trans. Gene J. Lund. St. Louis, MO: Concordia Publishing House.

Hill, Jonathan. 2003. *History of Christian Thought*. Downers Grove, IL: InterVarsity.

Kärkkäinen, Veli-Matti. 2009. *The Spirit in the World: Emerging Pentecostal Theologies in Global Contexts*. Grand Rapids, MI: Eerdmans.

---

45. An excellent study of Luke's approach to the Spirit in the Church.

Lane, Tony. 2006. *A Concise History of Christian Thought*. Rev. ed. Grand Rapids, MI: Baker Academic.

Macchia, Frank. 2009. *Baptized in the Spirit*. Grand Rapids, MI: Zondervan.

McGrath, Alister. 2012. *Historical Theology: An Introduction to the History of Christian Thought*. 2nd ed. Malden, MA: Wiley-Blackwell.

Meister, Chad and Stump, James. 2010. *Christian Thought: A Historical Introduction*. New York: Routledge.

Nichols, Aiden. 1991. *The Shape of Catholic Theology: An Introduction to Its Sources, Principles and History*. Collegeville, MN: Liturgical Press.

Oden, Amy. 1994. *In her Words: Women's Writings in the History of Christian Thought*. Nashville, TN: Abingdon.

Olsen, Roger. 1999. *The Story of Christian Theology*. Downers Grove, IL: InterVarsity Press.

Pelikan, Jaroslav. 1975-1991. *The Christian Tradition: A History of the Development of Christian Doctrine*, 5 Volumes. Chicago: University of Chicago Press.

_____. 1998. *Mary through the Centuries: her Place in the History of Culture*. New Haven, CN: Yale University press.

_____. 1999. *Jesus through the Centuries: His Place in the History of Culture*. New Haven, CN: Yale University press.

_____. 2005. *Credo: Historical and theological Guide to Creeds and Confessions of Faith in the Christian Tradition*. New Haven, CN: Yale University Press.

Placher, William, and Nelson, Derek R. 2013. *A History of Christian Theology*. 2nded. Louisville, KY: Westminster/John Knox Press.

Snyder, C. Arnold. 1997. *Anabaptist History and Theology: Revised Student Edition*. Kitchener, ON: Pandora Press.

Wells, David. 2009. *Reformed Theology in America: A History of Its Modern Developments*. Grand Rapids, MI: Eerdmans.

SYSTEMATIC THEOLOGY RESOURCES

General

Davis, John Jefferson. 1981. *Theology Primer.* Grand Rapids, MI: Baker.

Elwell, Walter A., ed. 1984. *Evangelical Dictionary of Theology.* Grand Rapids, MI: Baker.

Enns, Paul. 1989. *The Moody Handbook of Theology.* Chicago, IL: Moody.

Grenz, Stanley J., David Guretzki, and Cherith Fee Nordling. 1999. *Pocket Dictionary of Theological Terms.* Downers Grove, IL: InterVarsity.

Leith, John H., ed. 1982. *Creeds of the Churches.* 3rd ed. Louisville, KY: John Knox.

Arminian

Carter, Charles W., ed. 1983. *A Contemporary Wesleyan Theology.* 2 Vols. Grand Rapids, MI: Francis Asbury.

Finney, Charles G. 1887. *Lectures on Systematic Theology.* Oberlin, OH: E. J. Goodrich.

Grider, J. Kenneth. 1994. *A Wesleyan-Holiness Theology.* Kansas City, MO: Beacon Hill.

Oden, Thomas C. 1987–1992. *Systematic Theology.* 3 Vols. New York, NY: Harper & Row.

Wiley, H. Orton. 1960. *Christian Theology.* 3 Vols. Kansas City, MO: Beacon Hill Press.

Lutheran

Jenson, Robert W. 1997–1999. *Systematic Theology.* 2 Vols. New York: Oxford University Press.

Thielicke, Helmut. 1974. *The Evangelical Faith.* Trans.Geoffrey W. Bromley. 3 Vols. Grand Rapids, MI: Eerdmans.

Neo-Orthodox/Modern Continental

Barth, Karl. 1932–1967. *Church Dogmatics.* 13 vols. Trans. Geoffrey W. Bromley et al. London: T & T Clark.

Brunner, Emil. 1949–1962. *Dogmatics.* 3 Vols. Trans. Olive Wyon (Vols. 1 and 2) and David Cairns with T. H. L. Parker (Vol. 3). Philadelphia: Westminster.

Pannenberg, Wolfhart. 1991–1997. *Systematic Theology*. 3 Vols. Trans. Geoffrey W. Bromiley. Grand Rapids, MI: Eerdmans.

Tillich, Paul. 1951–1963. *Systematic Theology*. 3 Vols. Chicago: University of Chicago Press.

Pentecostal/Charismatic

Arrington, French L. 1992–1994. *Christian Doctrine: A Pentecostal Perspective*. 3 Vols. Cleveland, TN: Pathway.

Dayton, Donald W. 1987. *Theological Roots of Pentecostalism*. Grand Rapids, MI: Zondervan.

Grudem, Wayne. 1994. *Systematic Theology: An Introduction to Biblical Doctrine*. Grand Rapids, MI: Zondervan.

Higgins, John R., Michael L. Dusing, and Frank D. Tallman. 1993. *An Introduction to Theology: A Classical Pentecostal Perspective*. Dubuque, IA: Kendall/Hunt.

Warrington, Keith. 2008. *Pentecostal Theology: A Theology of Encounter*. New York, NY: T & T Clark.

Williams, J. Rodman. 1996. *Renewal Theology: Systematic Theology from a Charismatic Perspective*. Grand Rapids, MI: Zondervan.

Reformed/Baptistic/Dispensational

Berkhof, Louis. 1941, 1949. *Systematic Theology*. Grand Rapids, MI: Eerdmans.

Berkouwer, G. C. 1952–1976. *Studies in Dogmatics*. 14 Vols. Grand Rapids, MI: Eerdmans.

Bloesch, Donald. 1978–1979. *Essentials of Evangelical Theology*. 2 Vols. San Francisco, CA: Harper and Row.

———. 1992. *Christian Foundations*. 7 Vols. Downers Grove, IL: InterVarsity.

Erickson, Millard J. 2013. *Christian Theology*. 3rd ed. Grand Rapids, MI: Baker Academic.

Grenz, Stanley. 1994. *Theology for the Community of God*. Nashville, TN: Broadman & Holman.

Grudem, Wayne. 1994. *Systematic Theology: An Introduction to Biblical Doctrine*. Grand Rapids, MI: Zondervan.

Henry, Carl F. H. 1976–1983. *God, Revelation, and Authority*. 6 Vols. Waco, TX: Word.

Hodge, Charles. 1975. *Systematic Theology.* 3 Vols. First published in 1872. Grand Rapids, MI: Eerdmans.

Lewis, Gordon R., and Bruce Demarest. 1987–1994. *Integrative Theology.* 3 Vols. Grand Rapids, MI: Academic/Zondervan.

Strong, A. H. 1962. *Systematic Theology.* First published in 1907. Valley Forge, PA: Judson.

BIBLICAL COMMENTARIES

Carson, D. A. 2013. *New Testament Commentary Survey.* 7th ed. Grand Rapids, MI: Baker Academic.

Glynn, John. 2007. *Commentary and Reference Survey: A Comprehensive Guide to Biblical and Theological Resources.* 10th ed. Grand Rapids: Kregel Academic & Professional.

Longman, Tremper III. 2013. *Old Testament Commentary Survey.* 5th ed. Grand Rapids, MI: Baker Academic.

Helpful Sets[46]

Expositor's Bible Commentary, 13 Vol. set.

Hermenia[47] 68 Vol. set.

International Critical Commentary, 59 Vol. set[48]

New International Commentary, (OT 23 Vol. set—NICOT; NT 18 Vol. set—NICNT)

New International Greek Testament Commentary (NIGTC) 13 Vol. set.

The NIV Application Commentary (NIVAC) 20 Vol. set.

Tyndale New Testament Commentary, 20 Vol. set.

Word Biblical Commentary,[49] 58 vol. set.

---

46. Some sets are still in the process of putting out volumes or revising volumes for their respective sets.

47. Great exegesis, but tends to liberal interpretations. Commentaries on OT, NT, Intertestamental, Pseudopigraphical, and early church works.

48. Older; classically Evangelical.

49. Often very good but sometimes too liberal.

The key question we must ask to interpret a passage of the Scriptures and understand what God is saying through it is this: What did the Bible writer, led by the Holy Spirit, mean in that context to those people? To get at that meaning, one of the basic questions to ask is this: How did the writer use the key words or phrases, given how they were used in that world? The answer to this second question is found by doing word studies because we have not grown up in their world, speaking their language. However, there is a temptation in doing word studies that we must avoid: treating Bible words as though they have magical power waiting to be discovered, especially by tracing their roots. Words, including those used in the Bible, are just symbols, used in human language to communicate truths and concepts. God speaks to humanity clearly, not in secret codes. He gave us His written Word through real people in real human language—the way those people actually spoke.

Therefore, the goal of a word study should be to understand the meaning the Bible writer intended by the word or phrase in the passage under study. This goal is best accomplished by presenting *the evidence of all the possible uses/meanings* of the word or phrase in the world of that Bible writer and then *choosing the meaning that best fits the particular context*. It is important to always remember that words are used, and are to be understood, in combination with other words. Nevertheless, the tool one must use to find every use in the Old or New Testaments—the data base for any word study—is an exhaustive concordance.[2] Old Testament (OT) words must be studied from the Hebrew text of the OT (or Aramaic, as in parts

---

1. Roger D. Cotton is professor of Old Testament at the Assemblies of God Theological Seminary, Springfield, Missouri.

2. A wonderful, unique, ability of computers is to search combinations of words, quickly and thoroughly.

of Ezra and Daniel). New Testament (NT) words must be studied from the Greek NT, but can also be connected to usage in the ancient Greek translation of the OT, used by first-century Christians, called the Septuagint. A concordance is the key tool for any word studies.

The first step in an OT or NT word study is to find the Hebrew or Greek word behind the English word that the translators chose and that represents an idea we want to understand better from a certain passage. We can then look up the original word in a Hebrew or Greek concordance and see *every place* it was used in the OT or the NT. After reading those references, we should list the various meanings for the word in the OT or NT that are possible in our passage, followed by choosing the meaning that *best fits this context.* Finally, after doing this work ourselves, from the biblical data, we then need to (1) read the word studies done by OT or NT scholars, and (2) draw our own conclusions on the best understanding of the word in question. Just because a person is a scholar does not mean he or she is right about the meaning of every Bible passage.

For English-speaking Bible students who do not know Hebrew or Greek, numerous tools can empower their word studies. Obviously, various computer programs can provide needed information. When doing word studies through computer programs, one must ensure the software is searching on the Hebrew words, not just the English. Among printed books, concordances to particular versions of Scripture use a numbering system for identifying the Hebrew or Greek words behind the English words. In addition, Hebrew and Greek concordances use numbering systems so that we can go to a particular Hebrew or Greek word and see a listing of every place it is used. For the King James Version, Strong's concordance and its numbering system is useful; that numbering system is used by the Englishman's Hebrew or Greek Concordances. The NIV Exhaustive Concordance, with its unique numbering system, supports NIV users. Hebrew-English or Greek-English Concordances are available for use with the NIV.[3]

After we do this study implied in the preceding paragraph, we should read the article on the word in either the *New International Dictionary of Old Testament Theology and Exegesis* for a Hebrew word, or the

---

3. See those listed in Appendix 18 "Selected Bibliography for Biblical and Theological Research."

corresponding dictionary for a NT Greek word.[4] Finally, we should write our own summary of the meaning with our reasons for our conclusions, based on the best Bible references that illustrate that meaning in similar situations elsewhere in the Scriptures.

An example is the word for "kill" in Exodus 20:13 in the KJV; the Hebrew term is translated "murder" in the NIV. Through the concordances for either version, we can get a number that leads us to the Hebrew word *ratsach* and the list of its every occurrence in the Old Testament. From this list, we can determine that *ratsach* is not a general word for killing but is used only of killing people. Furthermore, it is sometimes used of accidental killing, especially in Numbers. Thus, we may conclude that the basic idea represented by this word is the act, not authorized by God, of taking a human life. Certainly, in the context of the Ten Commandments, this word refers to a willful choice that is prohibited (Ex 20:13) and is, thus, best translated as *murder*. However, God may authorize a government to execute capital punishment or warfare; killing in those cases does not break this commandment.

Anyone can do this kind of study and come to an accurate and insightful understanding of the Bible writer's message, and be equipped to evaluate what scholars are saying. Thank the Lord for the many tools we have. Let us diligently examine the Scriptures, as the Bereans did (Acts 17:11), and be workmen who do not need to be ashamed (2 Tim 2:15). See the Flow Chart for Doing Word Studies on the Bible next page.

---

4. Likewise see those listed in Appendix 18 "Selected Bibliography for Biblical and Theological Research."

1. ENGLISH WORD

Begin with a verse that deals with a concept that you want to understand better. What did
the Bible people mean by the words they used about it? Identify the English word chosen to express the concept by the translators of a version for which there is a concordance that has a number system designate the Hebrew words.

2. FIND HEBREW WORD THROUGH THE NUMBER IN AN ENGLISH CONCOR-DANCE

Go to the exhaustive English concordance for the translation. It must have a number system to designate the Hebrew word behind the English word so you can study the actual Hebrew idea that you want to understand better. Find your verse under the English word in the concordance and get the number for

3. LOOK AT EVERY USE THROUGH A HEBREW CONCORDANCE

Go to that number—the Hebrew word—in an exhaustive Hebrew-English concordance
for that version, keyed to that number system, and find the Hebrew word. Then look at every place it is used in the OT. List the various uses you find and lay out the range of usage. Propose where your verse fits in that range.

4. READ SCHOLARY WORD STUDIES

Go to scholarly word studies on the Hebrew word through the number system. Modify your understanding as you find compelling points made in the scholarly studies.

5. WRITE SUMMARY

Finally, write your own summary essay on the use of this word in God's teachings and

Flow Chart for Doing Word Studies on the Bible

APPENDIX 20
How to Do a New Testament Word Study
James D. Hernando, PhD[1]

INTRODUCTION

A serious Bible student will do a careful study of every word that is crucial to the understanding of his/her passage, recognizing that words have more than one sense or meaning. The study must attempt to determine what meaning the author had in mind when he used that word.

GUIDELINES FOR WORD STUDIES

1. Determine the word's "semantic range": that is, all possible senses or meanings to a word.

    Note 1: The interpreter cannot assume that because a particular sense of the word is found to fit in one text, he or she can transport that same sense to its use in another text. Neither should he or she assume that the safe interpretation is to interpret the whole of the semantic range into the meaning of that word in a particular text (e.g., The Amplified Bible translations).

2. Examine the immediate context to see which meaning the word carries in that particular text.

    Note 2: The interpreter must not simply determine the semantic range and then pick a preferred meaning. The possibility that more than one sense will fit the passage and "make sense" does not legitimize every sense or meaning that does.

    Note 3: Remember that biblical words can have special or technical meanings (*terminus technicus*). In such cases, we can expect that meaning

---

1. James D. Hernando is professor of New Testament at the Assemblies of God Theological Seminary, Springfield, Missouri. This document was provided by the author with permission to use.

to be fuller and sometimes at variance with the meaning(s) derived from a historical-lexical study of the word (e.g., *musterion*).

APPROACHES TO WORD STUDIES

3. **Etymologically:** by examining the way the word is formed, its component parts, and its origin or derivation from root words.

    This is sometimes helpful (e.g., Gk. *Episcopos*).

    By and large, however, this is of limited value (e.g., Eng. *awful;* Gk. *anaginosko*).

    Note 4: Usage/context, NOT etymology, determines meaning. For example, *homologeo* ("confess") is composed of two parts: *homos* ("same") and *lego* ("to say"). It is, however, incorrect to say that to confess is to "say the same thing as."

    Note 5: Most Greek words in the NT are not used often (5436 words in NT of which 3246 are used three or fewer times), and many have obscure origins and complicated histories. Students conducting this area of study must rely on lexicons, word books, theological dictionaries, and similar resources.

4. **Comparatively:** by examining how the word is used in the Bible. The interpreter must study:

    all citations

    all literary contexts: biblical genre and literary forms (e.g., "flesh" in the Gospels; "fool/foolish" in the Wisdom Literature)

    all biblical contexts in the Bible. Note how the various biblical authors (NT or OT) use your word, and how sections of the canon may use the word (Torah, Prophets [both Major and Minor], Wisdom Literature, Gospels, Acts, Epistles, and Revelation). Note any differences.

    parallel passages:

    verbal cross-reference (same word/words used in two verses)

    conceptual cross-reference (same thought/topic using different words) parallel cross-reference (two accounts of the same event: cf. the Gospels)

synonyms (see Trench's *Synonyms*: e.g., *phileo/agapao*)

equivalent expressions ("kingdom of God/kingdom of Heaven")

5. **Culturally**: gives insight into the scope and content of a word.

    oikos/oikia ("house/household"): the latter term could refer to all that a person possesses, but usually referred to the adult members (Consider the untenability of arguing for "infant baptism" from the use of *oikia* in Acts 16:31.)

    Matthew 5:41: the "compelled" Roman practice of enscripted service

    all items of physical culture e.g., tools, money, furniture

    all terms related to social or religious culture (e.g., *mnēsteutheisēs*"pledged to be married" or *hilasmos* "sin offering")

6. *Historically–Developmentally:* deals with the historical circles of context having a bearing on the Bible's use of a particular word; it overlaps with cultural study.

    Note 6: What constitutes the closest literary usage (chronologically) may not necessarily be the most germane to your study (e.g., Philo's use of a Greek word as opposed to the same word's usage in the LXX.)

    Historical Contexts of a NT Word[2]

    Koine. See BDAG: *A Greek-English Lexicon of the New Testament*[3]

    LXX. For a lexicon, see Lust, Eynikel, and Hauspie, eds. *A Greek-English Lexicon of the Septuagint.*

---

2. The reason why these historical contexts are studied is to explore the full semantic range carried by a particular word (all possible meanings). It also lets us see what meanings or connotations a word might have had with various audiences. It is not done so that you can uncritically import those meaning into the biblical text. The biblical author may have used the word in such a way as to reflect one sense of the word or another, but this has to be determined by contextual usage not by arbitrary assignment.

3. For the bibliographical details of cited sources see Appendix 18 "Selected Bibliography for Biblical and Theological Research."

For a concordance, see Hatch and Redpath's *Concordance to the Septuagint.*

Patristic Greek. Depending on the date of the Church Father cited, this usage could be very helpful, since the Fathers are often paraphrasing and quoting biblical material in their writings and could reflect the NT usage in their exegesis or commentary. See Lampe's *Patristic Greek Lexicon.*

Classical Greek. This usage could be very helpful, since the classical period contains the literary heritage of most NT words. The problem with the use of classical Greek is to determine if the NT writer knew and employed such usage, or if they opted for a different sense. See Liddell and Scott's *Greek Lexicon.*

Note 7: Greek students should do their own word studies, using the above lexicons and tools. The non-language student can still study the word historically by using theological dictionaries (e.g., Kittel's TDNT) and other word books (e.g., Balz and Schneider's *Exegetical Dictionary of the New Testament*).

7. *Use of Historical Word Study:* by examining the entire semantic range of the word gleaned from all of the historical contextual uses.

Note 8: It will be your job to discern which particular historical use or context informs the biblical author's use of that word. Now read your verse or passage in light of the meaning determined by your historical word study.

1. Maintain sound hermeneutical, exegetical thinking.

   A. Keep asking: What was the author's intended meaning?

   B. Consider all the contextual evidence for the meaning, from language, history and culture, literary features, and theology in context. Prioritize in circles of context: (1) the surrounding literary unit, (2) the book, (3) the same author, (4) the same genre, (5) the same subject, (6) the same time period, (7) the rest of the Testament, (8) the whole Bible.

   C. Seek to understand the significance of what is written for the people then, culturally and theologically, and state it in terms of principles. Then propose the significance for us today in terms of theological principles. Finally, identify specific applications.

2. Answer the major questions from the basic resources.

   A. Study the most probable meanings of the major terms and phrases. Read in various versions including NIV, ESV, CEV, NLT, NET, and NASB. Use lexicons (e.g., BDAG, HALOT); concordances (e.g., *New Englishman's Hebrew or Greek Concordance* or *The Hebrew-English Concordance to the Old Testament*); wordbooks (e.g., NIDOTTE, TWOT, TDNT, and abridged NIDNTT).[2] Study cross-references and parallel passages.

---

1. Roger D. Cotton is professor of Old Testament at the Assemblies of God Theological Seminary, Springfield, Missouri.

2. For the bibliographical details of cited sources see Appendix 18, "Selected Bibliography for Biblical and Theological Research."

B. Determine the meaning and significance for the Bible writers of essential historical and cultural points at the time of writing. Use encyclopedias, surveys, background books, and exegetical commentaries.

C. Analyze the flow of thought within the passage by diagramming it.

D. Place the passage within the document by outlining the latter and comparing yours to the outlines in the best exegetical commentaries.

E. Note what the genre characteristics and literary devices indicate about the author's intent. See what the best exegetical commentaries and literary scholars say about them. Check the *Dictionary of Biblical Imagery*.

F. Read the studies available on the passage by other exegetes, especially on the theology of it. See the best exegetical commentaries especially in the series: New International Commentary, Tyndale, Expositor's, and Word. See also relevant academic journals; specialized studies (e.g., Stanley Horton, *What the Bible Says About the Holy Spirit*); OT theologies (e.g., [OT], Goldingay, House, Martens, and Waltke; [NT] Ladd.)[3]

G. Draw conclusions on the meaning and significance then and the significance now. Meditate and "principlize."

3. For a given topic, bring together the above results for each of the passages pertaining to it and synthesize the Bible teaching on the topic.

A. Let each Bible writer give his unique contribution to the topic.

B. Do not force any categories on the data; rather, seek those of the Bible writers themselves.

---

3. See Appendix 18, "Selected Bibliography for Biblical and Theological Research."

APPENDIX 22
STUDYING A THEME IN BIBLICAL THEOLOGY[1]

Roger D. Cotton, ThD[2]

Biblical theology has a thematic component for the whole Bible, but below I will focus on the Old Testament for my description.

1. Ensure you have narrowed the theme down to a manageable size for your purpose, and have clearly restricted it to the specific aspects you are really interested in.

2. Identify the key words and phrases from the major passages that deal with the theme, as well as the images, metaphors, and cultural comparisons, used to describe the truths associated with it.

3. Find every passage in the Old Testament that makes any significant contribution to the understanding of your theme, using concordances and various sources of cross-references. Use the *New Englishman's Hebrew Concordance*, the *NIV Hebrew-English Concordance.*, or another that lists every place a Hebrew word is used, or a computer program that does the same, for *all the references to the key Hebrew words and phrases* involved in your theme.[3]

4. List the *principles* you see in each of the passages, distinguishing the contexts of the various writers, genres, and time periods as you do. The objective is to recognize

---

1. For an excellent summary of the principles and process of doing Old Testament theology, with illustrations, see Richard Schultz, "Integrating Old Testament Theology and Exegesis: Literary, Thematic, and Canonical Issues," in NIDOTTE, 1, 185–205; see Appendix 18, "Selected Bibliography for Biblical and Theological Research."

2. Roger D. Cotton is Professor of Old Testament at the Assemblies of God Theological Seminary, Springfield, Missouri.

3. For the bibliographical details of cited sources see Appendix 18, "Selected Bibliography for Biblical and Theological Research."

the different purposes and angles being stressed by each writer: let each writer speak his own contribution in his own context. You must do quick but accurate exegesis of each passage.

5. Read the word studies done in *NIDOTTE*; also may want to check *TWOT*, and *TDOT* (*TDOT* requires knowledge of Hebrew).

6. Research the key words, phrases, and the theme topic in other *scholarly literature* including: Bible encyclopedias (new *ISBE*, and *ABD*); *New Dictionary of Biblical Theology*; IVP Dictionaries of the OT: Pentateuch, History, etc.; *Dictionary of Biblical Imagery*; monographs; journals; the best exegetical commentaries; Old Testament Theologies (Dyrness, Eichrodt, Goldingay, House, Martens, Payne, Von Rad, and Waltke); and *NIDOTTE*, vol 4, Topical Dictionary).[4]

7. Compile all the principles or truths involved in your theme as you have studied all the significant passages and what the scholars have observed. Then find a few basic, natural groupings of the principles in order to organize your material. Be aware of the Bible writers' categories versus your own.

8. Outline the presentation simply, clearly, logically, and consistently. Use either a natural topical order or the order used in the canon; in the latter case, show any progressive revelation. Be sure to cite all major supporting Scriptures.

9. Draw conclusions about what God was saying to Israel. Then identify what principles He wants us to apply to the church today.

---

4. See Appendix 18, "Selected Bibliography for Biblical and Theological Research," for the bibliographical information on these.

APPENDIX 23
Types/Genres of Ritual:
A Suggestive List
Daniel E. Albrecht, PhD

The following suggestive list of rites and rituals is not exhaustive and many categories and types overlap. Types or genres of ritual includes:

Rites of passage are a major category of ritual. These rites mark a transition from one stage of life to another—a change of status e.g., birth, initiation, puberty rituals, marriage ceremonies, funerary rites.[1]

Calendrical and commemorative rites denote rituals celebrated on a cycle e.g. annually, seasonally, monthly, or weekly. Often, they celebrate an important historical event in the community's life, for Christians Easter, Christmas and communion remember with rituals. Americans celebrate the 4th of July and Thanksgiving annually. Calendrical and commemorative ritual can include festival rites, ritual drama, rites of feasting, and fasting. *Pilgrimages* can signal a cycle of life, a calendrical commemoration or other.

There are numerous rites of *worship/liturgical/devotional rites* and forms of micro-rites within them, e.g. varieties of worship services, liturgical and sacramental rites, rites of consecration and ordination, repentance rites, interaction and communion rites, sacrificial worship, purification rituals, healing and exorcism rites, meditative rites, and various personal and corporate religious disciplines and devotions.

Examples of *civic and socio-political rites* include graduation/commencements ceremonies, coronations and presidential inaugurations, symbolic demonstrations of support, oaths of allegiance or conversely resistance rites, rites of inversion, marches symbolizing discontent etc.[2]

---

1. Turner's work described and analyzed the processual nature of rites of passage, as well as *communitas,* liminality, and anti-structure, of this genre, largely in the liminal (middle) phase. See *Ritual Process,* and *Forest of Symbols.*

2. For a list of Charismatic/Pentecostal rites (foundational, liturgical, and micro) see Albrecht 1999, 254–59.

REFERENCES

Albrecht, Daniel E. 1999. *Rites in the Spirit: A Ritual Approach to Pentecostal/ Charismatic Spirituality.* Journal of Pentecostal Theology Supplement Series 17. Sheffield, UK: Sheffield Academic Press.

Turner, Victor. 1967. *The Forest of Symbols.* Ithaca, NY: Cornell University Press.

———. 1969. *The Ritual Process: Structure and Anti-structure.* Chicago: Aldine Publishing.

Andrews University Seminary Studies
Asia Journal of Theology
Asian Journal of Pentecostal Studies
Biblica
The Bible Translator
Biblical Archaeology Review
Biblical Archaeologist (now Near Eastern Archaeology)
Biblical Theology Bulletin
Bibliotheca Sacra
Bulletin for Biblical Research
Bulletin of the John Rylands University Library
Calvin Theological Journal
Canadian Journal of Theology
Catholic Biblical Quarterly
Christian History
Christian Scholar's Review
Church History
Communio
Concordia Theological Quarterly
Currents in Biblical Research
Evangelical Quarterly
Expository Times
Harvard Theological Review
Horizons in Biblical Theology
International Journal of Systematic Theology
Interpretation

---

1. It is understood that this list is not exhaustive, but is a good start for those not familiar with the field.

Journal for the Scientific Study of Religion
Journal for the Study of the New Testament
Journal for the Study of the Old Testament
Journal of Biblical and Pneumatological Research
Journal of Biblical Literature
Journal of Ecclesiastical History
Journal of Biblical Literature
Journal of Pentecostal Theology
Journal of the European Pentecostal Theological Association
Journal of the Evangelical Theological Society
Journal of Theological Studies
Modern Theology
New Testament Abstracts
New Testament Studies
Novum Testamentum
Old Testament Abstracts
Pneuma
Religious and Theological Abstracts
Review and Expositor
Revue Biblique
Scottish Journal of Theology
Semeia
St. Vladimir's Theological Quarterly
Southwestern Journal of Theology
TC: A Journal of Biblical Textual Criticism
The Journal of the Evangelical Society
Theological Studies
Theology Today
Toronto Journal of Theology
Trinity Journal
Tyndale Bulletin
Vetus Testamentum
Zeitschrift für die Alttestamentliche Wissenschaft
Zeitschrift für die Neutestamentliche Wissenschaft

APPENDIX 25
Major Journals in Missions and Related Disciplines[1]

American Ethnologist
Currents in Theology and Mission
Dharma Deepika: A South Asian Journal of Missiological Research
Ethne: Online Journal for Pentecostal and Missional Leadership
Evangelical Missions Quarterly
Exchange: A Journal of Missiological and Ecumenical
Global Missiology
International Bulletin of Missionary Research
International Journal of Frontier Missiology
International Review of Mission
Journal of Asia Mission
Missiology
Missionalia
Mission Frontiers
Mission Studies
Occasional Bulletin of the Evangelical Missiological Society
Southern Baptist Journal of Missions and Evangelism
Transformation
Zeitschrift für Missionswissenschaft und Religionwissenschaft

---

1. It is understood that this list is not exhaustive, but is a good start for those not familiar with the field.

GLOSSARY*

Contextualization: broadly embraces the challenge of relating the gospel to culture. As a process, it includes endeavoring to communicate faithfully and relevantly God's revelation of his Word, works, and person into a new cultural setting in ways that help people respond to Christ, have their worldview transformed, and obey him in their social worlds.

Cross-cultural: the description of moving from one culture to another.

Culture: the symbolic system by which meanings are expressed in both tangible (e.g., art, gesture, rituals) and intangible (e.g., speech) forms that are socially acquired, learned behaviors, and transmitted inter-generationally. Culture provides the tools people use to navigate complex social interactions and fosters a sense of corporate shared identity through language, religion, ethnicity, and other interpersonal domains.

Emic: a culture-specific approach to knowing in anthropological and similar social science research in which researchers explore the beliefs, values and rules of behavior of a culture or society from the perspective of those who live within it; an insider's view.

Etic: a culture-general approach to knowing in anthropological and similar social science research in which researchers explore the beliefs, values, and rules for behavior of a culture or society from the perspective of an outsider; an outsider's view.

---

* Resources for additional missiology terms:
http://www.aibi.ph/missions/glossary.pdf
https://quizlet.com/198400/miss-325-missiological-terms-flash-cards/
Winter, Ralph D. "The Two Structures of God's Redemptive Mission." In *Perspectives on the World Christian Movement: A Reader*, edited by Ralph D. Winter and Steven C. Hawthorne, 3rd ed. 220–30. Pasadena, CA: William Carey Library Publishers, 1999.

Empirical: a way of knowing that is based on data from the senses, usually by experiment, and evidence discerned by the senses.

Epistemology: the study of knowledge; seeking an answer the question, "How do we know anything?"

Exegesis: the critical analysis and interpretation of a text (particularly the Bible in this context) or a culture.

Hermeneutic: the art and science of interpretation which highlights exegesis, but also includes (especially in biblical hermeneutics) the movement from exegesis ("what it meant") to contextual application ("what it means today)."

Heuristic: a method, process, or function by which researchers intuitively explore phenomena in order to discover or learn something for themselves that aids the larger process of problem solving and decision making in the research process.

Interdisciplinarity: an approach to research that draws from the concepts, theories, and bodies of knowledge of two or more academic disciplines or fields of study, and integrates their empirical toolsfor the purpose of new data gathering and understanding that could not be gained through single-discipline research. This approach to inquiry requires ongoing dynamic integration of research methodologies, resulting data, and concluded findings from multiple disciplines.

Interdisciplinary: the crossing and integrating of two or more academic disciplines, including their tools, concepts, theories, and related bodies of knowledge for the purpose of gaining new knowledge and understanding that is beyond the scope of one traditional academic discipline.

Memoing: the process of reflective record keeping about what a researcher is learning from raw data that aids to make conceptual leaps in understand analytical themes and their relationships.

Modality/Sodality: Based on an essay by Ralph D. Winter (1974) with missiological implications, *modality* refers to local church structure without age or sex distinctions and composed of families across generations, which is in contrast to *sodality* which is a structure that is different than groups that include whole families such as specialized groups that work on special functions in a local church context, perhaps along age, sex, or task lines.

Mono-cultural: the awareness or parameters of people from a single culture with a non-cross-cultural perspective or understanding.

Ontological: that which is related to the metaphysics of ontology, or the nature of existence or being.

Qualitative coding: Qualitative coding is an analytical process in which qualitative data, such as the words in verbatim interview transcripts, are systematically classified and categorized into "codes" that summarize and capture the important content of the data. That analysis can be completed manually or with the aid of computer software, and often focuses on identifying major themes and concepts and their relationships running through the data.

Theologizing: the process of working through one's theology within their own (or in a missional context their recipient) culture

Theory: a comprehensive integrative explanation of known research-generated facts, capable of generating hypothetical statements that can be tested in future research.

Triangulation: the process which involves utilizing multiple research methods to produce a richer account of phenomenon by examining and interpreting data through different viewpoints. Commonly viewed as a means to test validity, qualitative researchers make use of triangulation to facilitate a robust and fuller understanding of data, and to provide illumination into the interpretive process.

CPSIA information can be obtained
at www.ICGtesting.com
Printed in the USA
JSHW051353180723
44978JS00006B/69